BEYOND LEADERSHIP

The governmental role of
the attendants of the bride

GREG HASWELL

Deep Roots Press

2013

"This book is a big treasure chest. Profound and in my opinion it is currently unique. Greg is a big picture man with an apostolic wisdom that makes complicated things simple. The powerful perceptions in this book will resonate with the readers and awaken much needed discernment in our day. Hope deferred makes the heart sick, but so does the presumption of immediacy without the means! It is possible to precipitate a premature peak of revival. Our Father allows this in His love of passion and zeal but He knows that such peaks lack the means to produce sustainability. The hopes that such peaks would be the answer for the Church percolate through history as eloquent monuments calling out and appealing to a generation to go "beyond leadership". There is a heavenly pattern of government. God has ordained for His Church to manifest His majesty, not just in short peaks of revival but by coming to the stature of all the fullness of Christ! The spectrum of ingredients needed to see the Church revealing the manifold wisdom of God are presented in a simple, practical and accessible way in this book. It is written for this generation now!

I congratulate you Greg for your patience, courage and wisdom in waiting to write this book at the right time.

I wish you every success for this book!"
Your friend,
Rob Rufus

Greg is an exceptional leader and is more than qualified to write on the subject of leadership. Like the David he writes about, Greg is a 'Man with a heart after God'

I was on a pastoral team in a mega church with Greg where he proved to be an exemplary team player. I have served on a team led by him where he was an outstanding leader, visionary and Bible teacher. This all spans over 25 years. After all this time I regard him as one of the best friends a man could have. May those who read this book benefit from each chapter as much as I have from your example of leadership.

Steve Wheeler
(Author 'Highway to Grace')
Lead elder Highway Christian Community

"As we move into the administration phase of the grace revolution it is absolutely vital that we hold onto and capitalize on authentic church government. There is no substitute for that which Christ has ordained in His Church for biblical leadership and authority to keep the Church healthy and on track with His purposes. Greg has done a thorough job in expositing biblical Church government from many insightful and inspiring angles. You will be blessed as you read and meditate on his writings. May the Church of Jesus Christ rise in these days to see the greatest awakening mankind has ever known!"

Ryan Rufus
Founder of New Nature Publications
www.newnaturepublications.com
Author of "Extra Virgin Grace" and "After the Revolution".
Pastor at City Church International

"A phrase by Greg Haswell that has had a deep impact on my leadership and Church is 'where does the grace flow?'. Greg has in a profound way unpacked in this book the idea that grace needs to flow the 'right' way. That when the Church is led well the 'grace gifts' of God to the Church are working at all levels. This is a profoundly deep theological work yet accessible to the casual reader."

Peter Rasmussen
Leader of City Hill

THIS BOOK IS DEDICATED TO

Jesus

My Lord, the consummate shepherd of Your sheep,

"Our highest praise, deepest honor, most earnest thanks, greatest aspirations, most steadfast service - You are worthy of it all, Lord"

Michelle

My great love,

"You are a gift beyond measure and still the only woman I want to be in covenant with. A great beauty who has born the weight of our ministry with tremendous grace"

Nicole

Our most amazing daughter,

"As promised you are clothed in splendor, and I couldn't be more proud of you. I love you beyond the singing of it"

Tyler

A man of honor who won all of our hearts,

"My true son, whom I admire in our common faith. Remember, your futures so bright you'll have to wear shades and that I knew you before you were famous."

Acknowledgments

All the eldership teams we have served in, every saint we have watched over, and each year in ministry, have added their shaping touch to what is written in these pages. To each we are grateful and indebted. What joy we will share together before the throne, when the King is acknowledged as supreme. Finally the lamb will receive His full and due adoration and we will confess that He is worthy of everything we were able to give.

The following people deserve special acknowledgement for their affect in our lives; Our families, whose early and unrelenting love for us, and whose joyful belief in us, is still a source of life. The elders of Northlands Church, whom we honor as people worthy of the name, Ed Roebert and David Griffiths, fathers in the faith whose belief in us gave us roots and wings. Dudley Daniel, an apostolic pioneer and the first of the new breed of leaders known to me. The leaders and members of Highway Christian Community who believed when it wasn't convenient.

Additionally this is a respectful acknowledgment to all those who preach God's gospel in the many churches we have visited, faithful servants who labor in God's word. I cannot name all of you, but the revelation from God's word that you have unearthed to me is eternally precious and deserves thanks.

May this book bring life and freedom to God's bride!

Amen

INTRODUCTION

Thank you for getting this far. The fact that you opened a book this size on this topic means that you are bolder than most. We the church, and our generation, are slaves to the lack of what is described in these pages. We are made poor in its absence and will be explosively launched by its proper functioning. **We need people to govern the church as God intended.** We need people to go beyond leadership into biblical governance. Don't misunderstand the very high opinion I have of leaders and the leadership gift. It is an indispensable need in the church and a valuable gift of God. Yet leadership principles deal with the relationships between groups of people and those who would lead them. Governance encompasses these two groups and also responds to the eternal God as a dynamic participant with both. An atheist with a great leadership ability cannot stand in front of, or govern the organism called the body of Christ. In other words, governing Gods people demands incredibly more than mere leadership prowess. It requires prepared servant leaders able to hear His voice and usher His people into all of its beauty.

Psalm 78:72 And David shepherded them with integrity of heart; with skillful hands he led them. (NIV11)

In my experience in the ministry the scripture above has proven itself true. People will let you shepherd them, care for them, pray for them, and fuss over them if they believe you have integrity. Yet that integrity, sincerity and purity will not be enough if you expect them to follow you. To get people to follow where you lead, you must also have skillful hands. Too often I have felt like a man with a pure heart and ten thumbs. Fumbling with good intentions yet unskilled hands and under developed leadership potential. Additionally and perhaps more importantly, without an accurate sense of God's design for how His church is to be led or an accurate sense of His particular guidance. This often leads to more frustration than release for God's people. As leaders in God's household, we owe our generation a debt to maximize our leadership and governance gifts so that we can offer ourselves as useful instruments, ready to begin the job of governing God's people. This is the "leadership" paradigm the Scriptures reveal.

Our skill in this essential role ushers in great blessing for the entire church. Where we settle for dull edges in leadership grace, we minimize one of the essential tools of governance and a far greater effort is required from the people to achieve the same results.

Ecclesiastes 10:10 If the ax is dull and its edge unsharpened, more strength is needed, but skill will bring success.(NIV11)

The history of the world is shaped by people who have functioned in the call of God on their lives. God's design for those who govern His church is that they create space for His people to develop in all God has called them to. Liberty is evident in every area of the lives of those who are governed by godly leadership. The church is God's great plan for man, the pillar and foundation of truth (1 Timothy 3:14-16). When we embrace a scriptural church leadership, a style of government is practiced that creates life in those it oversees and fashions wide open spaces for them to flourish. God gives His church a great "gateway gift" that is redeemed, servant leaders. These gifts have within their grasp the ability to change history. Through them, great doorways are opened for us all. In their example and in their gifting, they carry the potential to inspire, equip and release redeemed people to God-dreamed destinies. All of creation waits for the sons and daughters of the kingdom to be revealed

I believe that in anticipation of the greatest days of God's glory yet experienced, the Holy Spirit is hard at work, preparing and teaching a new set of governors. He is training them to watch over God's people with His heart. These governors are going to be the prepared sons and daughters, mature and ready to oversee the greatest period of man's history on this globe.

Their lips are full of the gospel of God's grace, their hearts are saturated in genuine humility, their spirits are full of a hunger for God to be glorified, and their lives are given to be poured out on behalf of His bride. Their minds are free from selfish ambition and the love of money. They are consumed with love for Jesus Christ, and more importantly they know about His love for them. They are not small people, either in mind or spirit.

These are huge capacity people with a sober view of themselves and a firm grasp on who their God is. This book is written with the hopes that it might stir some of you into that kind of biblical governance.

God measures the days of this planet by His agenda and plan. When He has accomplished what He desires, He will wrap up history and we will be gathered to meet Him. Yet the world goes on as Jesus said, oblivious, engaged in normal human endeavors, unaware that the stopwatch set by God's agenda races to its own ticking conclusion. God's church will be glorious; there will be latter rains on the church greater than the first-fruits of Pentecost. There is going to be a greater glory at the end of this church age than there was at the beginning. To help guide, oversee and shepherd this move, the Holy Spirit appoints human overseers or governers to co-labor with His purposes. They will be rescued from the oblivion of this world and placed by the Holy Spirit on the ticking agendas of heaven. In this, they become bearers of revelation and light, able to be creative originals in a world flooded by copies and fakes.

They will no doubt be scorned, persecuted, mistreated and hated by this world, but they will also usher in God's kingdom to this earth while seeing unbelievable glories not yet known on this earth. Of them it will be written, as it is of all the heroes of faith, that this world was not worthy of them.

If your heart does not beat faster at this prospect, and if there is no longing in your soul to be part of this revolution, then the rest of this book isn't for you. If your soul aches for a new day in the church, then I believe it will do you some good to read on. At the very center of what God is going to do on this planet in the last days, are prepared sons and daughters of the King of Kings. They have been tested and have proven true, they are qualified by the work that Jesus did on the cross and by how He has worked that work in them. Do not get weary in the process of His development of your governing ability. It is a prize work with eternal potential.

As someone who has been in ministry for years, I know how pastors and elders read books. They get the highlights of the most impacting parts from their diligent spouses who read the interesting parts to them. These chapters are written to be relatively short, self-contained topics that are relevant to leaders. I know you aren't going to read the entire book in one sitting. I expect you will read the relevant chapters to your situation or interest and will hopefully find this text an interesting and informative start. I have kept the language basic and have added the scriptures from which the points are derived in full to save you from having to look them up. In some cases the points are self explanatory, and overall, I have tried to keep the explanations to a minimum and the scriptures maximized.

I hope this book fuels your ministry and stirs your leadership gift. My prayer is for those who have given themselves to God's sheep, whether you are celebrated or full of sheep bites, that you never forget that He who called you is faithful. I hope you also remember that for all eternity you will be thankful for every sacrifice, offering, step of obedience and prayer you gave, to see Him glorified and His bride prepared.

Grace and peace is yours in abundance.

Gregory Haswell

Table of Contents

Section 1-A case for Biblical Governance.21

Section 3 Releasing God's life into churches through spiritual gifts.102

10.Spiritual Gifts 103

Section 3.1 - Ascension Gifts.113

11.Ascension Gift Ministries 114

12.Apostles 125

Section.181

3.2 Manifestation gifts.181

22. The gifts of Healing 216

23. The Gifts of Healing and their hindrances 225

Section 1

A CASE FOR BIBLICAL GOVERNANCE

GOING BEYOND LEADERSHIP

*T*here are many leaders in churches who are brilliantly gifted. They can move crowds with their communication. They seem to have an almost inhuman clarity and confidence about them. They can plan, cast and administrate vision ferociously. They appear to have the pressures of life mastered or at least under a firm leash. Things go well for them and this is good for us. They are the disciplined, hardworking, and respectable people that it is appropriate that we follow. Their leadership gift is of great worth to the kingdom and vital to the success of our lives. People who function at this level of leadership have usually paid their dues, worked hard and honed their leadership gift. Like all the other grace gifts God gives, leadership pours His grace into our lives. When leaders are faithful to administrate their gift, we all benefit. This is why leadership training for church leaders is vitally important.

Yet if we do not also inspect the limitations of leadership within a church context we will remain locked in a diminished inheritance, asking leadership to accomplish what it cannot. This chapter seeks to outline what is necessary beyond the scope of leadership. I want to investigate governing the church, of which leadership gifting is a needed subset.

WE SERVE IN A KINGDOM

Lets first recognize that we serve in a kingdom and not a democracy. A kingdom's focus is the pleasure and comfort of the king. In a democracy, the comfort and will of the people takes center stage. In this kingdom leaders or governors derive their authority from the king and not the vote or opinion of the people. They are not set into their roles by the will of the governed, but by the appointment of the king. Granted their job will be made exponentially easier if they win the support and consent of the people, which is where developing their leadership gift comes in.

In a kingdom, my favor and inheritance in the kingdom, are dependent on my relationship to the king. In this kingdom, I come to give an account to the One before whose eyes all things are uncovered and laid bare. No public relations firms can clean up my image, represent me with a more professional or polished facade before the Faithful and True witness. Only the blood of Jesus, embraced and believed, can present me pleasing in His sight and qualified to share in my inheritance. You see, here I am primarily concerned with what He thinks and wants. My goal is to please Him, with appropriate awe and fear of the greatness of my king. I understand that it is to Him I give account. I do not trust my own works to please Him, but I do offer Him my good works because He has loved, chosen, qualified and appointed me to office. My business as a governor appointed in His kingdom, is to see His kingdom established on the earth. My release in public places will for the most part be dependent on my private relationship with Him.

2 Corinthians 5:9 Therefore we make it our aim, whether present or absent, to be well pleasing to Him. 10 For we must all appear before the judgment seat of Christ, that each one may receive the things done in the body, according to what he has done, whether good or bad. (NKJV)

In a democracy my favor depends on how I can present myself to the people. My public image is more important than my private practices which are for the most part hidden. I am concerned with pleasing the people I lead. Their comfort and perspective must be served. I trade my efforts to see them comforted, for their support and "follower-ship". This is a subtle point easily missed. Leaders must learn to navigate the course their vision has mapped out for them while simultaneously satisfying the stated needs of those following. This makes the focus of leadership more earth bound and people centered than that of governing. Again let me say that God loves people and especially those who make up His bride, so a grand concern for people pleases Him. It is in the absence of an understanding of the king and His kingdom that the emphasis of leadership tends toward imbalance.

The distinction about whether I answer primarily to the Lord or the people is an important one. If to the Lord then I must forego some pragmatic solutions based on my understanding of human nature for a more godly minded approach. I cannot for example use flattery, nor appeal to the basic greeds of people's hearts or their rampant self interest, as a motivational technique, I do not trumpet my own accomplishments or employ some of the more brutal but effective Machiavellian style pragmatisms of cynicism, dominance and merciless combat. My actions are tempered constantly by my recognition that my authority is derived by the appointment of my king and not the popular vote of the people. I become more aware of His eye on me than of the people I serve.

1 Thessalonians 2:5 You know we never used flattery, nor did we put on a mask to cover up greed—God is our witness. (NIV11)

If I know I answer primarily to the Lord then I govern God's people in the fear of God and rule over them in righteousness. I withhold myself from engaging in behaviors which even though may be tried and effective leadership strategies are unbecoming my king. Kingdom governors are "hampered" and "weakened" in their leadership by their call to govern. We cannot excuse character drift through strength of gifting or excellence in execution. We will never rise above servant status and in fact will learn to serve with greater abasement as we assume greater governance. We cannot use the momentum of our leadership success and the adulations of the young followers to draw attention away from a current mistake or abuse we perpetrated. As Paul said we let people's opinions about us be constrained to what can be plainly seen in us right now. We are never allowed to dominate and Lord it over God's people for Jesus called this pagan. Even though many people clamor to be dominated through their desire to be absolved of responsibility, we do not sit on the thrones they offer, nor will we wear a crown that was not fashioned in heaven. As Paul demonstrates, when he is forced to appeal to the human nature of the Corinthians, it is foolish even though they have stopped up their ears to any spiritual argument.

> *2 Corinthians 11:20 For you put up with it if one brings you into bondage, if one devours you, if one takes from you, if one exalts himself, if one strikes you on the face. 21 To our shame I say that we were too weak for that! But in whatever anyone is bold—I speak foolishly—I am bold also. 22 Are they Hebrews? So am I. Are they Israelites? So am I. Are they the seed of Abraham? So am I. 23 Are they ministers of Christ?—I speak as a fool—I am more: in labors more abundant, in stripes above measure, in prisons more frequently, in deaths often.(NKJV)*

> *2 Corinthians 12:6 Even if I should choose to boast, I would not be a fool, because I would be speaking the truth. But I refrain, so no one will think more of me than is warranted by what I do or say.*

GOVERNANCE IS SPIRITUALLY MINDED

For the purposes of this book let me give simple definitions to leadership and governance. Leadership is the effective rallying of people and resources behind a cause. Governance is the practice of seeing that God's will is done in and through His people on the earth. In order to govern, in addition to maximizing our leadership ability, we must also maximize our spirits and walk with God.

Leadership training is concerned with honing the gift of leadership resident on many peoples lives. It is simply true, that some of the best leaders around are not believers. Therefore we can learn some great principles of leadership from great leaders, some of whom have no idea about Jesus Christ or His kingdom. They can help us hone a desperately needed gift in the body of Christ, but they cannot teach us about Biblical governance. By Biblical definition they are enemies of the kingdom and darkened in their understanding. They cannot understand the things the Spirit of God is about in the earth, and in fact they will find His work and workers foolish.

25

Now if we are going to govern the church of God we need to go beyond leadership into governance. The wisdom that is sourced from this world is a poor substitute for the glorious, multi-faceted wisdom God wants to demonstrate through His church. Although leadership can be learned from many sources, wisdom to govern God's people is a gift from God alone. The "spiritual" leaders at the time of Jesus' crucifixion did not understand heaven's agenda and pressed for His crucifixion. Their wisdom was earthly, unspiritual and driven by demons. So the fallacy that leadership presents, is that leadership that is not fueled and sourced from heaven, can accomplish heaven's agenda on the earth. History proves that effective leaders move nations and fill in the details of the earths history. God's agenda on the earth is fulfilled by ignorant and unwitting rebels, as well as by submitted and willing servants who co-labor with God.

Ephesians 3:8 To me, the very least of all saints, this grace was given, to preach to the Gentiles the unfathomable riches of Christ, 9 and to bring to light what is the administration of the mystery which for ages has been hidden in God who created all things; 10 so that the manifold wisdom of God might now be made known through the church to the rulers and the authorities in the heavenly places. 11 This was in accordance with the eternal purpose which He carried out in Christ Jesus our Lord, 12 in whom we have boldness and confident access through faith in Him. (NASB)

1 Corinthians 2:6 We do, however, speak a message of wisdom among the mature, but not the wisdom of this age or of the rulers of this age, who are coming to nothing. 7 No, we speak of God's secret wisdom, a wisdom that has been hidden and that God destined for our glory before time began. 8 None of the rulers of this age understood it, for if they had, they would not have crucified the Lord of glory. (NIV1984)

James 3:13 Who is wise and understanding among you? Let him show by good conduct that his works are done in the meekness of wisdom. 14 But if you have bitter envy and self-seeking in your hearts, do not boast and lie against the truth. 15 This wisdom does not descend from above, but is earthly, sensual, demonic. 16 For where envy and self-seeking exist, confusion and every evil thing are there. 17 But the wisdom that is from above is first pure, then peaceable, gentle, willing to yield, full of mercy and good fruits, without partiality and without hypocrisy. 18 Now the fruit of righteousness is sown in peace by those who make peace. (NKJV)

THE SKILLS OF GOVERNORS

People committed to governing God's people in His fear, will have to go beyond all the leadership skill that can be taught, into a much more important class where the tools of government are taught. Here are a few examples;

HEARING GOD'S VOICE

Of greatest importance is that we hear from Jesus directly and often. If your leadership hinges on how well your lines of communication function, then it stands to reason that how well and often you hear from God is at least equally vital and probably even more so. Governors act on what God has said both through His word but also through His direct communication with them. Everyone who the scriptures hold up as an example of government, heard directly from heaven. When they stopped hearing directly from the Lord they found themselves in trouble. It involves learning to speak the many languages God uses to speak to His governors. Dreams and visions, signs, repetition, unusual circumstances, multiple input sources saying the same thing, deep convictions in the leader, atypical emotion and compassion among many others. Lets face it, most of the ways recorded in the scriptures that God used to communicate would cause severe discomfort to most churches today. That is to say that if God remains consistent, we are in for an uncomfortable ride, too often unfortunately foreign to our preferred religious practice. Do you want to go beyond leadership into governing? Strap in for the adventure of your life.

DISCERNING OF SPIRITS

This is an added discernment, that comes not with experience, but through the Holy Spirit. It is a supernatural gift given by God which becomes the highly valued gift of those who seek it out. "Jesus knew what they were thinking" and so will His governors. The inner witness of the Holy Spirit regarding suggestions made, motives proffered, leaders potentially appointed. It is a massively unfair advantage about which leaders outside this arena can only dream. Imagine a team of leaders schooled in this and working together, not in judgment of others, but sensitive enough to the Holy Spirit's Lordship to make decisions as directed by Him.

LIVING DEAD LEADERS

Governors called to office, have the power of the cross demonstrated in their lives. They know that they were crucified with Christ, that their old sinful self was circumcised off of them, they were washed, cleansed, justified, sanctified, declared holy and blameless and are completely forgiven, highly favored and greatly loved. They have died to this world. They are not motivated by selfish ambition, arrogance or favoritism. They await their applause from heaven, convinced that their reward is with their God. Their treasure is waiting in heaven where Christ is seated at the Father's right hand. They have settled that they are not their own but were bought at a price and they know that promotion comes from the Lord. They know that a man can only receive what is given him from above. People dead to their old life and the applause of this world are exceedingly dangerous people and God's government is built upon them.

PRAYER

Prayer is indispensable to a governor whereas it is often a nagging afterthought for gifted leaders. After all, who needs to pray when what you want to accomplish is easily within the realm of your gifting. Governors have the same sense as Paul that they are not equal to the task they have been called to. This is an important and often defining sign of whether someone is acting as a governors or as a leaders. That is not to say that leaders don't pray, merely that they often don't feel the need to.

2 Corinthians 2:16 To the one we are the smell of death; to the other, the fragrance of life. And who is equal to such a task? 17 Unlike so many, we do not peddle the word of God for profit. On the contrary, in Christ we speak before God with sincerity, like men sent from God.

FAITH

All good leaders will aim high and many will accomplish what seemed to be impossible in team with their followers. Good leadership can achieve remarkable things. Governors are called to achieve the impossible. Our primary objective is not to deliver completed projects or services but to train God's people to believe in Him. Governors will be required to demonstrate their faith which those who follow are commanded to emulate. Your Red Sea will come, your 5,000 needing food, your cancer sufferer, destroyed marriage, hopeless victim or underfunded dream. Governors will discover the constant invitation to demand that impossibilities also bow their knee to Jesus Christ. Without this war, or if we surrender the fight, we reduce the church to what is natural, earthly and, despite our religious sounding words and buildings, what is unspiritual.

This book is written to investigate these issues. To call the church and its leaders to a deeper look into scripture and a more Biblical practice in governing God's people. Both our orthodoxy and our ortho-praxis need help. We have become far too smug for people who seem to be losing the battle for the soul of our generation. The book outlines some of the issues that are indispensable if we are to move beyond leadership into governing God's people. Its focus is on these issues and less on developing the leadership gift. I know that there is a governmental style, the key of David, that is part of the answer. I hope I can uncover some of its secrets here.

THE LAST WORDS OF A GREAT GOVERNOR

*W*hat will you say to your children, grandchildren and good friends on your deathbed? Imagine that you have a few minutes left and they are all gathered to say goodbye to you. What will you say to them? You will most likely speak words of love, gratitude and affection. Maybe you will add some instructions on what to do about your goods and estate, or perhaps even a few words of advice or admonition. Those families who are accustomed to it, might join in prayer or worship. If you had seen the day coming for a while, those last few words will probably be thought through. They will be significant to you and to those in attendance as they are the words most likely to be remembered and quoted by loved ones. The scripture records the remarkable last words that David uttered on his deathbed. Surprisingly they fall into none of the usual categories we might expect. So what was it that he felt compelled to whisper to them with his last breath?

David's last words were about a style of godly leadership over God's people, which was a dominant theme in his life and writings. I'm sure David had blessed his family and made peace with them. As he was king, I'm sure he had fully discussed all the issues relating to his estate. Yet David saved his last words on this earth to speak out a dream that had consumed his life. The Holy Spirit had embedded a vision into his David's heart, and he died still longing to see it completely fulfilled. God had promised David that this longing would be fulfilled through one of his descendants. Let's take a look at his last words.

2 Samuel 23:1 These are the last words of David: "The inspired utterance of David son of Jesse, the utterance of the man exalted by the Most High, the man anointed by

30

the God of Jacob, the hero of Israel's songs: 2 "The Spirit of the LORD spoke through me; his word was on my tongue. 3 The God of Israel spoke, the Rock of Israel said to me: 'When one rules over people in righteousness, when he rules in the fear of God, 4 he is like the light of morning at sunrise on a cloudless morning, like the brightness after rain that brings grass from the earth.' 5 "If my house were not right with God, surely he would not have made with me an everlasting covenant, arranged and secured in every part; surely he would not bring to fruition my salvation and grant me my every desire. 6 But evil men are all to be cast aside like thorns, which are not gathered with the hand. " (NIV11)

David's last words were about the Spirit-given dream of a style of leadership that brings growth and life to everything it oversees. The Holy Spirit used a simile to explain to David how He views those who govern in the fear of God and in righteousness. He said, "They will be like the light of morning at sunrise on a cloudless morning, like the brightness after rain that brings grass from the earth." What a picture of beauty, serenity, freshness and hope for all who live under this government. The wonderful promise from God is that there is a style of leadership that evokes this kind of fresh life and hope for everyone it oversees. There is a style of government that the Holy Spirit loves, and is still working to see manifest among His people. My hope is that this book may act as an agent of change to usher in "the light of the morning at sunrise, the brightness after rain that brings forth growth."

GOD'S FAVORITE GOVERNOR

When it comes to government, David is the biblical character that stands out far beyond any other. His leadership style and heart towards the people of God impressed and moved God. Many people remember David as the man after God's heart, full of passionate praise and a heart for worship. Some will attribute God's fondness of David to his fully committed heart towards God. Careful investigation of scripture shows that David was accorded this approval because of his leading and governing style. God was watching when David went after the lion and the bear that attacked the sheep under his care. He noticed that

David would place his own life in danger to secure their safety. When the time came for God to choose a new monarch to watch over His people, He knew David was the right man. David was no hired hand who would run away from predators, but a man who had proven his commitment to the sheep at the risk of his own blood. David was a man after God's heart, a man of sacrificial, servant leadership, and was therefore God's choice of a leader for His people.

Acts 13:22 After removing Saul, he made David their king. God testified concerning him: 'I have found David son of Jesse, a man after my own heart; he will do everything I want him to do.'

1 Samuel 15:27 As Samuel turned to leave, Saul caught hold of the hem of his robe, and it tore. 28 Samuel said to him, "The LORD has torn the kingdom of Israel from you today and has given it to one of your neighbors—to one better than you. (NIV 11)

GOD'S COVENANT OF GOVERNMENT

God so approved of David's rulership that He made a covenant with David that his sons would always rule. The covenants cut before the New Covenant were all foreshadowings of the New. Each one contained an aspect that would be incorporated into the New. The covenant God cut with David was one of rulership or government. God swore to David that his style of government would be established forever by one of his sons seated eternally on the throne. By making this covenant with David that was a foreshadowing of the New Covenants leadership style, God left an emphatic portrait of the leadership He approves of. In other words, New Covenant leaders can learn from David's leadership over God's people, because God liked it so much that He incorporated it as a type for the New Covenant. Lets examine the details of the covenant as spoken by Nathan the prophet to David and then as remembered later by the Psalmist Ethan.

2 Samuel 7:8 "Now then, tell my servant David, 'This is what the LORD Almighty says: I took you from the pasture, from tending the flock, and appointed you ruler over my people Israel. 9 I have been with you wherever you have gone, and I have cut off all your enemies from before you. Now I will make your name great, like the names of the greatest men on earth. 10 And I will provide a place for my people Israel and will plant them so that they can have a home of their own and no longer be disturbed. Wicked people will not oppress them anymore, as they did at the beginning 11 and have done ever since the time I appointed leaders over my people Israel. I will also give you rest from all your enemies. "'The LORD declares to you that the LORD himself will establish a house for you: 12 When your days are over and you rest with your ancestors, I will raise up your offspring to succeed you, your own flesh and blood, and I will establish his kingdom. 13 He is the one who will build a house for my Name, and I will establish the throne of his kingdom forever. 14 I will be his father, and he will be my son. When he does wrong, I will punish him with a rod wielded by men, with floggings inflicted by human hands. 15 But my love will never be taken away from him, as I took it away from Saul, whom I removed from before you. 16 Your house and your kingdom will endure forever before me; your throne will be established forever.'"

Psalm 89:28-39 28 I will maintain my love to him forever, and my covenant with him will never fail. 29 I will establish his line forever, his throne as long as the heavens endure. 30 "If his sons forsake my law and do not follow my statutes, 31 if they violate my decrees and fail to keep my commands, 32 I will punish their sin with the rod, their iniquity with flogging; 33 but I will not take my love from him, nor will I ever betray my faithfulness. 34 I will not violate my covenant or alter what my lips have uttered. 35 Once for all, I have sworn by my holiness— and I will not lie to David— 36 that his line will continue forever and his throne endure before me like the sun; 37 it will be established forever like the moon, the faithful witness in the sky."

JESUS ON DAVID'S THRONE

The immediate fulfillment of the promises of David's covenant was found in Solomon, who was his son with Bathsheba. Solomon established the temple with the design David had received from God, and for which David had made complete provisions. Yet a far greater son of David, Jesus Christ, is meant by these covenant promises and He fulfills them completely. The promise that one of David's sons would remain on the throne forever, finds its completion in Jesus the King of the Kings. Jesus is clearly meant as is shown in Acts 2 by Peter and Acts 13 by Paul.

Acts 2:29 "Brethren, I may confidently say to you regarding the patriarch David that he both died and was buried, and his tomb is with us to this day. 30"And so, because he was a prophet and knew that God had sworn to Him with an oath to seat one of His descendants on His throne, 31he looked ahead and spoke of the resurrection of the Christ, that He was neither abandoned to Hades, nor did his flesh suffer decay. 32 "This Jesus God raised up again, to which we are all witnesses. (NASB)

Acts 13:32 "We tell you the good news: What God promised our ancestors 33 he has fulfilled for us, their children, by raising up Jesus. As it is written in the second Psalm: "'You are my son; today I have become your father.' 34 God raised him from the dead so that he will never be subject to decay. As God has said, "'I will give you the holy and sure blessings promised to David.' 35 So it is also stated elsewhere: "'You will not let your holy one see decay.' 36 "Now when David had served God's purpose in his own generation, he fell asleep; he was buried with his ancestors and his body decayed. 37 But the one whom God raised from the dead did not see decay. 38 "Therefore, my friends, I want you to know that through Jesus the forgiveness of sins is proclaimed to you.

The well known passage of Isaiah 9 again speaks to this continuation of Jesus style of government on the foundations of his father David. Fascinating that Jesus rules on the throne of David, who as to His human ancestry was the leader God wanted emulated. It is also worthy to note that God has placed on His shoulders all government.

> *Isaiah 9:6 For a child will be born to us, a son will be given to us; and the government will rest on His shoulders; and His name will be called Wonderful Counselor, Mighty God, Eternal Father, Prince of Peace. 7There will be no end to the increase of His government or of peace, On the throne of David and over his kingdom, to establish it and to uphold it with justice and righteousness from then on and forevermore. The zeal of the LORD of hosts will accomplish this. (NASB)*

In the book of Revelation, Jesus mentions to the church at Philadelphia that He will give them a gift which will open and shut great blessings. He calls it the key of David. Primarily this key will open the way into the glory of God. As we have discovered, the key of David is a style of government that brings life and fruitfulness to everyone it serves.

> *Revelations 3:7 "To the angel of the church in Philadelphia write: These are the words of him who is holy and true, who holds the key of David. What he opens no one can shut, and what he shuts no one can open.*

The first time we hear about the key of David is in Isaiah when God prophesies that a king's steward would be ruler and he would bear the key of David on his shoulders. This speaks of David's government.

> *Isaiah 22:20 "In that day I will summon my servant, Eliakim son of Hilkiah. 21 I will clothe him with your robe and fasten your sash around him and hand your authority over to him. He will be a father to those who live in Jerusalem and to the people of Judah. 22 I will place on his shoulder the key to the house of David; what he opens no one can shut, and what he shuts no one can open.*

SHARING THE PASSION FOR GOVERNORSHIP

It is my belief that through the church, the last days of history will be full of the greatest works of God ever seen on Earth. Before those majestic days, the development of leaders fashioned to handle the profound glory must surely be the highest priority. The Holy Spirit is preparing a Davidic government that will bring freedom to everyone it serves. Good and godly government of God's people will open doors of blessing and opportunity previously shut and close doors of evil and harm that have previously remained open.

David's obsession with correct government was so pronounced and obvious that when Solomon his son succeeds him to the throne of Israel, and he is offered any gift that heaven can give, he requests wisdom to govern. "Since I am to be part of the covenant of ruler-ship over God's people give me that ability my father had"

2 Chronicles 1:7 That night God appeared to Solomon and said to him, "Ask for whatever you want me to give you." 8 Solomon answered God, "You have shown great kindness to David my father and have made me king in his place. 9 Now, LORD God, let your promise to my father David be confirmed, for you have made me king over a people who are as numerous as the dust of the earth. 10 Give me wisdom and knowledge, that I may lead this people, for who is able to govern this great people of yours?" 11 God said to Solomon, "Since this is your heart's desire and you have not asked for wealth, possessions or honor, nor for the death of your enemies, and since you have not asked for a long life but for wisdom and knowledge to govern my people over whom I have made you king, 12 therefore wisdom and knowledge will be given you. And I will also give you wealth, possessions and honor, such as no king who was before you ever had and none after you will have."

From that day onward Solomon's wisdom in leadership and justice was legendary. David had modeled this value so well that Solomon had it as his highest prayer priority. During his reign Solomon and his kingdom prospered greatly, like brightness after rain that brings forth growth.

1 Kings 10:27 The king made silver as common as stones in Jerusalem, and he made cedars as plentiful as sycamore trees that are in the lowland.(NASB)

DAVID'S LAST PSALM

David's last Psalm was a prayer for Solomon and includes the God-given simile of godly government as well as a plea for righteousness and justice. The next chapter will include more detail on this.

Psalm 72:1 Endow the king with your justice, O God, the royal son with your righteousness. 2 May he judge your people in righteousness, your afflicted ones with justice. 3 May the mountains bring prosperity to the people, the hills the fruit of righteousness. 4 May he defend the afflicted among the people and save the children of the needy; may he crush the oppressor. 5 May he endure as long as the sun, as long as the moon, through all generations. 6 May he be like rain falling on a mown field, like showers watering the earth. 7 In his days may the righteous flourish and prosperity abound till the moon is no more . . . 18 Praise be to the LORD God, the God of Israel, who alone does marvelous deeds. 19 Praise be to his glorious name forever; may the whole earth be filled with his glory. Amen and Amen. 20 This concludes the prayers of David son of Jesse.

David's plea is for righteousness and justice to be established in Solomon. David knew that righteousness and justice were foundational to godly government and the establishment of a throne and he prays for these two qualities to be given his son. He prays for them so that Solomon would be like rain falling on a mown field, like showers watering the earth. This is the God-given picture of leaders who bring life and growth to everyone under their oversight.

The Queen of Sheba shares her encounter with Solomon. She speaks with him, investigates his entire kingdom, and recognizes his desire to lead in righteousness and justice.

1 Kings 10:9 Praise be to the LORD your God, who has delighted in you and placed you on the throne of Israel. Because of the LORD's eternal love for Israel, he has made you king to maintain justice and righteousness."

Coming over into the New Testament we find in Acts 15 one of the most significant early meetings takes place in Jerusalem. It is convened to discuss whether the gospel was equally for Jew and Gentile alike. After much discussion, James quotes a prophecy from the prophet Amos which speaks to the restoration of David's tabernacle so that Jew and Gentile alike will be blessed by it. The prophecy concerns the establishment of the church, which emulates much of the Davidic worship. Yet the restoration of David's tabernacle is not merely a restoration of spiritual sacrifices but it is also the reestablishment of David's government under God.

Acts 15:15 The words of the prophets are in agreement with this, as it is written: 16 "After this I will return and rebuild David's fallen tent. Its ruins I will rebuild, and I will restore it, 17 that the rest of mankind may seek the Lord, even all the Gentiles who bear my name, says the Lord, who does these things'

There is a call for the restoration of government that rules in righteousness and in the fear of God. Like rain falling on a mown field and like the brightness after the rain may it rise across the earth to bring universal growth! While this chapter has served as a brief introduction to the leadership of David, I hope it has also communicated God's passion for good government and the tremendous potential for blessing that it possesses. God has been clear about the kind of leadership He sanctions over His people. When this is in place, everybody prospers because that leadership maintains justice and fosters righteousness. The kingdom of God is best established on Jesus' leadership and a Davidic model.

DAVID'S HEART

*G*od found David's governance attractive, and to understand why, let's look at some specifics. It is noteworthy that of all the biblical characters, we know more about the thoughts and musings of David than of any other person. This is the product of the many Psalms he wrote before the ark and Presence of God. They show us what he was going through and how he reasoned. I believe God left this treasure in scripture for leaders to unearth.

Let's examine some aspects of David's life that moved God's heart.

PERSONAL WHOLEHEARTED DEVOTION

David is esteemed because of his devotion to the Lord. This wholehearted passion for God set him apart from other kings. His devotion remained consistent throughout his life. When he was a young shepherd out in the fields he became a skilled musician and developed a heart for worship before he was ever anointed king. He first earns access to Saul's court because of his skill as a musician. In scripture, he is called Israel's beloved singer or Israel's singer of songs. What a great reputation for a leader, marked by His worship leading and praise to God.

We similarly have the great privilege of the Holy Spirit lighting fires of passion for God in our lives. When we celebrate and stoke the fires He starts we likewise exhibit a deep passion for God.

1 Thessalonians 5:19 Do not put out the Spirit's fire. (TNIV)

Romans 12:11 Never be lacking in zeal, but keep your spiritual fervor, serving the Lord.

There are many Scriptural examples of David's wholehearted devotion to the Lord which makes highlighting a few verses difficult. In his actions, and in the Psalms he wrote, David's passion for God is unmistakable. From his earliest days, David demonstrated that he had set his heart on God as his refuge and strength. His eyes looked to the Lord for help and he longed for the courts of the Lord.

Psalm 27:1 The LORD is my light and my salvation— whom shall I fear? The LORD is the stronghold of my life — of whom shall I be afraid? . . . 8 My heart says of you, "Seek his face!" Your face, LORD, I will seek. 9 Do not hide your face from me, do not turn your servant away in anger; you have been my helper. Do not reject me or forsake me, God my Savior. 10 Though my father and mother forsake me, the LORD will receive me.

As he hands the kingdom over to Solomon, in the presence of Israel, David's parting advice to him is to wholeheartedly serve the Lord.

1 Chronicles 28:9 "As for you, my son Solomon, know the God of your father, and serve Him with a whole heart and a willing mind; for the LORD searches all hearts, and understands every intent of the thoughts. If you seek Him, He will let you find Him; but if you forsake Him, He will reject you forever.(NASB)

David's devotion to the Lord was a safeguard for him when his men began to praise him beyond what he was due. David expressed thirst and, three of his mighty men risked their lives to secure him a drink. When they came back, David realized that he held a place of devotion in their hearts that God alone deserved and he refused the sacrifice of water and poured it out as a drink offering to the Lord. Effectively David said," this is too costly a sacrifice for human leaders, I am not worthy of it; God alone deserves this kind of devotion." The Holy Spirit's work in David's heart was to not accept undue devotion but to deflect and point these to the Lord. O that more governors of God's people would pour out these cups of devotion that their followers offer. That would help destroy the cult of leadership veneration so rampant in our generation. Submission, devotion and loyalty are all good fruit in those who follow, and are the work of the Holy Spirit in them, but these must be balanced by a wholehearted devotion to Jesus Christ. This wholehearted devotion is the capstone that holds the rest in balance.

2 Samuel 23:16 So the three mighty warriors broke through the Philistine lines, drew water from the well near the gate of Bethlehem and carried it back to David. But he refused to drink it; instead, he poured it out before the LORD. 17 "Far be it from me, LORD, to do this!" he said. "Is it not the blood of men who went at the risk of their lives?" And David would not drink it.

2 Corinthians 8:5 And not only as we had hoped, but they first gave themselves to the Lord, and then to us by the will of God. (NKJV)

PASSION FOR GOD'S PRESENCE

David spent much of his lonely time tending the sheep and worshiping God. His heart longed to be near the Lord and His Presence which, at that time, meant approaching the tabernacle. When he fell out of favor with Saul and was forced to leave Israel, David's greatest lament was that he had been removed far from the Presence of God. As Saul pursued him, David spared Saul's life and afterwards, made the following appeal:

1 Samuel 26:18 And he added, "Why is my lord pursuing his servant? What have I done, and what wrong am I guilty of? 19 Now let my lord the king listen to his servant's words. If the LORD has incited you against me, then may he accept an offering. If, however, people have done it, may they be cursed before the LORD! They have driven me today from my share in the LORD's inheritance and have said, 'Go, serve other gods.' 20 Now do not let my blood fall to the ground far from the presence of the LORD.

Although there is no introduction that indicates David's authorship, most commentators believe that the 84th Psalm is the work of David. In this Psalm, as David pours out his longing for God's Presence, he seems envious of a sparrow that had made a nest for herself near the tabernacle.

> *Psalm 84:1 How lovely is your dwelling place, LORD Almighty! 2 My soul yearns, even faints, for the courts of the LORD; my heart and my flesh cry out for the living God. 3 Even the sparrow has found a home, and the swallow a nest for herself, where she may have her young — a place near your altar, LORD Almighty, my King and my God. 4 Blessed are those who dwell in your house; they are ever praising you. . . . 10 Better is one day in your courts than a thousand elsewhere; I would rather be a doorkeeper in the house of my God than dwell in the tents of the wicked.*

Soon after his ascent to the throne, David orders the Ark of the Covenant, the dwelling place of God's presence, to be moved to Jerusalem. In Psalm 132:1-5 we are reminded that David made an oath to the Lord, such was his determination that he would not go home or go to sleep, until he had found a place where God's presence could rest. Some cynics say that it was merely a political move to take control of the Ark. I believe that David could not bear to forego the opportunity of being so close to the Lord, so he set up a tent in Jerusalem, probably on the slopes of Mount Moriah, where the Ark could be housed. Now David appointed priests to offer spiritual sacrifices of praise and thanksgiving before this tent he had established. He instigated many different expressions of praise in the Presence of God. He sanctioned the clapping of hands (Psalm 47:1), shouting (Psalm 47:1), singing (Psalm 47:6-7), dancing (Psalm 149:3), hand waving (Psalm 134:2), displaying banners (Psalm 20:5). Every type of musical instrument was employed, including the trumpet, harp, lyre, timbrel, strings, pipe, cymbals, resounding cymbals and everything that could draw breath.

Previously, unauthorized entry into the Ark of the covenant was immediately punished and could only be done by the high priest and only once a year. However, David entered with confidence and did not bear these consequences. In the other tabernacles there were no chairs for priests, but David finds a place to sit, perhaps even lounge, while he expresses his thanks to God

1 Chronicles 17:15 According to all these words and according to all this vision, so Nathan spoke to David. 16 Then David the king went in and sat before the LORD and said, "Who am I, O LORD God, and what is my house that You have brought me this far? (NASB)

A HEART FOR RIGHTEOUSNESS AND JUSTICE

David had a well developed heart to do what was right and just. He longed for a lawful state, obedient to the laws of God. He refrained from killing Saul, who had attempted to kill David twice. Although he was already anointed by God to be Saul's successor, he did not pick up a spear to kill Saul in retaliation. Rather, he ran away. He prohibited his men from killing Saul, twice when Saul was given into his hands. He had a heart for justice. In one instance, David crept forward in a cave and cut off the fringe of Saul's garment, the tassels that signify government. David had symbolically cut the kingdom from Saul. Afterwards he was conscience stricken and repented before his men, and prohibited them from taking Saul's life when they had the chance.

1 Sam 24:4 The men said, "This is the day the LORD spoke of when he said to you, 'I will give your enemy into your hands for you to deal with as you wish.'" Then David crept up unnoticed and cut off a corner of Saul's robe. 5 Afterward, David was conscience-stricken for having cut off a corner of his robe. 6 He said to his men, "The LORD forbid that I should do such a thing to my master, the LORD's anointed, or lay my hand on him; for he is the anointed of the LORD." 7 With these words David sharply rebuked his men and did not allow them to attack Saul. (NIV11)

When some of his men were too exhausted to continue and stayed behind to watch the baggage, others who did continue sought to preclude them from sharing in the spoils. David institutes an equal share for all.

> *1 Samuel 30:24 The share of the man who stayed with the supplies is to be the same as that of him who went down to the battle. All will share alike." 25 David made this a statute and ordinance for Israel from that day to this.*

When David sinned with Bathsheba and had her husband killed, Nathan the prophet reveals God's anger by telling David a story. In the story he tells of a great injustice done by a rich man to a poor man. David's heart is stirred and he cries out for justice.

> *2 Samuel 12:5 David burned with anger against the man and said to Nathan, "As surely as the LORD lives, the man who did this must die! 6 He must pay for that lamb four times over, because he did such a thing and had no pity." 7 Then Nathan said to David, "You are the man!*

This theme of righteousness and justice is constantly connected to good government as is demonstrated in the following scriptures.

> *Psalm 89:13 Your arm is endowed with power; your hand is strong, your right hand exalted. 14 Righteousness and justice are the foundation of your throne; love and faithfulness go before you.*

> *Psalm 97:1 The LORD reigns, let the earth rejoice; Let the many islands be glad. 2 Clouds and thick darkness surround Him; Righteousness and justice are the foundation of His throne. (NASB)*

David understood that God-given authority must be tempered with righteousness and justice. Without these, any kingdom would crumble because leaders would be tempted to use their authority towards selfish purposes and not to protect the people. This most often leads to the people's harm and thereby incurs the removal of God's sanction.

Isaiah focused on these traits and prophesied that Jesus would fulfill them all. The kingdom of God and the throne of Jesus are established on righteousness and justice. New Covenant leaders, born to lead like David and Jesus, should practice these as a matter of habit. Isaiah ties these attributes to Jesus and His continuation of David's throne.

Isaiah 9:7 Of the greatness of his government and peace there will be no end. He will reign on David's throne and over his kingdom, establishing and upholding it with justice and righteousness from that time on and forever.

Isaiah 16:5 In love a throne will be established; in faithfulness a man will sit on it— one from the house of David— one who in judging seeks justice and speeds the cause of righteousness.

Godly leaders who aim to have lasting impact must embrace righteousness and justice. It is not a bad thing for leaders to gain a reputation for being passionate about doing the right things and who are angered by injustice. These leaders are reflecting the throne of David upon which Jesus reigns.

A LOVE FOR GOD'S PEOPLE

As we have already seen David exemplified Jesus words in John 10 about being a good shepherd. Jesus said that a hired hand runs away at the first sign of a predator. In other words, when it is no longer advantageous or convenient, they will abandon the sheep. David had killed a lion and a bear in defense of the few sheep under his care. When God was looking for a shepherd for His people He called on David. David loved God's people. God reminded David that it was his love for the sheep that qualified him for Kingship.

1 Chronicles 17:7 "Now then, tell my servant David, 'This is what the LORD Almighty says: I took you from the pasture, from tending the flock, and appointed you ruler over my people Israel.

It was often David's prayer that God would watch over Israel. It is fascinating that God's promise to bless David and establish his kingdom forever comes with an assurance that it would go well with the people. The well-being of God's people is a value to both God and the shepherds He appoints.

Psalm 28:9 Save Your people, And bless Your inheritance; Shepherd them also, And bear them up forever. (NKJV)

1 Chronicles 17:8 Now I will make your name like the names of the greatest men on earth. 9 And I will provide a place for my people Israel and will plant them so that they can have a home of their own and no longer be disturbed. Wicked people will not oppress them anymore, as they did at the beginning 10 and have done ever since the time I appointed leaders over my people Israel. I will also subdue all your enemies.

Near the end of his life, David offends the Lord by taking a census. He is offered three types of judgments to choose from. He chooses the judgment at the hand of the Lord. While God is executing this punishment, His mercy "triumphs over His judgment" and He relents. To illustrate David's love for God's people notice his response to God's judgment on them. True to form David places their safety above his own.

2 Samuel 24:16 When the angel stretched out his hand to destroy Jerusalem, the LORD relented concerning the disaster and said to the angel who was afflicting the people, "Enough! Withdraw your hand." The angel of the LORD was then at the threshing floor of Araunah the Jebusite. 17 When David saw the angel who was striking down the people, he said to the LORD, "I have sinned; I, the shepherd, have done wrong. These are but sheep. What have they done? Let your hand fall on me and my family."

David's heart of sacrifice on behalf of God's sheep remained with him all the days of his life. He and His Great Son are Israel's beloved shepherds. There is so much to say about the tremendous preparation process that God employed to ready David for kingship. We strive to learn at least those traits mentioned here and hopefully we can join the procession of godly leaders being established in these last days.

It is always what is secret and hidden in the heart that has the most opportunity for blessing or wounding. Anyone who has held a ministry position of authority will have seen people whose gifting made a way into a place their character could not sustain. God is committed to preparing the natures and character of those who are called to govern His people. Working with Him in our lives is a vital habit to develop so that our public ministry rests on our private development. Where this is true of those who govern a great sense of security comes on God's people. Where gifting outstrips character a quiet unease slowly settles on them. Lets make sure we tend to God's work inside us, working out His glorious salvation in awe and respect for Him.

LEADERSHIP MISCONCEPTIONS

$\mathscr{T}$here are universal issues that seem to transcend our differences of culture, theological persuasions, socio-economic realities or geographic boundaries and tap into our shared humanity. In Christian church life, this means that despite our differences, there are certain challenges common to all of us who aspire to lead God's people well. Leaders will exist because people respond to them. Good church leaders must be developed therefore, to fill this leadership need. Where good leadership does not emerge poor leadership will rule because it is a universal truth that people respond to leadership.

First let's get some erroneous thinking out of the way. These next two chapters will aim to do this by engaging and annulling some leadership myths that hover around this topic. The answers to these myths will serve to annunciate our presuppositions.

WE DON'T NEED LEADERS IN THE CHURCH

Every so often this cry arises from well meaning and often sincere people in the church. "We are all of equal worth before God" they say. "Each of us has a part to play in the body." "You are no better than I am!" All of these statements are truth gleaned directly from the pages of the scriptures but as my father used to say, "Half the truth is a lie." All of us equally share the distinction of being valued trophies, purchased by the precious blood of Christ, and as the scriptures say we are the ones for whom Christ died. It is because He created us, then redeemed us and included us into His body that He assumes the right to arrange the parts of the body as He determines.

1 Corinthians 12:17 If the whole body were an eye, where would the sense of hearing be? If the whole body were an ear, where would the sense of smell be? 18 But in fact God has placed the parts in the body, every one of them, just as he wanted them to be. 19 If they were all one part, where would the body be?

Our Father gifted (graced) the lives of some for leadership, furnishing leaders with the necessary raw materials. It is Jesus who gives some people great authority as they serve to prepare the bride for His return. The answer to the accusation "Who died and put you in charge?" is Jesus. When He ascended, He appointed some to be leaders of His people. It is the Holy Spirit who anoints leaders with wisdom, discernment and the ability to inspire others. In other words, leadership is a God-ordained and God-appointed role.

The truth is that while we all bear the same call to heavenly dwellings, we do not share the same specific callings to the particular joys, opportunities, service, sacrifice and sufferings that make up the individual races God has marked out for us. All believers; while beloved by God, bought by Jesus and anointed by the Spirit, are not equally gifted, nor do we bear the same capacity. We are not equal in faithfulness, or obedience, or in faith and responsiveness to God's words. We each have distinct roles in the body just as Paul said. Here, there exists no fairness as some understand it. There are parts of the body that are up front and in the spotlight and there are those that are behind the scenes and less presentable as Paul says;

1 Corinthians 12:20 As it is, there are many parts, but one body. 21 The eye cannot say to the hand, "I don't need you!" And the head cannot say to the feet, "I don't need you!" 22 On the contrary, those parts of the body that seem to be weaker are indispensable, 23 and the parts that we think are less honorable we treat with special honor. And the parts that are unpresentable are treated with special modesty, 24 while our presentable parts need no special treatment. But God has put the body together, giving greater honor to the parts that lacked it,

Notice again how it is God's role to put His body together according to His plan, a plan designed to bring maximum glory to Jesus.God chooses, calls, appoints, anoints and equips those He wants to lead His Church. He delegates degrees of authority to them as He wills.

DO WE NEED A SPECIFIC LEADER, WHY NOT SHARE THE LEADERSHIP AMONG US?

We will discuss the plurality of leadership as the distinct scriptural model for local churches in greater detail later, but for now we will focus on the fact that God appoints one among them to lead. This mantle of leadership is both necessary and natural to human beings. This leadership responsibility causes that person to be a first among equals. Recognizing their unique role does not require the people to always agree with them. There are many Scriptural examples of set-apart leaders. Here are a few;

MICHAEL IS CALLED CHIEF ANGEL

(Daniel 10:13 But the prince of the Persian kingdom resisted me twenty-one days. Then Michael, one of the chief princes, came to help me,)

THERE WERE CHIEF MUSICIANS AND CHIEF LEVITES IN DAVID'S TABERNACLE

(1 Chronicles 15:22   Kenaniah the head Levite was in charge of the singing; that was his responsibility because he was skillful at it. - For the chief musician Psalm 4,5 and 6)

In Jesus' day He recognized the chief priests (Luke 9:22), Chief Pharisees (Luke 14:1), Rulers of the synagogue (Acts 18:8, 17). Paul recognized the high priest and apologized for criticizing him. (Acts 23:1-5)

THE EARLY CHURCH RECOGNIZED LEADERSHIP AMONG THEMSELVES.

(Acts 15:22 Then the apostles and elders, with the whole church, decided to choose some of their own men and send

them to Antioch with Paul and Barnabas. They chose Judas (called Barsabbas) and Silas, two men who were leaders among the brothers.)

Moses (Exodus 18:17 - 26), Joshua (Josh 7:6, 8:10, 20:4) Samuel (1 Sam 15:30) David (2 Sam 5:3, 1 Chron 11:3) Solomon (1 Kings 8:1,2 Chron 5:2,4) and many more. There were head Levites, chief priests, heads of tribes, heads of clans, leaders of tens, hundred and thousands.

NEW TESTAMENT EXAMPLES INCLUDE:

Peter, who clearly assumed a leadership role. (Matt 16:18,19 see also Acts 1:15, 2:14, 3:4 - 25, 4:8 - 12 etc.) James, who raps up the council in Jerusalem vital to the future of the gentiles and the faith (Acts 12:17, 15:1, 13 - 22), Paul and the Ephesian Church who recognize his right to lead (Acts 19:10 - 11, 18:11, 20:17 - 35). Timothy, whom church history accords as the leader of the Ephesian Church. Titus, ordained the leader of the church of Crete when Paul exhorted him to continue in his leadership role (Titus 1:5) and many more. God has always used leaders and holds them personally to account for the way they lead.

There are also the various single messengers to each of the churches in the book of Revelation. The form of the address they used mirrored the games of Domitian, in which he would have the leader of a portion of his kingdom report to him. Domitian used the speech patterns of "I commend you for the following but have the following against you." The first century Christians reading the book of Revelation would have understood the analogy equating the leaders of the regions to God-appointed leaders in the church. While no one is consummately gifted with all truth, wisdom or ability, there is one person that God appoints and who He holds responsible for the execution of His will in a given context. The manner in which they exercise that authority is vitally important in helping people follow and grow.

GOVERNMENT IS UGLY AND UNGODLY

Sometimes, those who are not comfortable with confrontation or not aware of dangers to the flock, react badly when governors have to exercise decision-making authority, especially in correction and rebuke. In those people's defense, sometimes it is just overbearing leaders displaying personal weaknesses. Some of these leaders are drunk with the use of authority God gave them to build the church up. Governors have no authority to harm the church or to lord it over her. This is covered in greater detail later in this book but let's take time now to read Paul's assertion of the limits of His God-given authority.

2 Corinthians 10:8 For even if I boast somewhat freely about the authority the Lord gave us for building you up rather than pulling you down, I will not be ashamed of it.

2 Corinthians 13:10 This is why I write these things when I am absent, that when I come I may not have to be harsh in my use of authority—the authority the Lord gave me for building you up, not for tearing you down.

For whatever reason, some people reject leadership and church government because it seems ugly or ungodly as it sometimes has to deal with the ugly side of human nature and of life. The "why can't we all just get along" crowd will not easily agree with the necessary use of authority leaders are often forced to exercise in defense of the flock.

THREE DANGERS TO THE FLOCK

Shepherds usually have to watch for three destructive foes. First, they must watch for predators whose primary desire is the destruction, devastation and devouring of sheep. Next they have to deal with sheep who have a contagious disease and lastly, and perhaps the most dangerous, are errant shepherds.

Lets look at predator first. These wolves, in rebellion to God and His appointed leaders, will seek the destruction of the flock. Their attitude comes from a devilish source and mirrors the rebellion of God's enemy. Scripture shows the devil's rebellion against God's government and how, in his arrogance, he aimed to defy God and deify himself. (Isaiah 14:12 - 14, Ezzekial 28:1 - 19; John 8:44; 2 Peter 2:4; Jude 6). Finding himself on earth, the enemy preyed on man to join him by choosing rebellion against the explicit command of God (Genesis 3:1-6). That rebellion against authority remains a significant force of the enemy who tries, whenever possible, to bring destruction to order and government because it benefits his kingdom of anarchy.

Each form of legitimate government will be attacked by the enemy because he is called the lawless one. Jesus said that a house divided against itself cannot stand, and so it is the primary goal of the enemy to bring division. The greatest preventive force to this division is the mature functioning of God-ordained government. Let me say it again, the enemy's plans are thwarted when there is good government, as it is the best protection against division and destruction. It is the responsibility of shepherd leaders to put the wolves to flight or to destroy them. Their influence on God's sheep must be removed. Often this means that a confrontation is necessary. Nowhere in history have tyrants responded to gentle requests and diplomacy. Aggressors must be confronted and resisted. This confrontation falls to leaders and shepherds of God's flock.

In most cases, the person who supports and affirms government, is allied to the will of God who establishes government. Those who constantly reject, question or fight government, ally themselves with the devil's purposes. People who do not submit to an authority set themselves up as an authority. A rejection of God's government in its various forms is a vote for self-government.

Continuing to speak of wolves, the problem often comes when the wolves have put on sheep's clothing, feigning submission to leadership and yet insidiously trying to weed out the weak sheep from the flock. Paul put it this way;

Acts 20:29 For I know this, that after my departure savage wolves will come in among you, not sparing the flock. 30 Also from among yourselves men will rise up, speaking perverse things, to draw away the disciples after themselves. 31 Therefore watch, and remember that for three years I did not cease to warn everyone night and day with tears. (NKJV)

Some people, who have not yet seen through the wolves' disguise, are shocked with the necessary violence against what is a terrible threat to the flock of God. Often these wolves' level accusations and half truths against shepherds in whispered slights to other sheep. Eventually, to deal with them leaders must bring into the open the things being said. Paul had to do this with the Corinthian church where "super apostles" were maligning him and his ministry. Paul had to become "worldly" in his defense of himself, justifying, promoting and validating his ministry, the very thing he did not want to do.

2 Corinthians 12: 11 I have made a fool of myself, but you drove me to it. I ought to have been commended by you, for I am not in the least inferior to the "super-apostles," even though I am nothing. (NIV11)

Yet a potentially more dangerous threat needs to be dealt with by God's shepherds. This is the threat of sheep who bear a contagious virus. They are sick, bound up with a potentially destructive disease. It may be a festering hurt they incurred a long time ago, under other leadership, in different circumstances, but without healing, it can become a festering sore and a bitter root spread to the flock. It may be a cherished unbelief or a nursed cynicism, a sinful hatred or a personal evaluation which is not sober. If these diseased sheep are not being healed then they need to be isolated and attended to before their infectious disease infects the whole flock. Described in a different metaphor, these diseased sheep are like a little leaven that will spread through all the dough. The writer of the book of Hebrews admonishes;

Hebrews 3:12 See to it, brothers and sisters, that none of you has a sinful, unbelieving heart that turns away from the living God. 13 But encourage one another daily, as long as it is called "Today," so that none of you may be hardened by sin's deceitfulness.

Hebrews 12:15 See to it that no one misses the grace of God and that no bitter root grows up to cause trouble and defile many. 16 See that no one is sexually immoral, or is godless like Esau, who for a single meal sold his inheritance rights as the oldest son.

1 Corinthians 5:1 It is actually reported that there is sexual immorality among you, and such sexual immorality as is not even named among the Gentiles—that a man has his father's wife! 2 And you are puffed up, and have not rather mourned, that he who has done this deed might be taken away from among you. . . 6 Your glorying is not good. Do you not know that a little leaven leavens the whole lump? 7 Therefore purge out the old leaven, that you may be a new lump, since you truly are unleavened. (NKJV)

Shepherds step in to lovingly confront these diseases of the mind or heart. This intervention is for the healing of both the sick sheep and the rest of the flock. Often, when there is rebellion, the sick sheep will protest, most times loudly and publicly, proclaiming the injustice of the leaders. Very seldom will those receiving correction embrace it willingly even when they know it is right. Many times a correction brought to these people in private, will become a twisted one sided version that favors them. This happens because they have rebellious hearts and refuse to submit to leadership. They will often broadcast their half-truths throughout the flock, positioning the leadership as brutal and as uncaring overseers in the eyes of the sheep. Although Proverbs cautions us against listening to only one side of a story many people in the congregation will listen and believe stories they hear from disgruntled church members. The New Testament suggests that accusations against elders should be disregarded when they originate from a single source. If multiple testimonies are brought against an Elder, he must be dealt with publicly.

1 Timothy 5:18 For Scripture says, "Do not muzzle an ox while it is treading out the grain," and "The worker deserves his wages." 19 Do not entertain an accusation against an elder unless it is brought by two or three witnesses. 20 But those elders who are sinning you are to reprove before everyone, so that the others may take warning. (NIV11)

Often, protection of the sheep through rebuke is mistaken for harshness. Yet Paul charges Timothy to embrace correction. Correction is to be done with great patience and careful instruction. Leaders inflict the most pain when they do not use patience and care in rebuke.

2 Timothy 4:1 In the presence of God and of Christ Jesus, who will judge the living and the dead, and in view of his appearing and his kingdom, I give you this charge: 2 Preach the word; be prepared in season and out of season; correct, rebuke and encourage—with great patience and careful instruction. 3 For the time will come when people will not put up with sound doctrine. Instead, to suit their own desires, they will gather around them a great number of teachers to say what their itching ears want to hear.

When God created humans beings, He created government for their protection and welfare. Scripture teaches that government is ordained by God. Without government, lawlessness and anarchy prevail and produce destruction. People were created to be governed in the home, in the church, and in the nation they live in.

1 Corinthians 11: 3 But I want you to realize that the head of every man is Christ, and the head of the woman is man, and the head of Christ is God.

1 Corinthians 12:28 And in the church God has appointed first of all apostles, second prophets, third teachers, then workers of miracles, also those having gifts of healing, those able to help others, those with gifts of administration, and those speaking in different kinds of tongues.

Romans 13:1 Everyone must submit himself to the governing authorities, for there is no authority except that which God has established. The authorities that exist have been established by God. Rom 13:2 Consequently, he who rebels against the authority is rebelling against what God has instituted, and those who do so will bring judgment on themselves.

Last we need to confront and teach our people to avoid errant shepherds. Those once faithful leaders of God's flock who have turned away to error with a continuing passion for more. Many such examples exist in scripture and we are warned about many in the New Testaments pages. People like; Nicolas of the Nicolaitans of Rev 2:6, Balaam of Jude 1:11, 2 Peter 2:15, Rev 2:14, Jezebel of Rev 2:18-29 as well as groupings like the Pharisees, Sadducees and teachers of the law.

Those who are not ready to govern in the Spirit will be ill equipped to deal with these people who represent essentially a spiritual onslaught to the church.

We will discuss some myths in the next chapter.

MORE MISCONCEPTIONS

THE SCRIPTURES ARE NOT CLEAR ON CHURCH GOVERNMENT.

*S*ome suggest that the scriptures are not clear about God's desire for the government of His church. We should not fall into the illusion that Jesus is nonchalant about how His church should be led. This view of an ambivalent God who sets things in motion and then removes Himself, has sadly crept into the operational philosophies of many churches. If God has been silent on leadership, and assuming we accept the need for leaders, we must then seek input elsewhere. The "it's up to us" philosophy tends to look to the most modern leadership trends for the solution. While there are tremendous truths to be learned and examples to be admired, the scriptures offer a consistent and timeless wisdom set apart from popular culture.

The leadership of the church must continue in the revealed wisdom of God and not the cheap wisdom of the world. The church is God's dwelling place, His tabernacle. It is the mystery long kept hidden in God, whose beauty prophets only longed to see. Even the angels longed to look into this mystery. In time, God revealed His eternal plan through revelation. It seems now that the modern church says, "Thanks Lord for this revelation, we'll take it from here. We have excellent leadership manuals and procedural courses. We have leadership experts who will whip the church into shape." This lack of humility before the eternal plan of God is shocking to those who see some of the bigger picture. It assumes that leaders, not filled and led by the Holy Spirit, can lead the church.

GOD DOESN'T MIND HOW WE BUILD THE CHURCH AS LONG AS WE DO IT.

The scriptures show that God who has always presided over the creation and administration of His tabernacles with the greatest care. Each of the major tabernacles had the following similar elements. They had a careful pattern which had been prescribed by God. They were built by Holy Spirit appointed craftsmen. They were filled or 'staffed' by a priesthood and were instituted by the consuming of sacrifices by heavenly fire. Let's examine each of these elements in the different tabernacles God established.

MOSES TABERNACLE PLANS

God was insistent that the Tabernacle of Moses be built according to His specific pattern. It was to mimic the real tabernacle in heaven. The following scriptures show God's instruction.

Exodus 25:9 Make this tabernacle and all its furnishings exactly like the pattern I will show you.

Exodus 25:40 See that you make them according to the pattern shown you on the mountain.

Exodus 26:30 "Set up the tabernacle according to the plan shown you on the mountain.

Numbers 8:4 The lamp stand was made exactly like the pattern the LORD had shown Moses.

Acts 7:44 "Our forefathers had the tabernacle of the Testimony with them in the desert. It had been made as God directed Moses, according to the pattern he had seen.

Hebrews 8:5 They serve at a sanctuary that is a copy and shadow of what is in heaven. This is why Moses was warned when he was about to build the tabernacle: "See to it that you make everything according to the pattern shown you on the mountain."

In addition to supplying the plan for the tabernacle God also chose the builders. He anointed these people with the skills to work with various mediums. This special God anointed ability in order enabled the tabernacle 's completion. Here is what the Lord said to Moses;

Exodus 31:1 Then the LORD said to Moses, 2 "See, I have chosen Bezalel son of Uri, the son of Hur, of the tribe of Judah, 3 and I have filled him with the Spirit of God, with skill, ability and knowledge in all kinds of crafts-- 4 to make artistic designs for work in gold, silver and bronze, 5 to cut and set stones, to work in wood, and to engage in all kinds of craftsmanship. 6 Moreover, I have appointed Oholiab son of Ahisamach, of the tribe of Dan, to help him. Also I have given skill to all the craftsmen to make everything I have commanded you: 7 the Tent of Meeting, the ark of the Testimony with the atonement cover on it, and all the other furnishings of the tent-- 8 the table and its articles, the pure gold lampstand and all its accessories, the altar of incense, 9 the altar of burnt offering and all its utensils, the basin with its stand-- 10 and also the woven garments, both the sacred garments for Aaron the priest and the garments for his sons when they serve as priests, 11 and the anointing oil and fragrant incense for the Holy Place. They are to make them just as I commanded you."

MOSES TABERNACLE PRIESTS

After Israel refused God's offer to be a kingdom of priests, God commanded Moses to choose priests from the tribe of Levi. The Levites displayed their zeal for the Lord when Moses came down from Mount Sinai and killed the three thousand who would not obey the word of the Lord. On that day, the Levites became the priesthood of blood and death. Here are the relevant scriptures;

Exodus 19:5 Now if you obey me fully and keep my covenant, then out of all nations you will be my treasured possession. Although the whole earth is mine, 6 you will be for me a kingdom of priests and a holy nation.' These are the words you are to speak to the Israelites."

Exodus 32:25 And when Moses saw that the people were naked (for Aaron had made them naked unto their shame among their enemies), 26 then Moses stood in the gate of the camp and said, "Who is on the Lord'S side? Let him come unto me." And all the sons of Levi gathered themselves together unto him. 27 And he said unto them, "Thus saith the Lord God of Israel: 'Put every man his sword by his side, and go in and out from gate to gate throughout the camp, and slay every man his brother, and every man his companion, and every man his neighbor.'"28 And the children of Levi did according to the word of Moses, and there fell of the people that day about three thousand men. 29 For Moses had said, "Consecrate yourselves today to the Lord, even every man upon his son and upon his brother, that He may bestow upon you a blessing this day." (NKJV)

MOSES TABERNACLE FIRE

The last element of this tabernacle was the consuming of sacrifices by Holy fire. On the day it was dedicated, Moses' tabernacle was ratified by fire from God's Presence. In that moment, a fitting dwelling place for the Lord Almighty was established.

Leviticus 9:22 Then Aaron lifted his hands toward the people and blessed them. And having sacrificed the sin offering, the burnt offering and the fellowship offering, he stepped down. 23 Moses and Aaron then went into the Tent of Meeting. When they came out, they blessed the people; and the glory of the LORD appeared to all the people. 24 Fire came out from the presence of the LORD and consumed the burnt offering and the fat portions on the altar. And when all the people saw it, they shouted for joy and fell facedown.

Later in Israel's history we see the tabernacle of Solomon being established with similar instruction.. David received the plans from the Lord and made all the provisions for it's establishment. It is clear from both of these examples that God desires to be the chief architect of His dwelling place. In the New Testament this means He watches over His church and is very interested in the exact details of her establishment.

1 Chronicles 28:11 Then David gave his son Solomon the plans for the portico of the temple, its buildings, its storerooms, its upper parts, its inner rooms and the place of atonement. 12 He gave him the plans of all that the Spirit had put in his mind for the courts of the temple of the LORD and all the surrounding rooms, for the treasuries of the temple of God and for the treasuries for the dedicated things. 14 He designated the weight of gold for all the gold articles to be used in various kinds of service, and the weight of silver for all the silver articles to be used in various kinds of service: 15 the weight of gold for the gold lampstands and their lamps, with the weight for each lampstand and its lamps; and the weight of silver for each silver lampstand and its lamps, according to the use of each lampstand; 16 the weight of gold for each table for consecrated bread; the weight of silver for the silver tables; 17 the weight of pure gold for the forks, sprinkling bowls and pitchers; the weight of gold for each gold dish; the weight of silver for each silver dish; 18 and the weight of the refined gold for the altar of incense. He also gave him the plan for the chariot, that is, the cherubim of gold that spread their wings and shelter the ark of the covenant of the LORD. 19 "All this," David said, "I have in writing from the hand of the LORD upon me, and he gave me understanding in all the details of the plan."

SOLOMON"S TABERNACLE ARTISANS

As we have seen, God not only gave the details of the plan but also selected the skilled craftsmen that would execute the plan.

1 Kings 5:18 The craftsmen of Solomon and Hiram and the men of Gebal cut and prepared the timber and stone for the building of the temple.

1 Kings 7:13 Now King Solomon sent and brought Huram from Tyre. 14 He was the son of a widow from the tribe of Naphtali, and his father was a man of Tyre, a bronze worker; he was filled with wisdom and understanding and skill in working with all kinds of bronze work. So he came to King Solomon and did all his work.(NKJV)

SOLOMON"S TABERNACLE PRIESTS

David instructed Solomon in the divisions of priests and on their duties in the tabernacle. This included the musicians and the service they were to render.

1 Chronicles 28:13 He gave him instructions for the divisions of the priests and Levites, and for all the work of serving in the temple of the LORD, as well as for all the articles to be used in its service.

SOLOMON'S TABERNACLE FIRE

On the day of dedication, the Lord again sanctions his house with fire from heaven that consumes the sacrifices.

2 Chronicles 7:1 When Solomon had finished praying, fire came down from heaven and consumed the burnt offering and the sacrifices; and the glory of the Lord filled the temple.[a] 2 And the priests could not enter the house of the Lord, because the glory of the Lord had filled the Lord's house. 3 When all the children of Israel saw how the fire came down, and the glory of the Lord on the temple, they bowed their faces to the ground on the pavement, and worshiped and praised the Lord, saying: "For He is good, For His mercy endures forever." (NKJV)

The New Testament tabernacle is a different tabernacle altogether. No longer is God's dwelling a residence of wood and stone, but it is in the living stones of a new tabernacle. It is a tabernacle built for the presence of God in the hearts of men. Paul makes it clear that this new tabernacle has been part of God's elaborate plan but only recently revealed through apostles and prophets. These Scriptures depict Paul's revelation of God's New Covenant plan.

Ephesians 3:4 In reading this, then, you will be able to understand my insight into the mystery of Christ, 5 which was not made known to people in other generations as it has now been revealed by the Spirit to God's holy apostles and prophets. 6 This mystery is that through the gospel the Gentiles are heirs together with Israel, members together of one body, and sharers together in the promise in Christ Jesus. 7 I became a servant of this gospel by the gift of God's grace given me through the working of his power. 8 Although I am less than the least of all the Lord's people, this grace was given me: to preach to the Gentiles the boundless riches of Christ, 9 and to make plain to everyone the administration of this mystery, which for ages past was kept hidden in God, who created all things. 10 His intent was that now, through the church, the manifold wisdom of God should be made known to the rulers and authorities in the heavenly realms, 11 according to his eternal purpose that he accomplished in Christ Jesus our Lord.

NEW TESTAMENT TABERNACLE ARTISANS

For this new tabernacle, God appointed skilled craftsmen to equip and build the church upon the foundations of Jesus Christ and His work on the cross. These master builders, as Paul called himself, are outlined in Ephesians.

Ephesians 4:11 It was he who gave some to be apostles, some to be prophets, some to be evangelists, and some to be pastors and teachers, 12 to prepare God's people for works of service, so that the body of Christ may be built up 13 until we all reach unity in the faith and in the knowledge of the Son of God and become mature, attaining to the whole measure of the fullness of Christ.

NEW TESTAMENT TABERNACLE PRIESTS

The priesthood of this tabernacle is made up of believers who have accepted Jesus' salvation and work on the cross. We are all called to be priests in this priesthood, and as such, we each have a specific role.

1 Peter 2:9 But you are a chosen people, a royal priesthood, a holy nation, a people belonging to God, that you may declare the praises of him who called you out of darkness into his wonderful light.

1 Peter 2:5 you also, like living stones, are being built into a spiritual house to be a holy priesthood, offering spiritual sacrifices acceptable to God through Jesus Christ.

NEW TESTAMENT TABERNACLE FIRE

Fire from heaven consumed the sacrifices in this new tabernacle, just as it did in the Old Testament tabernacles. Three thousand men were killed on the day of Pentecost in Moses' time, but the latter Pentecost brought life and the Spirit to three thousand. This is a beautiful picture of the death brought by the onset of the Law and the life brought by the outpoured Spirit.

2 Corinthians 3:6 He has made us competent as ministers of a new covenant—not of the letter but of the Spirit; for the letter kills, but the Spirit gives life.

Acts 2:1 When the day of Pentecost came, they were all together in one place. 2 Suddenly a sound like the blowing of a violent wind came from heaven and filled the whole house where they were sitting. 3 They saw what seemed to be tongues of fire that separated and came to rest on each of them. 4 All of them were filled with the Holy Spirit and began to speak in other tongues as the Spirit enabled them. . . . . 41 Those who accepted his message were baptized, and about three thousand were added to their number that day.

God's intent has always been the diligent execution of an eternal plan, perfectly accomplished in Christ and now to be demonstrated through the church. He is specific about how the church is to be built and led. He appoints people carefully to see that it is done in accordance with His word. He is not a distant creator, but a great monarch vested in His promise to build His prevailing Church.

Section 2

ESSENTIAL INGREDIENTS FOR
HEALTHY CHURCHES
- THE BUS ANALOGY

WHERE IS THIS BUS GOING?

$\mathcal{I}$ believe that more damage is done in churches through poor governance than by any other factor. I also believe that more blessing is ushered into the lives of church members by good governance than any other single factor. Biblical governance is the greatest source of the liberation of members and is the first line of defense against everything that assails the church. It is of crucial importance that we co-labor with God in the development of leaders within a servant leadership governance model.

I will use the analogy of a bus to emphasize the importance of godly church leadership. I hope to supply some practical clarity on how to get your bus speeding down the road of God's calling. God is clear in scripture about how His church should be led. We will study the passages that share this in great detail, and will also discuss the areas in which the scriptures are silent.

3 THINGS NEEDED FOR A GOOD BUS RIDE

If we are going to go on a bus ride, there are three things we need to clarify in order for the journey to be smooth and enjoyable. The first thing that needs to be clear is the final destination of the bus. Buses advertise their destinations clearly so that all can see the destination and decide whether to get on or not. No-one willingly gets on a bus that is headed in a direction they don't want to go. If, by some mistake, they end up on a bus headed away from their destination, they will ring the bell and get off as soon as they are able. Passengers who find themselves on the wrong bus, but who don't want to leave, often want to suggest "helpful" direction changes from the back. This only hinders the journey, because the other passengers are supportive and desirous to reach the end point, and the bus driver has a duty to take the passengers to their final destination.

MAKE THE VISION CLEAR

A clearly stated destination equates to vision casting in churches and is the first essential piece of clarity that church leaders need to supply. A church that has no clear vision is like a bus that has no final destination. A clearly stated church vision is integral to the purpose of the individual church and is a necessary step toward gaining supportive and motivated church members. Clear vision is the greatest motivating factor for members and validates their decision to make a church their spiritual home. A defined vision also acts as a buffer against hurt and bitterness when someone decides to step off the bus. Clear vision gives them reasons for their discomfort and allows them to define those aspects of the church's vision that they don't agree with. Those people who disagree with this bus's direction have only to ring the bell, and they will be let off with blessing and love. In our own church experience, we bless those who leave, but also encourage them to find a bus that is headed in the right direction for them. This freedom to find the right bus for them allows us all to recognize that our church will not be for everyone. When someone steps off the bus, a church vision emphasizes neither a deficiency in that person nor the church, but allows for a peaceful separation and positively reinforces the need for clarity.

Discovering, enunciating and maintaining the clarity of a church's vision is the responsibility of its leadership team. This is part of the unique role that leaders play. In fact many believe, and I agree, that vision casting is their primary role. It should not be neglected by leadership nor left to other people. The casting of vision for your members should be the most prepared sermon of the year and should remain the highest priority for leaders. Vision casting should be discussed, planned and prayed over in an ongoing pursuit, because it is vital to church life.

Church leaders should not shy away from vision casting merely because it has been maximized by people that are chasing financial incentive. Leaders, who are able to clearly outline a preferred future (vision), discover that the people they lead are energized by it and they will work hard to see it accomplished. The ability to look into the future and see what the Holy Spirit is alluding to, and then to cast it into the present, in a way that seems attainable creates powerful momentum in our churches. People want to believe in a better future and we all like to hear stories. A leader who can make people believe in his story will discover a crowd of motivated followers eager to see it made a reality. This ability may come naturally to a few, but for most of us, it is the product of hours of prayer, discussion, dreaming, longing, talking to members and wrestling in leadership planning times. We are not talking about throwing out pretty pictures. Rather, knowing the Holy Spirit's heart for your church's future and articulating that to the members will make believers out of followers. This will take diligent attention from the leaders to dream the dream and to imagine it in their minds, visiting it there many times before articulating it to those who follow.

Let's discuss some essential elements of an inspiring church vision. The first is that leaders should create a vision in dependence on the Holy Spirit. It is inconceivable to me that some church leaders consider doing this without any consultation with the Lord of the church.

Proverbs 29:18 Where there is no revelation, people cast off restraint; but blessed is the one who heeds wisdom's instruction. (NIV 11)

Revelation from heaven is the primary and only legitimate ignition of church vision. Without it people will cast off restraint. Everyone longs for a cause and for something to give their lives to. If this cause is not a clear revelation of heaven, they will give themselves to lesser things. Sometimes they will give themselves to church vision that is not the substance of the breathed word of God, but only a whittled down version of one man's gifting. Again let me say that as profound as some leaders gifts are, their limits will eventually become evident to those who follow them. Churches led without distinct revelation tend to cause people to focus only on the giftedness of the leader. There is little equipping of individuals, in that scenario, towards their own calling, but often only an equipping of them to fulfill a role in the machinery. I know that people all have diverse roles to play in the body, but my point here is that their roles should be devised in such a way that brings growth.

TAKE NOTE OF THE WRITTEN MANDATE

The church's mission has already been set by the Lord Jesus Christ. Each local church must define its vision under the shadow of the mission of the church universal. As church leaders, we should be the people who have the greatest respect for God's word and His will. We are to model for our members a trembling at God's word.

Isaiah 66:2 Has not my hand made all these things, and so they came into being?" declares the LORD. "These are the ones I look on with favor: those who are humble and contrite in spirit, and who tremble at my word.

It was this issue that disqualified Moses from entering the Promised Land. He did not regard God's word as sacred and holy.

Numbers 20:8 "Take the staff, and you and your brother Aaron gather the assembly together. Speak to that rock before their eyes and it will pour out its water. You will bring water out of the rock for the community so they and their livestock can drink." 9 So Moses took the staff from the LORD's presence, just as he commanded him. 10 He and Aaron gathered the assembly together in front of the rock and Moses said to them, "Listen, you rebels, must we bring you water out of this rock?" 11 Then Moses raised his arm and struck the rock twice with his staff. Water gushed out, and the community and their livestock drank. 12 But the LORD said to Moses and Aaron, "Because you did not trust in me enough to honor me as holy in the sight of the Israelites, you will not bring this community into the land I give them."

The second element in creating and casting a clear vision, after hearing from the Lord, is working with the current leadership team to clarify what the Lord has said. If we have the right people in the room it will be a productive and enjoyable process. If we have the wrong people in the room it often becomes frustrating and mired in unnecessary details. Generally those people who are gifted to govern will measure things primarily by their impact on the church. Those without government ability tend to measure new ideas by how they have an impact on them personally. Leaders usually have an ability to prioritize things in order of importance. They tend to see the big picture, a 50,000 foot view. They can usually step back and see the current idea against a large picture. People of capacity in specific areas know what is crucial and what is just noise. Those without this leadership function see most things as of equal importance and therefore tend to insert irrelevant detail into strategic conversations. If this happens too often, and if they insist on their voice being heard, the planning breaks down into a quagmire of frustration. With the right people in the room, however the conversation crackles with energy, creativity and a leap-frogging from one possibility to another. Before you call a planning meeting, take time to think through which people should be involved. We don't allow anyone to lead worship and play any instrument. Not everyone is equally gifted in children's church. Why do we presume that big picture strategic thinking and planning is any different? When we ignore this practical truth, the meetings go about as well as if we had got volunteers to play instruments they weren't good at and appointed them to lead worship for the next year.

This basic skill of gift recognition cannot be overstated and is of primary importance for each leader. A clear understanding and statement of someone's current grace, gifting, appointment or anointing is not arrogant or limiting. It allows us to follow the biblical injunction to give them the respect and honor that is due.

Romans 13:7 Give to everyone what you owe them: If you owe taxes, pay taxes; if revenue, then revenue; if respect, then respect; if honor, then honor.

Somehow we have arrived at the belief that a declaration of the call of God on people's lives is somehow arrogant or limiting, or is unfair to others not similarly gifted. If God chooses to give grace and specific gifting to someone, then it is arrogant and immature to be vague about it, because it goes against the clearly stated will of God. Not everyone is gifted or called to lead. We need to deal with that truth and help others to recognize it as well. The recognition of those who have a leadership gift is key to the vision-casting process.

SEEK OUT SOBER THINKERS

Get the right people in the room, who are sober about themselves and able to recognize other people's gifts accurately. With this kind of team, your planning sessions will be a pleasure. Get it wrong, and you will develop a theology that makes strategic planning an act of the flesh just so you can get out of these soul draining meetings. It is essential that your leadership team develop sober views of themselves and do not think of themselves more highly than they ought. Drunken people tend to be loud and insensitive to others. Sober people demonstrate a lot more discretion. The scripture teaches that we should not think of ourselves more highly than we ought. A self referential person will often judge themselves more highly than they ought. The scriptures teach that this incorrect measuring of ourselves is not wise.

2 Corinthians 10:12 For we are not bold to class or compare ourselves with some of those who commend themselves; but when they measure themselves by themselves and compare themselves with themselves, they are without understanding (not wise). (NASB)

I can celebrate my gift soberly when I realize the diversity of gifting in the body. When I correctly discern the need for multiple gifts in the church, it gives me great freedom to celebrate someone else's strengths in an area of my weakness. I do not have to compete or try to equal them in their gifting,

73

aiming to be more than one part of the body. I gain a proper perspective when I measure my gifts in the context of the entire body of Christ.

If we cannot declare that we are part of the eye (as a particular part of the body), but can only declare that we are part of an amorphous body, we tend not to celebrate specific graces and God-given gifts. A lack of sobriety also comes from a lack of recognition of gifting. It is precisely in this grey area that intoxicated and inflated views of ourselves are allowed to fester unchecked. Where the body and others in team with us are able to add perspective we find our most sober and useful service. Sober leaders know when they have something to add. They know when their voice will be helpful to the discussion.

Romans 12:3 For by the grace given me I say to every one of you: Do not think of yourself more highly than you ought, but rather think of yourself with sober judgment, in accordance with the faith God has distributed to each of you.(NIV11)

The leaders that you invite into strategic conversations will be the leaders who support, translate, and lead the vision into the future. (People who make a nuisance of themselves in these meetings should be taught what they could do to help or they should be invited to be elsewhere when these planning and discussions are being held.

INCLUDE THE OPINION MAKERS

Those people who are supportive of the vision should be plugged in. The compelling nature of the vision can be determined by the reaction of the members. If they engage, their eyes will shine and their energy will be high. If the vision is not compelling, their hearts will not be gripped with excitement. The goal is not to get people all going in a direction, it is to get them going in the direction that God indicates with passion and joy. If people share in the creation of a dream, they are far more likely to give themselves to its accomplishment. A shared vision becomes one that is adopted by a large group of people. Members who feel that they are able to contribute to the vision by opinions or questions will become its most avid supporters. The outlines of the direction have previously been established by the right leaders in strategic planning sessions, now the members fill in the colors and the details as they catch the vision.

An important aspect to the culture a leader should develop is to allow and welcome relevant discussion and questions. This can be dangerous as sometimes it leads us on rabbit trails and wastes time, but the potential upside far outweighs this danger. The leadership teams' culture, is primarily crafted by the leader of that team. Even when boundaries and expectations are not clearly stated, as the team function together they will become aware of these. Many church leadership cultures allow a first question to clarify what the leader just stated. In many leadership spheres if the same person asks a second question, the prevailing culture developed by that leader lets them know in very clear yet often intangible ways that they are now out of line. The second question intimates dissent, non-agreement and promises comment and debate on the leaders direction. Many leaders will not accept this kind of question and will create a culture hostile to these questions. "Don't mess with me or my vision!" is what the culture shouts at them. In this environment, the strength and creativity of the team is often limited to the skills of one charismatic leader. The innate protection, creativity and common sense inherent in many eyes watching, multiple minds engaging and a team functioning in all of their strength is lost.

To develop a culture of the second question means that we allow people their questions that are clarifying and also probative. Genuine differences of opinion motivated by a passion for truth and good intentions for the church must be encouraged. Again this is balanced by an understanding that we all need a great dose of sobriety. When the vision is emerging, times of open discussion with both leaders and opinion-makers are vital. Not all opinion-makers are in our leadership teams. There are often high capacity marketplace members in churches who embrace their call to the marketplace. This means that they cannot often spare the time to be in every meeting. However, their opinion is still valuable and needed, because usually their success in the marketplace has given them the ability to recognize the underlying structure of an issue very quickly. A meal, an office appointment or a cup of coffee with them, enables you to glean from their gift of clarity This involves them in a high level of participation that fits their schedules. It's a win-win for the church and these opinion leaders, but will only be accomplished when capacity church leaders take the initiative to set it up. These opinion leaders share our joint destiny and will in many cases be the catalysts to bring about the proposed future, as the rest of the congregation look to them for their approval or skepticism of the cast vision. Their leadership from the pews can be a powerful source of momentum. Their support when others are indecisive makes a profound difference. Ignore them at your peril.

Often there will be a capacity person in your congregation who has specific aptitude in establishing clarity and important fundamentals. Utilize their gift, send them an email listing the issues at hand, and ask for their opinion. They will usually ask the hard and penetrating questions. It is not negative, but rather helpful if you do not have all the answers yet. You are not handing leadership over to them, that remains your responsibility, but their valuable gift to you is their hard earned gift of perspective. I have seldom walked away from one of these discussions without being positively stretched and challenged. Personal growth is one of the greatest gifts a leader can give his people.

After the vision is clear to the leaders, it must be made clear to the members so that they can support and share it with ease. To do this we must create our own language. Speak out your dreams in language and handles that people will resonate with and use themselves. Much of this will emerge in the discussions that you have, but leaders should make specific effort to create these language handles. This process does not happen overnight and is seldom completed in a single session. Rather, it is usually the synthesis of months of thought, prayer and vibrant discussion. When you can articulate the vision, using carefully crafted language, the vision is ready to be shared with all the passion and conviction it has stirred in you. If you are not ready to give yourself to see its fulfillment, don't ask this of anyone else. Share the vision with the conviction that it is something worth giving your life to.

WHO IS DRIVING THE BUS? ELDERS ROLE

*T*he bus driver is vitally important in this analogy. Passengers will always assess the skill of the driver. Is he qualified, alert and knowledgeable? After the assessment that he or she is competent, no one assumes the right to take hold of the steering wheel. Such behavior would risk the safety of everyone on board. In the case of gross negligence, a driver may be asked to stop the bus and disembark but we don't allow a group of people to all have their hands on the wheel.

Whatever leadership model you follow, whether eldership leading, congregational leadership, or a more executive-like leadership model, the members of your church will decide whether they like and trust the existing leadership. If they mistrust the driver, they will most likely attempt to steer the bus themselves. This most often does not go well. A large number of hands on the wheel is chaotic and unfeasible in any church. People need to ascertain and trust those who hold the decision-making power for the bus to run smoothly. It's usually when people who want leadership start grabbing for the wheel that many people in the church get hurt. It is the responsibility of the leadership team to employ a servant-leadership style that draw the members closer to Jesus.

APPOINT GOOD DRIVERS

I believe in the "Presbyterian" style of government, meaning that elders take responsibility under God for the leadership of each local church. Three Greek words are used almost interchangeably when speaking about the roles of elders. These words are;

"Presbuteros" - which is a senior; an Israelite Sanhedrist (also fig. member of the celestial council) or "presbyter", elder. (Strong's number 4245)

The next is "Episkopos" - who is a superintendent, officer in charge of a church: bishop, overseer. (Strong's number 1985)

The third is "Poimaino" - which is someone who tends as a shepherd (fig. superviser) feed, rule. (Strong's number 4165) These three words are used of the same persons in various scriptures.

Acts 20:17 From Miletus, Paul sent to Ephesus for the elders (Presbuteros) of the church. 18 When they arrived, he said to them: . . 28 Keep watch over yourselves and all the flock of which the Holy Spirit has made you overseers (Episkopos). Be shepherds (Poimaino) of the church of God, which he bought with his own blood.

In laymen's terms, I believe Paul says to the elders at Ephesus, "Watch over the flock that the Holy Spirit has appointed to you to (Bishop/oversee/watch over). Be shepherds to these precious sheep that He died to purchase."

Elders are to Bishop and Shepherd God's sheep. The three words are used here of the same group of elders. This is no hierarchy of authority as many modern churches suggest. There is no structure of shepherds, then Elders and then Bishops in escalating authority. Let's examine this idea again through Peter's eyes.

1 Pet 5:1 To the elders (Presbuteros) among you, I appeal as a fellow elder (Presbuteros), a witness of Christ's sufferings and one who also will share in the glory to be revealed: 2 Be shepherds (Poimaino) of God's flock that is under your care, serving as overseers (Episkopeo) not because you must, but because you are willing, as God wants you to be; not greedy for money, but eager to serve; 3 not lording it over those entrusted to you, but being examples to the flock

Peter says to the elders among you that you should shepherd God's sheep, and serve them with your Bishop-ing (oversight). In this, they emulate Jesus Christ who was and is called the shepherd and overseer of our souls (1Peter 2:25) and who called Himself the good shepherd (John 10:11), whom Hebrews 13:20 calls the Great Shepherd.

How then are elders supposed to execute their shepherding and oversight of God's people? They must be respected, honored, and trusted people. They must earn these not only from their position but also from the example personal life. They are supposed to lead by example and by the force of their personal walk with God. Their lives must be dedicated in service to the body. If this is not the case, they will most likely become dictators over God's people, which Jesus, Paul and Peter all forbade.

The scriptures show that elders are to govern, guard and guide the flock. All of these require leadership authority. Let's look at some Greek words again to help us here.

Elders are told to govern God's people. The Greek word "Proistemi" which means to rule, be over, to stand before, i.e. in rank, to preside, or (by impl.) to practice. It is used of elders in the following settings in the New Testament.

(Speaking of those who watch over the church) 1 Thessalonians 5:12 Now we ask you, brothers, to respect those who work hard among you, who are over you (proistemi) in the Lord and who admonish you.

1 Timothy 5:17 The elders who rule (proistemi) well are to be considered worthy of double honor, especially those who work hard at preaching and teaching. (NASB)

1 Timothy 3:1 Here is a trustworthy saying: Whoever aspires to be an overseer desires a noble task. . . 4 He must manage (proistemi) his own family well and see that his children obey him with proper respect. 5 (If anyone does not know how to manage (proistemi) his own family, how can he take care of God's church?)

Here the ruling over and standing before his family is the deal breaking signal whether he should be allowed to rule over and stand before God's family. A suggestion to leaders when thinking about the appointment of elders is that you watch how they deal with their families and consider the state of their wives and children. That is how they will deal with God's family and His sheep will begin to emulate their family after exposure to their oversight. Elders are supposed to rule over the church, but they must do so with all humility, in a spirit of servant-hood, with great patience and careful instruction.

Second, the New Testament shows that elders should be on guard for the church. Here the word used is "prosecho" which means to hold the mind towards, i.e. pay attention to, be cautious about, apply oneself to, attend unto, beware, be given to, give (take) heed to, have regard. This word is used in conjunction with elders in Acts.

Acts 20:18 Paul sent to Ephesus for the elders of the church . . 28 Keep watch (prosecho) over yourselves and all the flock of which the Holy Spirit has made you overseers. Be shepherds of the church of God, which he bought with his own blood.

Third, elders are supposed to guide God's people through careful instruction much like a shepherd carefully guides his sheep only to what is good. The word used in this regard is the Greek word didaskalia meaning instruction, doctrine, learning and teaching. It is used in the following scriptures relating to elders.

1 Timothy 5:17 The elders who direct the affairs of the church well are worthy of double honor, especially those whose work is preaching and teaching (didaskalia).

1 Timothy 3:2 Now the overseer must be - able to teach (didaskalia).

Titus 1:7 Since an overseer is entrusted with God's work, he must . . . 9 hold firmly to the trustworthy message as it has been taught, so that he can encourage others by sound doctrine and refute those who oppose it.

This instruction in sound doctrine demonstrates the need for governing authority on the elders. The role of elders will also be discussed further in the chapter of Pastors but let's focus now on the legitimate (biblical) expectations for elders. They are tasked with looking after God's sheep but what can they expect in return from the sheep?

RESPECT

1 Thessalonians 5:12 But we request of you, brethren, that you respect and appreciate those who diligently labor among you, and have charge over you in the Lord and give you instruction,(NASB)

LOVINGLY HELD IN HIGH REGARD

1 Thessalonians 5:13 Hold them in the highest regard in love because of their work. Live in peace with each other.

OBEDIENCE

Hebrews 13:17. Obey your leaders....Obey them so that their work will be a joy, not a burden, for that would be of no advantage to you.

SUBMISSION

Hebrews 13:17b and submit to their authority. They keep watch over you as men who must give an account.

ADEQUATE FINANCES AND DOUBLE HONOR FOR GOOD GOVERNANCE

1 Timothy 5:17 The elders who direct the affairs of the church well are worthy of double honor, especially those whose work is preaching and teaching. 18 For the Scripture says, "Do not muzzle the ox while it is treading out the grain," and "The worker deserves his wages."

*1 Timothy 5:19 Do not entertain an accusation against an
elder unless it is brought by two or three witnesses.*

PRAYER

*1 Timothy 2:1 Therefore I exhort first of all that
supplications, prayers, intercessions, and giving of thanks
be made for all men, 2 for kings and all who are in
authority, that we may lead a quiet and peaceable life in
all godliness and reverence. (NKJV)*

IMITATION

*Hebrews 13:7 Remember your leaders, who spoke the word
of God to you. Consider the outcome of their way of life
and imitate their faith.*

A LEADER OF THE TEAM

Having already understood that God will raise up a "set
man" or a "first among equals", or the person who is "most
accountable"; what are the Biblical checks and balances that God
establishes to ensure that this man does not become a dictator or
an autocrat?

The answer lies in the plurality of eldership. Elders are
equal in function i.e. they share the same responsibilities before
God and must join in executing God's manifest will. The New
Testament congregations at Jerusalem, Antioch, Phillipi,
Thessalonica and Ephesus all demonstrate plurality of eldership.
This safeguards a Church against dictatorship and creates an
avenue for the manifold wisdom of God to be released. It is also
simply a fact that people will naturally relate to different elders
and therefore a team of elders committed to one another, to God's
direction and to the peoples needs is the optimal solution. This
kind of team helps all the members feel connected to the elders,
it helps the elders have multiple touch points for their decisions

and affords the Lord many listening ears to hear what He is saying. This works well when the elders are in unity and are not competing for personal gain or running after selfish ambition. When elders seek to draw people after themselves it destroys the plurality of eldership causing division and destruction in the body. This was Paul's greatest concern for the Ephesian eldership team.

Acts 20:29 I know that after I leave, savage wolves will come in among you and will not spare the flock. 30 Even from among your own number men will arise and distort the truth in order to draw disciples after them. 31 So be on your guard! (NIV11)

ELDERS ARE EQUAL IN FUNCTION BUT ARE NOT EQUAL IN ABILITY

This is a perceivably obvious fact and yet many churches expect equal results and output from different people. This will lead to frustration and unreasonable pressures. God recognizes abilities because He gives them. He functions with us in line with what He has given. This truth calls for a sober view of ourselves as well as for others. Where I remain un-sober of my abilities, I exert pressure on the team and its leader by my unrealistic and therefore unrealized expectations.

Mat 25:15 To one he gave five talents of money, to another two talents, and to another one talent, each according to his ability. Then he went on his journey

ELDERS ARE NOT EQUAL IN GIFTING

God's grace on our lives is diverse. While there are many aspects of our mandate that we are all called to share, (evangelism, prophecy, hospitality, showing mercy) there are people who are particularly graced by God to do these. This does not exclude the rest of us from service in these areas but merely gives us models to follow.

Romans 12:6 We have different gifts, according to the grace given us...... Rom 12:8 if it is encouraging, let him encourage; if it is contributing to the needs of others, let him give generously; if it is leadership, let him govern diligently; if it is showing mercy, let him do it cheerfully

ELDERS ARE NOT EQUAL IN RESPONSIBILITY

God calls people to areas of responsibility according to His sovereign will. He created them, gifted them, called them and empowers them. They answer to Him and not us about His calling on their lives. While it is true that we can encourage and sometimes equip them for their race, we should always keep in mind that He who called them will be faithful.

Revelation 2:8 "To the angel of the church in Smyrna write: - Rev 2:12 "To the angel of the church in Pergamum write: - Rev 2:18 "To the angel of the church in Thyatira write: -Rev 3:1 "To the angel of the church in Sardis write: - ETC.)

ELDERS ARE NOT EQUAL IN FAITHFULNESS AND SERVICE.

We are not all equally faithful to God's calling. While I understand that our salvation does not rest on our efforts, the outworking of that salvation does have something to do with our progress on this earth. We do not all press forward in the call of God at the same rate.

Each of us find a specific mixture of each of the factors outlined above. When we function in a team of people who similarly have their own mixture of factors, one person will emerge to lead the team. Hopefully that person has leadership as their strongest grace and has the spiritual wisdom and understanding to know when best to release other team members. Each team will have a leader who is the leader because of the divinely given abilities and graces them, complimented by their own decision to faithfully serve Jesus and His bride. The one to whom much has been given, much will be demanded.

*Luke 12:41 Peter asked, "Lord, are you telling this parable to us, or to everyone?" 42 The Lord answered, "Who then is the faithful and wise manager, **whom the master puts*** *in charge of his servants to give them their food allowance at the proper time?. . . .47 "That servant who knows his master's will and does not get ready or does not do what his master wants will be beaten with many blows. 48 But the one who does not know and does things deserving punishment will be beaten with few blows. From everyone who has been given much, much will be demanded; and from the one who has been entrusted with much, much more will be asked.*

HELPING THE DRIVERS · DEACONS ROLE

*A*s we continue with our bus analogy, we need to include another group of people who aid the steering process. They are the other, of only two offices in the local church, that are recognized within the New Testament. Elders and deacons form a spiritually mature team who care for God's people. Unlike elders however, the role of deacons is not as clearly defined in Scripture. We can make a number of inferences from accounts of their appointment and from the lists of character accomplishments they should prove to have mastered. Yet the distinct silence in the scripture regarding their roles is stark by comparison. It is such a distinct difference to elders that it is in itself a shouted message. I believes it is because deacons have had to fill a diversity of roles across the ages and cultures that no one specific list of achievements can quantify their role. The name means servant. They are to be the primary servers in the church.

I believe that deacons are appointed to support the elders as they follow God's leading. They lead from the second chair. They are similar to a mother in a household, speaking, explaining, encouraging and listening to the children as they process something Dad has decided the family should do. Leaders in the second chair can move the cause downfield in ways that are difficult for those who lead from the front. In the same way deacons will be called on to fill the space created by the elders leadership. Deacons can support both the sheep and the elders and can promote the leadership team with humility and trust. They can say things about the elders that elders can't without appearing self serving. Deacons can say a well placed amen, or be the first to step up for duty in a new plan, or be the people who pray enthusiastically in the quiet prayer meeting. In short they fulfill a pivotal role as leaders in a supporting role. Deacons are eager to step up to a challenge, quick to get involved, supportive and serving. They meet a huge need in the church and fill the pivotal role of supporting leaders.

Deacons massage the Holy Spirit's spoken word into the church. They add practical applications to the teachings and vision, and act in response to the word of the Lord. Deacons are the kind of supporting leaders we all wish we had more of in our churches. We will discuss some of their inferred responsibilities a little later but first we will examine the requirements scripture speaks to and how they were appointed.

QUALIFICATIONS

There is only one standard of living to which all believers are held. Elders and deacons must adhere to this standard of living before their appointment. If we assume that there is a different standard for leaders that believers are not to held to, our assumption does the church a disservice. Its not as though elders and deacons are to be men worthy of respect, sincere, not indulging in much wine, and not pursuing dishonest gain but ordinary believers are welcome to be disreputable, given to too much wine and indulging in dishonest gain. No, these standards are for us all. In appointing leaders in the church we should ensure that they are keeping to the standards laid out for all. Here is what Paul says about deacons.

1 Timothy 3:8 Likewise deacons must be reverent, not double-tongued, not given to much wine, not greedy for money, 9 holding the mystery of the faith with a pure conscience. 10 But let these also first be tested; then let them serve as deacons, being found blameless. 11 Likewise, their wives must be reverent, not slanderers, temperate, faithful in all things. 12 Let deacons be the husbands of one wife, ruling their children and their own houses well. 13 For those who have served well as deacons obtain for themselves a good standing and great boldness in the faith which is in Christ Jesus. (NKJV)

From this list we can assume that deacons are to be respected as they should be worthy of respect. They are not to be malicious talkers or "double tongued" or of doubled speech as the literal translation indicates. From this stipulation, we infer that they will have extensive personal interaction with many people, and they are encouraged to avoid the temptation to take sides They should have the courage and character to speak the truth directly. They should be temperate and trustworthy in everything and especially in areas of potential excess like wine and food. The stipulation that they should not be pursuing dishonest gain implies they may have to manage portions of church finance and the, distribution of money to the poor. They should have strong convictions in the faith so that they can strengthen others in truth. They should be examined and questioned before appointment, and should have a clear conscience. Their marriages must be healthy and their children not wild or disobedient. If they do not have the personal wholeness or the spiritual maturity to secure a healthy, whole and stable family environment, then they are clearly not qualified to produce this in God's household.

Stephen and Phillip are two of the seven deacons believed to be the first deacons and their evangelistic office took them far beyond the borders of their local assembly. Although the Bible does not state that deacons should regularly teach, it must be assumed that some of them should be willing. Remember that we know the names of these first deacons but know none of the names of the elders of the same church. Through their faithful service in the local church some of these deacons were launched far beyond their local role. The role of a Deacon is not limiting or binding. In the book of Acts we see deacons traveling more frequently than any of the elders whose responsibility lay in looking after the sheep.

Deacons' Appointment

The following scripture describes how the first church went about appointing deacons or people called to serve.

Acts 6:1 In those days when the number of disciples was increasing, the Grecian Jews among them complained against the Hebraic Jews because their widows were being overlooked in the daily distribution of food. Acts 6:2 So the Twelve gathered all the disciples together and said, "It would not be right for us to neglect the ministry of the word of God in order to wait on tables. Acts 6:3 Brothers, choose seven men from among you who are known to be full of the Spirit and wisdom. We will turn this responsibility over to them Acts 6:4 and will give our attention to prayer and the ministry of the word." Acts 6:5 This proposal pleased the whole group. They chose Stephen, a man full of faith and of the Holy Spirit; also Philip, Procorus, Nicanor, Timon, Parmenas, and Nicolas from Antioch, a convert to Judaism. Acts 6:6 They presented these men to the apostles, who prayed and laid their hands on them.

This text presents a number of interesting pointers. The need for deacons arose out of a cultural misunderstanding. The Grecian and Hebraic Jews had a dispute among their widows regarding the allocation of food. This was not merely an administrative need to ensure equal distribution. Rather, this was a racially driven conflict with innuendo, complaints and accusations of favoritism.

(The Grecian Jews among them complained against the Hebraic Jews)

The commotion warranted the gathering of the apostles and all the believers to resolve the issue. The council decided to choose seven men known to be full of the Holy Spirit and wisdom, to resolve the issue and to discharge the tension. Here again we must surmise that if the issue was merely an equal distribution of food it would not have required such lofty prerequisites.

How did the church go about selecting these men? Some sort of consensus was used which the Bible is again specifically silent on. Did they vote or debate? How did people disagree with someone proposed? At what stage did they finally decide it was to be these particular seven? What we do know is that the church seemed to be pleased with the process. What is also clear is that much of the process for deacon selection involved members. Once

89

the church had selected the deacons, apostles laid hands on them and appointed them to the office of deacon.

Acts 6:3-5 So the Twelve gathered all the disciples together and said . . . Brothers, choose seven men from among you who are known to be full of the Spirit and wisdom . . .This proposal pleased the whole group

I believe that deacons should be appointed through the process of recognition (in that they are already filling the role in serving others as the scripture above shows) as well as the process of revelation (a clear sense from the Lord of the rightness of the decision).

The disciples laid out a few guidelines for the church to follow in finding these deacons. Its not out of place to tell the church how many deacons you expect to appoint. They said that the deacons must be from among them. No outside imports here. They were to be tested men who had a proven track record at the local church base. They were to be members of their own body.

Acts 6:3 Therefore, brethren, seek out from among you seven men of good reputation, full of the Holy Spirit and wisdom, whom we may appoint over this business (NKJV)

They were to be men full of the Holy Spirit and wisdom. What outstanding people they must have been to be known by these two adjectives. Think for a moment about people you know that fulfill these requirements. (Known to be full of the Spirit and wisdom)

When they were presented to the apostles, they laid hands on them to set them aside for the office of servant (deacon) in the church. It was a particular role, with spiritual gravitas beyond a helpful hand or kind heart.

(They presented these men to the apostles, who prayed and laid their hands on them)

While in the specific passage we see only the appointment of seven men, it does not follow that all deacons are men. The scriptures and church history show that deacons can be men and women. A lady can serve as a deaconess in her own right as in the case of Phoebe. Many commentators believe that the scripture in 1 Timothy 3:11 which is sometimes translated "likewise their wives" which is often translated "likewise women" because there is no specific "their" in the Greek and the word for wife is the same as that for woman. If interpreted this way, it is a scripture speaking to women deacons.

> *Romans 16:1 I commend to you Phoebe our sister, who is a servant (diakonos – Greek word for deacon) of the church in Cenchrea. (NKJV)*

SO WHAT DO DEACONS DO? (HOW DOES ONE DEAC?)

I believe that deacons are in office to serve the body in spiritual and practical ways. They are appointed to enhance the proper functioning of the body, making up the difference in practical ways between what is being taught and what is being done. They will be as diverse in their giftings as is possible and should find areas in the church where their specific gift will best serve others. This is another reason why their specific functions are not clearly described in scripture. There are too many different places of important service to mention.

Deacons are full of the Holy Spirit and use their wisdom to keep the church together behind the vision of the Holy Spirit.. They do this by speaking and connecting to other members of the congregation. They take opportunities to re-enforce and remind people about where the church is going and what the Lord is doing. They absorb shock, and strive to maintain unity among the body. They squash rumors, smooth over misunderstandings, uproot potential bitterness, and clarify misunderstandings.

LIGAMENTAL FUNCTIONS

Deacons function like the ligaments of a body. Paul spoke of the body of Christ needing ligaments to hold it together.

Colossians 2:19 He has lost connection with the Head, from whom the whole body, supported and held together by its ligaments and sinews, grows as God causes it to grow.

Ephesians 4:16 From him the whole body, joined and held together by every supporting ligament, grows and builds itself up in love, as each part does its work.

Ligaments have three main functions in the body of Christ according to the scriptures above.. Firstly, they supply materials and nourishment that maintain unity in the body. Deacons are aware of those things that can cause potential disruption to the body. They supply nourishment to body part that needs it. This comes from the Greek word used in the previous scriptures called "epichoregeo" which means to furnish besides, fully supply, give nourishment to. Just as in an argument the two parties seek out ammunition against one another, so the deacon seeks out ammunition and supplies that will foster peace and unity among parties. Practically this means that they will speak words of reconciliation, love and honesty. They will focus people on viewpoints and perspectives that bring out the best in others. They constantly point out the nature of God and ascribe greatness and glory to Him.

Secondly, deacons in this ligamental role, drive unity. This comes from the Greek word "sumbibazo"-which is translated as "held together" in English, which means to force, to drive together, unite, knit together (it is a continuous action). They plan unity, organize it by deliberate action and will walk across rooms to facilitate connections between people. They foster acceptance and will never let someone be excluded.

Thirdly, deacons organize people and cultivate systems that maintain healthy relationships amongst members. We see this in the Greek word "sunarmologeo" which means to render close-jointed, together, or to organize compactly. It is their job to entrench a culture and structure where people do life together. They consider how to aid people in loving one another deeply. They mingle well at meetings and are constantly connecting joints to muscle and holding seemingly opposite strong forces in balance which allows the body to move forwards.

To be made an elder or a deacon is not a "promotion" as the world would view it, but rather the assumption of more responsibilities under God. They serve more, endure longer, pray more faithfully, stay later, think of themselves less, listen to more complaints, solve others problems and are thanked less. Those who accept this office serve as models for the rest of the body. Their actions are the standard for the members and should be exemplified. (see Heb 13:7). The appointment of deacons is not the primary mechanism of recognition for faithful service, If the appointment of deacons was the way to show appreciation for tremendous service, generous giving, or commitment to the church, wewould have to appoint 95% of members to the office for the effort they put in and continue to put into the life of each church.

In summary, deacons are a pivotal sustaining force in the church. They support the elders and serve the people. Their role is to love God's people and usher them into their calling in God. No eldership, however gifted, can fulfill the entire leadership role in a local church. People of integrity, who to serve by bringing their strengths, without needing the spotlight, are some of God's greatest gifts to the body of Christ. Deacons are to be honored and applauded when they fulfill the calling of their office.

WHICH SEAT ON THE BUS IS MINE?

*T*he third issue we must deal with is where is each person can find their seat on the bus. Finding the correct seat on the bus is important. Each person on the bus makes a contribution to our corporate success, welfare and enjoyment. We should all have the opportunity to bring our strength to make the journey more pleasant and productive. Finding each person a seat that utilizes their gifts is important for each member and for the body as a whole.

When each member is seated and serving in the right seat, peace and productivity in the church are the result. The right seat can turn a member from a disgruntled passenger to a bus-ride enthusiast. It is the responsibility of leadership teams to engage the gifts of all of their members. Everyone is gifted according to the scriptures and ought to be using their gifts to serve others. Leadership teams should ensure that 1 Peter 4:10 is enacted in their church by ensuring that each member faithfully administers their gifts in service of others.

A KEY TO PERSONAL GROWTH

Involving members in service and ministry and utilizing their strengths, causes individual and corporate spiritual growth. It is probably the single biggest key that we can offer to cause them to grow up in their faith. The New Testament resounds with this theme. Let's go through a few key scriptures to establish this truth in our hearts.

Ascension gift ministers of Apostles, Prophets, Evangelists, Pastors and Teachers are given to equip the saints, who in turn are built up through the exercise of the good works they have been equipped to do.

Ephesians 4:12 for the equipping of the saints for the work
of ministry, for the edifying of the body of Christ, (NKJV)

A few verses later, Paul mentions again that each part of the body builds itself up and grows by exercise within the context of a loving environment.

Ephesians 4:15 Instead, speaking the truth in love, we will
grow to become in every respect the mature body of him
who is the head, that is, Christ. 16 From him the whole
body, joined and held together by every supporting
*ligament, grows and builds itself up in love, **as each part***
does its work.

The activity of God's people is vital to the health of the body. This service produces healthy growth and fosters an understanding of the inheritance that is ours in Jesus. Our inheritance was secured by Jesus' sacrifice alone, but our understanding of it and access to its depths is made clear to us as we exercise effort and obedience.

Philemon 1:6 I pray that you may be active in sharing
your faith, so that you will have a full understanding of
every good thing we have in Christ.

Some truths we only learn in the fields of service or the plains of battle. No classroom environment provides the same urgency or clarity of the moment that practical service does. Are you teaching people how to lead? Have them start a small group and they will soon be eager to hear your input. Church leaders should think through what they are asking people to give at their church. By this I mean, what expectations are fundamental to this community? In some churches the "ask" is that members attend on a Sunday and give what they have in their pockets without any other involvement. This is a very low expectation that will likely produce anemic, disinterested Christians.

So what are the scriptural expectations of God's people? Many churches will have synthesized these to their own set of expectations for members. The expectancy bias in your church is an integral part of members' personal growth. If we accept that faithful service and dedication to the body is vital to personal spiritual growth, then we should have confidence in implementing the expectations of the Scriptures. The New commandment and the Great commission were Jesus-given mandates for everyone. These should be foundational expectations for all who serve in a local church.

John 13:33 Little children, I am with you a little while longer. You will seek Me; and as I said to the Jews, now I also say to you, 'Where I am going, you cannot come.' 34 A new commandment I give to you, that you love one another, even as I have loved you, that you also love one another. 35 By this all men will know that you are My disciples, if you have love for one another." (NASB)

1 John 3:23 This is His commandment, that we believe in the name of His Son Jesus Christ, and love one another, just as He commanded us. (NASB)

1 John 4:21 And this commandment we have from Him, that the one who loves God should love his brother also. (NASB)

Matthew 28:18 And Jesus came and spoke to them, saying, "All authority has been given to Me in heaven and on earth. 19 Go therefore and make disciples of all the nations, baptizing them in the name of the Father and of the Son and of the Holy Spirit, 20 teaching them to observe all things that I have commanded you; and lo, I am with you always, even to the end of the age." Amen.(NKJV)

USE YOUR STRENGTH TO ADD SOMETHING

Each believer should partake in the global calling of Jesus. He is not a respecter of persons as the King James Version puts it. There is so much that is wise and healthy for us to respond to. among others we are invited to draw near to God, be full of His word, offer up prayers and praises, to purify ourselves from things that contaminate, to engage in good works of charity, and surrender to the Holy Spirit's guidance. None of these important practices secures our place in heaven. That is done by the body, blood and resurrection of Jesus alone. When we believe on Him, the grace of God that we receive energizes us through our new nature to pursue godliness and to say no to ungodliness. The things mentioned above are just few things that God invites us to partake in. It is as we put them into practice and not only in the hearing and understanding of them that we are continually blessed, but it is in their execution that the real blessing accrues to our lives. James teaches us that there is a dangerous and distinctly religious deception that invades inactive hearts.

James 1:22 Do not merely listen to the word, and so deceive yourselves. Do what it says. 23 Anyone who listens to the word but does not do what it says is like someone who looks at his face in a mirror 24 and, after looking at himself, goes away and immediately forgets what he looks like. 25 But whoever looks intently into the perfect law that gives freedom, and continues in it—not forgetting what they have heard, but doing it—they will be blessed in what they do.

The operative word in the scripture above is to "Do what the word says." If you looked in a mirror and saw that you had a big black dot on the tip of your nose, it ought to prompt you to clean your face. Yet many people look into the word and discover their need for cleansing or direction but walk away without an appropriate action.

Jesus began the discussion of being deliberately diligent to do what we hear. He said;

Luke 6:46 "Why do you call me, 'Lord, Lord,' and do not do what I say? 47 As for everyone who comes to me and hears my words and puts them into practice, I will show you what they are like. 48 They are like a man building a house, who dug down deep and laid the foundation on rock. When a flood came, the torrent struck that house but could not shake it, because it was well built. 49 But the one who hears my words and does not put them into practice is like a man who built a house on the ground without a foundation. The moment the torrent struck that house, it collapsed and its destruction was complete."

A foundation of faith is built in our lives when we act on God's word. People who do this, are the kinds of people Jesus called to be a part of His family. When His mothers and brothers acted apart from His words, He adopted the crowd as His family.

Matthew 12:47 Then one said to Him, "Look, Your mother and Your brothers are standing outside, seeking to speak with You." 48 But He answered and said to the one who told Him, "Who is My mother and who are My brothers?" 49 And He stretched out His hand toward His disciples and said, "Here are My mother and My brothers! 50 For whoever does the will of My Father in heaven is My brother and sister and mother." (NKJV)

Jesus' highest priority was to do what the Father told Him to do. The smallest action is better than the greatest intention. We want every member using their strengths to better the church, not just coming along for the ride. It is the leaderships responsibility to make this happen.

Each member shares the mandate of 1 Peter 4:10 which we will deal with in more detail in the chapters on grace gifts. For now it is enough to be aware that each of us has a responsibility to faithfully administer the grace gifts that God has given to us.

Let me close this chapter with a quick review of the analogy of a body and each part of the body fulfilling an important yet diverse function. Corinthians provides the broadest overview of this analogy.

1 Corinthians 12: 12 Just as a body, though one, has many parts, but all its many parts form one body, so it is with Christ. 13 For we were all baptized by one Spirit so as to form one body—whether Jews or Gentiles, slave or free—and we were all given the one Spirit to drink. 14 Even so the body is not made up of one part but of many. 15 Now if the foot should say, "Because I am not a hand, I do not belong to the body," it would not for that reason stop being part of the body. 16 And if the ear should say, "Because I am not an eye, I do not belong to the body," it would not for that reason stop being part of the body. 17 If the whole body were an eye, where would the sense of hearing be? If the whole body were an ear, where would the sense of smell be? 18 But in fact God has placed the parts in the body, every one of them, just as he wanted them to be. 19 If they were all one part, where would the body be? 20 As it is, there are many parts, but one body. 21 The eye cannot say to the hand, "I don't need you!" And the head cannot say to the feet, "I don't need you!" 22 On the contrary, those parts of the body that seem to be weaker are indispensable, 23 and the parts that we think are less honorable we treat with special honor. And the parts that are unpresentable are treated with special modesty, 24 while our presentable parts need no special treatment. But God has put the body together, giving greater honor to the parts that lacked it, 25 so that there should be no division in the body, but that its parts should have equal concern for each other. 26 If one part suffers, every part suffers with it; if one part is honored, every part rejoices with it. 27 Now you are the body of Christ, and each one of you is a part of it.

Let's briefly examine this scripture for its message. All who believe in Jesus have been taken by the Spirit of God and submerged (baptized) into the body of Christ and we all share the nourishing streams of the Holy Spirit (v13). The idea is then re-stated that a body has many parts even though it functions as one body. If we become aware of unique and capacity gifting on others and assume that our relative deficiency is cause for exclusion from Christ's body, we are in error. The entire body is marked by its diversity. Neither should we say to any other part of the body "I don't need you!" because we are not the ones who design the body of Christ. There will be people in the body with radically different gifts and strengths to you. God arranges the body as He wills. Weaker parts of the body are indispensable says Paul and deserve particular honor and presentation. God does not want division in His body but desires for each member to have concern for others. We all rejoice and mourn together for we are one body and each of us has a part to play. Paul first introduced this theme in the book of Romans.

Romans 12:3 For by the grace given me I say to every one of you: Do not think of yourself more highly than you ought, but rather think of yourself with sober judgment, in accordance with the faith God has distributed to each of you. 4 For just as each of us has one body with many members, and these members do not all have the same function, 5 so in Christ we, though many, form one body, and each member belongs to all the others. 6 We have different gifts, according to the grace given to each of us.

Members will have different functions. Although all of these different functioning members form one body they each belong to the others. There is a sense of ownership, a degree of incorporation that allows for obligation on each members part. If I believe that I belong to the other members of the body, I must face my obligations to that body.

Many leaders, not convinced that finding everyone the appropriate seat is vital for growth, will find it difficult to make demands of the people. These leaders feel guilty that they must ask members to share in the service. They feel guilty as though somehow their actions mirror Tom Sawyers in the co-opting of his friends into doing his chores. Nothing could be further from the Biblical view. Leaders are to model, coach and equip people for works of service. When we realize that each person will be rewarded for the things they have done in obedience, faith and love, we are bold in urging people to give all they can, to serve when they can, and to bring all their strength to the task of serving Jesus. Part of the very last discourse that the scriptures give us of Jesus' words are found in Revelation 22 where Jesus promises to give accurate rewards to His people. Let's be clear that salvation and righteousness are free gifts that cannot be earned but a reward is something earned. When Jesus speaks of rewards it is in the arena of our service.

Revelation 22:12 "Look, I am coming soon! My reward is with me, and I will give to each person according to what they have done. 13 I am the Alpha and the Omega, the First and the Last, the Beginning and the End.

Make every effort to get your members up and serving, attending with great obedience to the call of God on their lives. This is a leader's primary calling along with equipping the body. These are practical necessities in helping people find effective places of ministry in your church. When people are on the right bus, with the right driver, and in the right seat, the journey is an adventure and delight. Leaders should take great care to ensure that their people understand these fundamentals. If they do, shiny eyed and wildly excited members will be the result.

Section 3

RELEASING GOD'S LIFE INTO CHURCHES THROUGH SPIRITUAL GIFTS

Spiritual Gifts

1 Corinthians 12:1 Now about spiritual gifts, brothers, I do not want you to be ignorant.

There are different kinds of spiritual gifts that have been given to all parts of the body of Christ. Ignorance of them is unhelpful and poor administration of them can lead to harm instead of blessing. The following chapters are going to focus on the different types of spiritual gifts and will hopefully provide some clarity on how to effectively administrate these gifts.

While it is true that all Christians are to embrace the great commission of evangelism, it remains that some are in the office of evangelist. We are all called to show hospitality without grumbling, yet some have the grace of hospitality on their lives. Hebrews tells us to encourage one another, yet we know that some are graced with the gift of encouragement. All members of the body are told to eagerly desire the gift of prophesy but some are called to the office of prophet. When we recognize our gifting, blessing not only flows into our lives, but an example is set for the believers in that gift. When we rub shoulders with people who function well in any of the spiritual gifts, some of their giftedness rubs off onto us. Anyone who has a gift from God has the ability to spread that gift throughout the body. Simply stated, spiritual gifts are infectious. When you press into the God-given gifts on your life, you will set an example for the rest of the body.

Basic principles

Each person of the Godhead has given a set of gifts to the body of Christ which we will mention according to the Greek word representing them. The Father has given grace gifts (Charisma gifts) to each person. Jesus gave some gifts as presents (Doma gifts) to the body and the Holy Spirit administers manifestation gifts (Phanerosis gifts) as He determines and as we desire them. Although different gift sets are given by different members of the Godhead, they all originate with the Father, are established in Jesus and are administered by the Holy Spirit. Through the diversity of expressions, all gifts are for the service of one Lord. Though they vary in ability and capacity, it is one Father who stirs them in each of us. This is the message of 1 Corinthians 12:4-5.

1 Corinthians 12:4 There are different kinds of gifts, but the same Spirit distributes them. 5 There are different kinds of service, but the same Lord. 6 There are different kinds of working, but in all of them and in everyone it is the same God at work.

There are six significant passages in the New Testament that speak about spiritual gifts. In one chapter of 1 Corinthians, Paul gives us three different lists of gifts and when added to other lists that appear elsewhere we find six different lists of spiritual gifts where no two lists are the same.

ARE THE LISTS ILLUSTRATIVE OR EXHAUSTIVE?

We can infer that these are the only valid spiritual gifts because they are the only ones God lists in the Scriptures. The question is whether the gifts listed are the only ones God uses, that is are they exhaustive or illustrative? If exhaustive, then we must take care to engage in only these. If illustrative, we must take time to investigate other areas of service where specific gifts can be recognized and released. I believe they are illustrative and not exhaustive, specifically when speaking about grace gifts. We may find significant God-given abilities in use today that are not mentioned in the New Testament. Song-writing is an example of this. Music and lyrics that accurately communicate truth and foster worship has blessed the church for years and some people are gifted to add life to the church in this way.

Some infer from these diverse lists that the subject is all too confusing and God did not intend for these lists to be clear. Paul wrote to the Corinthian church because he did not want them to be ignorant about spiritual gifts. Spiritual gifts are a part of our inheritance and can bring tremendous blessing into our lives. We must not back down from our inheritance merely because administration, accountability and clarification are required. We will elaborate on these lists in later chapters in more detail. Some say that the gifts existed for the early church era only. The dispensational view generally stated says that they were valid for the Jesus era believers only and were given as a stopgap until the scriptures were written. While this may sound fine, it is not in line with what the scriptures say. The one passage badly exegeted from 1 Corinthians has been the primary validating proof for a dispensational view of scripture. It is found in the great chapter on the supremacy of love as a foundation for all service including the use of spiritual gifts. Paul states that spiritual gifts used without love are useless and then goes on to say that prophesies, tongues and knowledge will all cease. The passage is relating to the present experience we have and juxtaposes it against how it will be when we are face to face with Jesus. Paul keeps referring to the "now"as an imperfect, incomplete and poor reflection of what is to come. When we stand face to face with Jesus, which is the "then" Paul sets against the "now" there will be no need for prophecies, tongues or words of knowledge, for we will have complete knowledge and will ourselves be complete. We have not yet attained these wonderful promises and therefore the need for and use of spiritual gifts is still valid.

These spiritual gifts are to be judged by everyone because they operate in this time the scriptures call incomplete, imperfect and seeing through a glass darkly. They are not perfect expressions of God's heart but if judged carefully will yield a beautiful picture of who He is.

1 Corinthians 13:8 Love never fails. But where there are prophecies, they will cease; where there are tongues, they will be stilled; where there is knowledge, it will pass away. 9 For we know in part and we prophesy in part, 10 but when completeness comes, what is in part disappears. 11

When I was a child, I talked like a child, I thought like a child, I reasoned like a child. When I became a man, I put the ways of childhood behind me. 12 For now we see only a reflection as in a mirror; then we shall see face to face. Now I know in part; then I shall know fully, even as I am fully known.

To start our journey we must understand three Greek words surrounding the concept of gifts mentioned in the New Testament. They will help us clarify the sets of gifts and their functions. The primary texts for each of these outline their category. They are then mentioned again in groupings together. Each of these areas of gifting is to be exercised in the church but it is the "doma" gifts that are uniquely designed to build unity and maturity in all of God's people. Here are the lists set out.

"charisma" – which means a divine gratuity, a spiritual endowment, religious qualification, miraculous faculty, or a free gift. (Strong's number 5486)

Romans 12:6-8 lists the following charisma under the explanation that we all have diverse charisma according to the grace God gives us.

1. Prophesying
2. Serving
3. Teaching
4. Encouraging
5. Giving
6. Leadership
7. Showing mercy

1 Corinthians 12:28 includes the following "charisma"

1. Administration
2. Helping

I Peter 4:9-11 uses the same word to describe the following gifts;
1. Hospitality
2. Speaking

3. Serving

Paul adds celibacy as one of these gifts in 1 Cor 7:7
1. Celibacy

The second set of gifts are called in Greek "phanerosis" – which means an exhibition, expression, a bestowment, and manifestation. (Strong's number 5321)

They are manifestations of the Holy Spirit that make the His presence, nature and will manifest, and are listed in 1 Corinthians 12 as;

1.Word of wisdom
2.Word of knowledge
3.Faith
4.Gifts of Healing
5.Miraculous power
6.Prophecy
7.Distinguishing of spirits
8.Tongues
9.Interpretation of tongues

The third set of gifts mentioned are the "Doma" gifts which means a present or gift. (Strong's number 1390)

They are found in Ephesians 4:11-13 listed as follows;

1.Apostles
2.Prophets
3.Evangelist
4.Pastors
5.Teachers

Now these three sets of gifts are thrown together by Paul at the end of 1 Corinthians 12.

The apostles expected all of these gifts to be operational within the church. Although the gift sets are different, they should all be in operation in a healthy church. The lists are found in 1 Corinthians 12:28-30 and are;

1.Apostles (doma)

2.Prophets (doma)
3.Teachers (doma)
4.Miraculous power (phanerosis)
5.Gifts of Healings (charisma)(phanerosis)
6.Helping (charisma)
7.Administration (charisma)
8. Tongues (phanerosis)

He then goes on to ask if everyone functions in all of the following gifts;

1.Apostles (doma)
2.Prophets (doma)
3.Teachers (doma)
4.Miraculous power (phanerosis)
5.Gifts of Healings (phanerosis)
6.Tongues (phanerosis)
7.Interpretation of tongues (phanerosis)

I will go into more detail on each set of gifts in later chapters, but let's talk briefly about the management of the gifts. Spiritual gifts, if poorly managed and immaturely expressed, will bring damage and disorder to the body. Each gift set contains different gifting and therefore must be managed differently.

Each set has a gift that is a "gateway gift," that is the gift which will make way for all the others. Each set of gifts require specific administrations and each time we are clear about the expectations of the gift, they tend to flourish in an atmosphere where they are celebrated. Let's examine the gateway gifts of each set.

GRACE GIFTS - GATEWAY GIFT

The "gateway gift" for grace gifts is leadership. Leaders who are not given to immature arrogance or self-interest create space for those around them to flourish. Leaders are the people given the authority to create a church-culture that can be either beneficial or detrimental to the body's spiritual growth. As we saw with David's style of leadership, everyone who lives under good and godly leadership prospers. I believe that this is the first fruit we should look for when measuring leaders. Do those who follow this leader have "shiny eyes" and are they growing and prospering in their walk with God? If we will attend to the recognition, growth and training of leaders, their gift will make a way for others. Good leaders are always gathering a team around them and assigning people to tasks that they are both skilled at and excited about. Good leaders are constantly encouraging others, always giving them opportunities to thrive. They goad us on into the calling of God on our lives by believing in us even if we don't.

Good leadership creates boundaries that act as a safety net for the church. Without these, most gifts will not be recognized nor will they be matured. People's freedom to try out their spiritual gifts is directly proportional to how secure they are made to feel. How the gifts are released and monitored; how corrections are made are important factors leaders must facilitate which create security for the body. Leadership is the key gift that must operate if we are to see all the gifts come to fullness.

CREATE A MECHANISM TO IDENTIFY GIFTS

If we want to see these grace gifts in mature manifestation in our churches, we must work with the church leadership in recognizing these gifts. This can be done informally in discussion with the people who desire to discover their gifts. It can be done in conjunction with prophetic voices who recognize and set people in certain gift spaces. It can also be done by the mechanism of various assessments available today. These helpful tools point someone in the right direction, but should be held lightly enough for the Lord's voice to be supreme. We should also be aware that people grow and develop and can therefore not be held in a one place forever.

PROVIDE PRACTICAL EXPRESSIONS

Once these gifts are recognized, we must provide practical expressions for their use within the church vision. This is hard work for the leadership team and requires diligent attention. Very seldom will people press past leadership to create for themselves an expression for their gift. When they do, it is most often because their grace is leadership. Most para-church organizations were founded by people who bore God's call but were not recognized, equipped and released to that call within the local church. Leaders must take it on themselves to create the structure and the opportunities for each member in the church to find a practical expression of God's grace on their lives. Encourage the use of gifts

Leaders should then place an emphasis on these gifts and their use. In my experience, when a leadership team gets this right, the church explodes forwards as we engage the revived passion and momentum of all our members. Most leaders are amazed at the forward surge in momentum that occurs and how excited their people are to be serving, when they make the space for their gifts to find expression. One of the greatest gifts leaders can give their people is to help them recognize, exercise and develop the areas that God has graced them with.

Manifestation Gifts - Gateway gift

The "gateway gift" for manifestation gifts is the gift of tongues. Not only is it the gift that most often accompanies the baptism of the Spirit but it is the gift that Paul said he used more in private than anyone else in the Corinthian church. It is the gift that builds us up in our faith. In its exercise we are likely to function easier in the others. Tongues stir our spirits, and establish them in communion with God. We can sing or pray or speak mysteries with the gift of tongues and it goes a long way in creating a strong spirit within us. This oneness with the Spirit allows clarity when He wants to use us in any of the other manifestation gifts.

Eagerly desire them

Manifestation gifts should be eagerly desired. In this, those who teach and preach should be careful to create this expectation. Those who forbid prophesying and tongues go directly against the what the New Testament preaches and are part of the group who put out the fires that the Holy Spirit starts (1 Cor 14:39). Stir up a hunger in your members to be used by the Holy Spirit in these gifts.

Seek to be normal in the expression of these gifts. The delivery is often a matter of the deliverer's choice. When it is possible for you speak the word of the Lord calmly and clearly, do so. Clarity is always helpful when exhibiting manifestation gifts. Remember that you are the delivery person between the Holy Spirit and the people. You need to learn to have maximum access to both at the same time when manifesting these gifts.

THE DOMA GIFTS - GATEWAY GIFT

The "gateway gift" for doma gifts is the prophet. If we will recognize the prophets they will help us recognize all the other doma gifts. Prophets have the ability to recognize and call out giftings in people. When a prophet is mature, he or she will be able to discern God's calling on an individual and be a major part in setting them into their office by revelation. We do not need any more leaders in the church who have not been appointed by revelation. Too many leaders have been appointed by recognition of their longstanding service, their faithfulness, their financial contributions, and their success in the community but the heart of God has not been sought. Prophets like Samuel will hear God's voice enough that they will let the Holy Spirit lead them in appointing the leaders God has chosen. Take care to recognize and befriend mature prophets.

HONOR AND RECEIVE THESE GIFTS

Learn to receive doma gifting and embrace them. Each eldership team must take care of the sheep God has given them, but they will enrich those same sheep by inviting and welcoming gifted doma gifts. Too much veneration is just as dangerous as too little for these gifts. Accurately reward them for their lives as they have not been appointed by man but by God. When we receive them in this way, their grace flows to us. Reward them financially in a way that demonstrates how much you honor them.

Let's now examine each of the three words for gifting along with its corresponding scriptures to investigate further.

111

We will start with ascension gifts (doma), then manifestations of the Spirit (phanerosis) and then motivational gifts (charisma).

Section 3. 1

ASCENSION GIFTS

ASCENSION GIFT MINISTRIES

*T*he Scripture uses an analogy to explain the purpose for the ascension gifts. Jesus' life and ministry bridged the gap between the fulfillment of the Old Covenant and the launching of the New. No-one but Jesus could navigate the details of such a pivotal time for all of us. Therefore, it is important to listen to how Jesus positioned Himself during that time, with the following analogy in mind.

AN ETERNAL CONSORT FOR THE KING

The eternal purpose of God for His Son is to prepare a spotless bride who will be the eternal consort for the King of kings. Jesus spoke to His disciples in language that referred to their marriage customs. If we said today "Who gives this woman to be married to this man?" most people in western culture would know that those words are used in a modern wedding ceremony. In the same way, when Jesus promised to go prepare a place for us, He was speaking the words that a potential groom would utter to his fiancé when they cut a covenant of engagement.

Let's examine the process of engagement and marriage in the Jewish culture to aid our understanding. When a family of means had a son of marriageable age, they would sometimes have trusted servants go look for a potential bride for him. This was true of Abraham who sent his servant to find an appropriate wife for Isaac (Genesis 24). Once a suitable woman had been found, negotiations began between the two families, in consultation sometimes with the bride and groom until an agreement was reached. They entered a binding covenant (engagement). Down through the ages God has sent many servants (the prophets) to find a bride for His son.

At the engagement before witnesses, the groom would offer the bride a cup of wine which was the official way he asked her to be his wife. If she accepted the cup he pushed across the table and drank from it, she was publicly accepting his proposal. If she did not drink, she was refusing his proposal. The couple celebrated with bread and wine to signify the covenant. Often they would link arms to eat and drink to their union. It was the third cup at the Passover meal, the one after the meal, the cup of salvation, which Jesus took and offered His disciples as the cup of a new covenant in His blood. I believe it was also the cup of betrothal where the king engaged in the covenant cup with His betrothed. In taking that cup, they accepted His offer of betrothal.

In Jesus' day, if a man was pledged to be married, it was a binding covenant. That is to say that the covenant was cut at the engagement ceremony. This made it even more binding than our engagements would be for us. Only later after certain preparations had been concluded, would the couple consummate their marriage at a marriage celebration. When Joseph heard that Mary was pregnant, after they had committed themselves to one another in engagement but had not yet consummated the covenant, he planned a quiet divorce. It is considered a divorce because the binding covenant was established between them at engagement.

Matthew 1:18 This is how the birth of Jesus the Messiah came about: His mother Mary was pledged to be married to Joseph, but before they came together, she was found to be pregnant through the Holy Spirit. 19 Because Joseph her husband was faithful to the law, and yet did not want to expose her to public disgrace, he had in mind to divorce her quietly. 20 But after he had considered this, an angel of the Lord appeared to him in a dream and said, "Joseph son of David, do not be afraid to take Mary home as your wife, because what is conceived in her is from the Holy Spirit.

Customarily the groom gave gifts to the bride-to-be. Usually this included rings and bracelets and other jewelry which not only served to beautify her but as a confirmation of

His intent to return for her. These gifts were a deposit, guaranteeing what is to come. It is the New Covenant church that Paul says was given the first fruits of the Spirit as a deposit to guarantee the return of our king.

Romans 8:22 For we know that the whole creation groans and labors with birth pangs together until now. 23 Not only that, but we also who have the firstfruits of the Spirit, even we ourselves groan within ourselves, eagerly waiting for the adoption, the redemption of our body.(NKJV)

2 Corinthians 1:21 Now it is God who makes both us and you stand firm in Christ. He anointed us, 22 set his seal of ownership on us, and put his Spirit in our hearts as a deposit, guaranteeing what is to come.

2 Corinthians 5:4 For while we are in this tent, we groan and are burdened, because we do not wish to be unclothed but to be clothed with our heavenly dwelling, so that what is mortal may be swallowed up by life. 5 Now it is God who has made us for this very purpose and has given us the Spirit as a deposit, guaranteeing what is to come.

At this time the prospective husband promises, "I go to prepare a place for you!" It was expected that after this, under his Father's supervision, the groom would leave to prepare their home so that when he returned to collect his bride, they had a place to live. The groom did not know when he would return because it was his father who determined when he had completed their home satisfactorily. When the father was satisfied, the son was given the go ahead to go back for his bride. Now when Jesus is talking to His own just before the Passover meal, he has predicted His betrayal by Judas and His denial by Peter and turns to give some comfort and hope to them. He is about to go into the wonderful promise of the Holy Spirit and their ability to dwell in Him but He first uses bridegroom language to bring them to a specific understanding. He uses this metaphor of a groom under the eye of his father preparing a place for his bride.

John 14:1 1 "Let not your heart be troubled; you believe in God, believe also in Me. 2 In My Father's house are many mansions; if it were not so, I would have told you. I go to prepare a place for you. 3 And if I go and prepare a place for you, I will come again and receive you to Myself; that where I am, there you may be also. (NKJV)

Matthew 24:36 "No one knows about that day or hour, not even the angels in heaven, nor the Son, but only the Father. . . 42 "Therefore keep watch, because you do not know on what day your Lord will come. . . . 44 So you also must be ready, because the Son of Man will come at an hour when you do not expect him.

In royal weddings, the prince or king would supply the future bride with attendants whose role it was to serve her by preparing her for his return. These were skilled servants who could equip her in specific arenas so that she was prepared to be a fitting consort to the king. Often male attendants of the bride, mostly those charged with her safety, had enough skill at war and physical strength to be able to defend her. However, there was always the possibility that they could act inappropriately with the bride. For this reason, they were made eunuchs so that they could not take their own pleasure with someone else's bride. There is a great lesson for us in this. All who are truly called as attendants of His bride will be shaped by this attitude and understanding. We exist to equip His bride but cannot be found to be taking advantage of her for our own pleasure. Listen to Paul's heart towards Jesus' bride.

2 Corinthians 11:2 I am jealous for you with a godly jealousy. I promised you to one husband, to Christ, so that I might present you as a pure virgin to him. 3 But I am afraid that just as Eve was deceived by the serpent's cunning, your minds may somehow be led astray from your sincere and pure devotion to Christ.

2 Corinthians 4:5 For we do not preach ourselves, but Jesus Christ as Lord, and ourselves as your servants for Jesus' sake.

2 Corinthians 8:5 And they did not do as we expected, but they gave themselves first to the Lord and then to us in keeping with God's will.

From the time of the groom's departure, the bride would have her dress ready and would keep extra oil and a trimmed lamp next to her bed, so she was always ready for his return which often happened in the evening. When it was time, the groom would gather friends and supporters at the outskirts of the town and with loud celebrations, shouts and trumpet calls, announce his return. This noise alerted the bride to her imminent wedding, and she would quickly prepare herself. Her friends and attendants would run out into the night with lamps to light the way for the groom as he neared her bridal chamber. Jesus and the New Testament writers followed this theme when describing His return;

1 Thessalonians 4:15 For this we say to you by the word of the Lord, that we who are alive and remain until the coming of the Lord will by no means precede those who are asleep. 16 For the Lord Himself will descend from heaven with a shout, with the voice of an archangel, and with the trumpet of God. And the dead in Christ will rise first. 17 Then we who are alive and remain shall be caught up together with them in the clouds to meet the Lord in the air. And thus we shall always be with the Lord. (NKJV)

Matthew 25:5 The bridegroom was a long time in coming, and they all became drowsy and fell asleep. 6 "At midnight the cry rang out: 'Here's the bridegroom! Come out to meet him!' 7 "Then all the virgins woke up and trimmed their lamps.

The scriptures say that when Jesus went back to heaven, He gave gifts to His bride. These skilled servants should equip and prepare His bride for His return. When they equip the bride and she does what they have equipped them to do, she makes herself ready.

Revelation 19:7 Let us rejoice and be glad and give him glory! For the wedding of the Lamb has come, and his bride has made herself ready. 8 Fine linen, bright and clean, was given her to wear." (Fine linen stands for the righteous acts of the saints.)

The "Doma" gifts are listed by Paul in Ephesians:

Ephesians 4:10 He who descended is the very one who ascended higher than all the heavens, in order to fill the whole universe.) 11 So Christ himself gave the apostles, the prophets, the evangelists, the pastors and teachers, 12 to equip his people for works of service, so that the body of Christ may be built up 13 until we all reach unity in the faith and in the knowledge of the Son of God and become mature, attaining to the whole measure of the fullness of Christ. 14 Then we will no longer be infants, tossed back and forth by the waves, and blown here and there by every wind of teaching and by the cunning and craftiness of people in their deceitful scheming. 15 Instead, speaking the truth in love, we will grow to become in every respect the mature body of him who is the head, that is, Christ.

This is the only New Testament Scripture that speaks to their establishment and purpose directly even though they are mentioned numerous times throughout the New Testament. Five answers emerge from this passage that are helpful to our discussion.

WHEN WERE THESE GIFTS GIVEN?

"Ephesians 4:8 This is why it says: "When he ascended on high, he led captives in his train and gave gifts to men."

They were given to the church when Jesus ascended. This is why some people call them ascension gifts or post ascension gifts, sometimes also referred to as five fold gifting. This differentiates them from similar gifts given before His ascension. Specific chapters are dedicated to ascension apostles and prophets later in this book which outline the many apostles recorded in the book of Acts who were appointed post ascension. These ascension apostles are different to the pre–ascension apostles whom Jesus appointed under His Father's direction during His ministry (Mark 3:13-15). Those were the apostles

119

whose role it was to attend the bridegroom while He was on earth. In this they were unique, they were the friends of the bridegroom, the best men in our understanding. This what Jesus called them.

Luke 5:33 And they said to Him, "The disciples of John often fast and offer prayers, the disciples of the Pharisees also do the same, but Yours eat and drink." 34 And Jesus said to them, "You cannot make the attendants of the bridegroom fast while the bridegroom is with them, can you? 35 But the days will come; and when the bridegroom is taken away from them, then they will fast in those days." (NASB)

If we continue the analogy we see that John the baptizer recognized his own role as the best man at the wedding. He had made the arrangements for the bride and the bridegroom to meet and come together and knew it was his time to back out of the limelight because the engagement feast had begun. When his disciples bemoaned the fact that the crowds that used to throng to John were now going over to Jesus, John gave this telling reply;

John 3:26 And they came to John and said to him, "Rabbi, He who was with you beyond the Jordan, to whom you have testified, behold, He is baptizing and all are coming to Him." 27 John answered and said, "A man can receive nothing unless it has been given him from heaven. 28 You yourselves are my witnesses that I said, 'I am not the Christ,' but, 'I have been sent ahead of Him.' 29 He who has the bride is the bridegroom; but the friend of the bridegroom, who stands and hears him, rejoices greatly because of the bridegroom's voice. So this joy of mine has been made full. 30 He must increase, but I must decrease. (NASB)

Those 12 pre-ascension apostles are sometimes referred to as the apostles of the lamb. They will have a specific role in judging the 12 tribes with Jesus (Luke 22:30). This is why it was important that there were 12, and after Judas was dead, they appointed Matthias by lot to ensure that 12 of them remained.

(Acts 1:12-26). The book of Acts is careful to record that Peter stood up on the day of Pentecost with 11 others (Acts 2:14).

Similarly, these ascension prophets are different to Old Testament prophets who were part of very few who heard God's voice. Modern prophets are tasked with equipping God's people to hear and respond to His voice.

WHO GIVES THESE GIFTS?

Ephesians 4:11 It was he who gave . . .

Jesus is the one who gives the gifts and the ability to function in these capacities. People cannot take up these positions by themselves, they are offices given by Jesus. They are not titles but gifts and roles. They are servants given as gifts to the bride by her bridegroom.

HOW MANY GIFTS DID HE GIVE?

Ephesians 4:11 Some to be apostles, some to be prophets, some to be evangelists, and some to be pastors and teachers

There are five specific gifts, each with a separate and specific function.

WHAT IS THEIR PURPOSE?

Ephesians 4:12 to prepare God's people for works of service, so that the body of Christ may be built up

The primary purpose for these gifts is to build God's people up, equipping them to serve Him. The bride makes herself beautiful for her King by doing the righteous works she has been equipped to do through these ascension gift servants.

Revelation 19:7 Let us rejoice and be glad and give the glory to Him, for the marriage of the Lamb has come and His bride has made herself ready." 8 It was given to her to clothe herself in fine linen, bright and clean; for the fine linen is the righteous acts of the saints. (NASB)

121

With their service and the brides willing obedience the entire body develops and emerges as a beautiful bride.

HOW LONG ARE THE VALID?

Ephesians 4:13 UNTIL we all reach unity in the faith and in the knowledge of the Son of God and become mature, attaining to the whole measure of the fullness of Christ.

The ministry of these gifts is valid until a specific set of goals have been accomplished. They will minister until;

- We all reach unity in the faith

- We reach unity in the knowledge of the son of God

- We all become mature

- We all attain the whole measure of Christ's fullness

Imagine the church of Jesus made up of believers of every tribe, tongue and nation in unity, and complete in the knowledge of Jesus, mature, and filled with all His fullness. That church will see the glory of the Lord cover the earth and all creation will see the fulfillment of the promises of God through that church. There is much work to be done to reach those goals and there is a greater glory yet to be revealed through these ascension gifts in the earth. They are central to the purposes of God on the earth. Ascension gifts are to equip the church for that kind of glory.

RESPONDING TO ASCENSION GIFTS

How we respond to people with ascension gifts is uniquely important and proportional to their effectiveness in our lives. If we receive them and the grace God has put on their lives, we receive the blessing that comes from their ministry. If we do not receive them, or worse dishonor or look down on them, their ministry is severely hampered in our lives. Jesus taught that when we receive a prophet because he is a prophet, we receive the reward of the prophet.

Matthew 10:41 Anyone who receives a prophet because he is a prophet will receive a prophet's reward, and anyone

122

who receives a righteous man because he is a righteous man will receive a righteous man's reward.

Remember how Jesus' ministry in His hometown was hampered by this very issue.

Mark 6:2 When the Sabbath came, He began to teach in the synagogue; and the many listeners were astonished, saying, "Where did this man get these things, and what is this wisdom given to Him, and such miracles as these performed by His hands? 3"Is not this the carpenter, the son of Mary, and brother of James and Joses and Judas and Simon? Are not His sisters here with us?" And they took offense at Him. 4 Jesus said to them, "A prophet is not without honor except in his hometown and among his own relatives and in his own household." 5 And He could do no miracle there except that He laid His hands on a few sick people and healed them. (NASB)

Paul the apostle experienced this negative response when people who opposed him taught that he was not a real apostle and had not been one of the 12. In some places where Paul ministered, he was rejected and scorned and despised, making the grace on his life of no effect in those places.

1 Corinthians 9:1 Am I not free? Am I not an apostle? Have I not seen Jesus our Lord? Are you not the result of my work in the Lord? 1 Cor 9:2 Even though I may not be an apostle to others, surely I am to you! For you are the seal of my apostleship in the Lord.

When we do not recognize or receive any of the ascension gift ministers we choose not to receive the reward of their ministry. This does not imply that we should embrace anyone who lays claim to a specific ministry. We are encouraged to test ministries, to examine them for their adherence to scriptural truth, and to watch their lives and doctrines closely. This is one of the encouragements given to the church at Ephesus.

Revelation 2:2 I know your deeds and your toil and perseverance, and that you cannot tolerate evil men, and you put to the test those who call themselves apostles, and they are not, and you found them to be false;(NASB)

In the next chapters, we will look at each of the ascension gifts individually in an effort to learn more about how each one equips the bride for her master.

APOSTLES

*A*postolic ministry was pivotal in the early church and the words "apostle or apostles" are mentioned 85 times in the New Testament The word "pastor or pastors" is mentioned only once. Our emphasis in the modern church does not reflect this. There is a far greater emphasis on pastors or shepherds than on apostolic ministry. Some say the reason for this turn around is that the apostolic age is finished. Considering the scripture in Ephesians 4 which was discussed above, we see that apostles are as relevant and vital in our days as they were in the early church. Scripture teaches that Apostles are the foundation and first line of leadership in the Church. This means that they are to be the humblest servants of all.

1 Corinthins 12:28 And in the church God has appointed first of all apostles, second prophets, third teachers, then workers of miracles, also those having gifts of healing, those able to help others, those with gifts of administration, and those speaking in different kinds of tongues.

As we mentioned earlier, Jesus appointed 12 apostles during His ministry on earth. We called them the apostles of the Lamb. They were His attendants and they therefore represented a distinct group of people whose dispensation ended when the last of them died. Yet we have seen also that when Jesus left to go and prepare a place for His bride, He gave gifts to His bride to help equip her. Among these gifts are ascension apostles whose job exists until we all reach unity in the faith and have fullness in Christ. In other words, this is still the dispensation of ascension gift apostles. Many argue that Matthias was wrongly chosen by the other 11 and a theory has emerged that Paul was actually the 12th apostle and they should have waited for him. This is taken from the scripture where Paul states that he has seen Jesus but his point in that passage is not that he was to be included in the 12, but that he too had seen Jesus alive post resurrection. However, the New Testament mentions a number of other ascension apostles, sometimes directly calling them apostles and other times by inference. Here a some examples.

ASCENSION GIFT APOSTLES MENTIONED IN THE NEW TESTAMENT

PAUL AND BARNABUS

Acts 14:3 Therefore they spent a long time there speaking boldly with reliance upon the Lord, who was testifying to the word of His grace, granting that signs and wonders be done by their hands. 4 But the people of the city were divided; and some sided with the Jews, and some with the apostles. (NASB)

Acts 14:14 But when the apostles Barnabas and Paul heard of this,

ANDRONICUS AND JUNIAS

Romonas 16:7 Greet Andronicus and Junias, my relatives who have been in prison with me. They are outstanding among the apostles, and they were in Christ before I was.

SILAS AND TIMOTHY

2 Thessalonians 1:1 Paul, Silas and Timothy - 1 Th 2:6 As apostles of Christ we could have been a burden to you,

Philemon 1:1 Paul and Timothy, servants of Christ Jesus,

JAMES THE BROTHER OF JESUS

Galatians 1:19 I saw none of the other apostles--only James, the Lord's brother.

1 Corinthians 9:5 Do we not have a right to take along a believing wife, even as the rest of the apostles and the brother (James) of the Lord and Cephas? (NASB)

APOLLOS

Placed at the same level as Paul and Peter - 1 Corinthians 1:12 What I mean is this: One of you says, "I follow Paul"; another, "I follow Apollos"; another, "I follow Cephas "; still another, "I follow Christ."

1 Corinthians 4:6 Now, brothers, I have applied these things to myself and Apollos for your benefit,

WHAT IS THE GIFT OF APOSTLES?

The word apostle in the original Greek means a delegate, a messenger, one that has been sent. Greeks and Romans used the word in a secular context to describe special envoys sent out to expand their empire. The word started out being used for the first ship in the armada sent out to conquer and train and then gradually came to represent the commander of those forces. Many of these envoys were military generals who were given authority and commissioned to establish Greek and Roman culture around the known-world. They were to teach and train new subjects in the laws and cultures of the kingdom. They were highly equipped and given everything they needed to accomplish their task. They bore the support of Rome and were thereby vested with great authority. They were told to go to new areas and subdue, conquer, convert, instruct and train. This contextual understanding would have given the early church a much clearer view of the role of apostles than our culture does today. As in their day, Church apostles are similarly sent to conquer new territories and win converts to Christ, establishing His kingdom in their hearts and teaching them the laws and culture of His realm. Without the ministry of apostles, pioneering, dominant and entrepreneurial, the church becomes institutional and ceremonial. Apostles tend to keep people's focus outward and global while ministering in local contexts.

Each of the five ascension ministries produce diverse fruit helpful to our growth and development. While all of the ministries share in the task of equipping of God's people, an apostle creates Biblical order, foundational perspective, sound doctrine and a fathering role. The prophet produces insight, revelation, order, encouragement and the fear of God. Evangelists stir us to a love of lost people and a passion for the gospel. Pastors produce comfort, peace, wholeness, security and community. Teachers produces the fruit of clarity, understanding, excitement and love for God's word. Apostles are foundational to the others.

HOW CAN WE KNOW THEM?

Not every apostle need be universally recognized for their ministry to be functional. Even legitimately appointed apostles, whose lives bear all the marks of an apostle can have detractors trying to undermine them just as Paul did. Therefore, unanimity across the body in recognition of each of these ministries is not a prerequisite for their release.

1 Corinthians 9:2 Even though I may not be an apostle to others, surely I am to you! For you are the seal of my apostleship in the Lord.

The signs of the apostle are clearly documented in scripture. We are taught in scripture to test everything and to cling to the good. This means that we are to test the legitimacy of the apostle as well.

1 Thessalonians 5:21 Test everything. Hold on to the good.

2 Corinthians 11:13 For such are false apostles, deceitful workers, transforming themselves into apostles of Christ. 14 And no wonder! For Satan himself transforms himself into an angel of light NKJV

Revelations 2:2 "I know your works, your labor, your patience, and that you cannot bear those who are evil. And you have tested those who say they are apostles and are not, and have found them liars; NKJV

THE SIGNS OR SEALS OF APOSTLESHIP

1. SIGNS, WONDERS AND MIRACLES

2 Corinthians 12:11 . . . for I am not in the least inferior to the "super-apostles," even though I am nothing. 2 Cor 12:12 The things that mark an apostle--signs, wonders and miracles--were done among you with great perseverance.

Although false apostles sometimes emulate these signs, they should be evident in the ministry of apostles. Signs and wonders and miracles were done often by Paul and the earlier apostles in Acts 2:43. If we ignore this mark of apostleship, we are saying that we can preach the gospel without demonstrating any of its power. We are called to break into the kingdom of darkness and turn people to serve the living God. Demonstrations of wonders and miracles are a key factor in accomplishing this. In fact, Paul said that he wanted the Corinthians' faith to rest on such demonstrations.

1 Corinthians 2:1 When I came to you, brothers, I did not come with eloquence or superior wisdom as I proclaimed to you the testimony about God. 2 For I resolved to know nothing while I was with you except Jesus Christ and him crucified. 3 I came to you in weakness and fear, and with much trembling. 4 My message and my preaching were not with wise and persuasive words, but with a demonstration of the Spirit's power, 5 so that your faith might not rest on men's wisdom, but on God's power.

When John the Baptist's faith began to waiver because of his circumstances, he sent his disciples to Jesus to ask Him if He really was the Messiah or if there was someone else. Jesus' answer demonstrated how much value He placed on the demonstration of signs, wonders and miracles.

Matthew 11:1 When Jesus had finished giving instructions to His twelve disciples, He departed from there to teach and preach in their cities.2 Now when John, while imprisoned, heard of the works of Christ, he sent word by his disciples 3 and said to Him, "Are You the Expected One, or shall we look for someone else?" 4 Jesus answered and said to them, "Go and report to John what you hear and see: 5 the blind receive sight and the lame walk, the lepers are cleansed and the deaf hear, the dead are raised up, and the poor have the gospel preached to them.

Every time Jesus sent people, (Apostello) He commissioned them with power and signs to accompany their preaching. This is especially true of apostles.

Matthew 10:1 He called his twelve disciples to him and gave them authority to drive out evil spirits and to heal every disease and sickness . . . 5 These twelve Jesus sent out with the following instructions: "Do not go among the Gentiles or enter any town of the Samaritans. 6 Go rather to the lost sheep of Israel. 7 As you go, preach this message: 'The kingdom of heaven is near.' 8 Heal the sick, raise the dead, cleanse those who have leprosy, drive out demons. Freely you have received, freely give.

Luke 10:1 After this the Lord appointed seventy-two others and sent them two by two ahead of him to every town and place where he was about to go. . . . 3 Go! I am sending you out like lambs among wolves. 4 Do not take a purse or bag or sandals; and do not greet anyone on the road. 5 "When you enter a house, first say, 'Peace to this house.' 6 If a man of peace is there, your peace will rest on him; if not, it will return to you. 7 Stay in that house, eating and drinking whatever they give you, for the worker deserves his wages. Do not move around from house to house. 8 "When you enter a town and are welcomed, eat what is set before you. 9 Heal the sick who are there and tell them, 'The kingdom of God is near you.'

Mark 16:15 He said to them, "Go into all the world and preach the good news to all creation. 16 Whoever believes and is baptized will be saved, but whoever does not believe will be condemned. 17 And these signs will accompany those who believe: In my name they will drive out demons; they will speak in new tongues; 18 they will pick up snakes with their hands; and when they drink deadly poison, it will not hurt them at all; they will place their hands on sick people, and they will get well." . . . 20 Then the disciples went out and preached everywhere, and the Lord worked with them and confirmed his word by the signs that accompanied it.

2. OTHER MATURE LEADERS RECOGNIZE THE GIFT BY REVELATION

Acts 13:1 In the church at Antioch there were prophets and teachers: Barnabas, Simeon called Niger, Lucius of Cyrene, Manaen (who had been brought up with Herod the tetrarch) and Saul. Acts 13:2 While they were worshiping the Lord and fasting, the Holy Spirit said, "Set apart for me Barnabas and Saul for the work to which I have called them." 3 So after they had fasted and prayed, they placed their hands on them and sent them off.

God's principle of establishing a matter on the testimony of two or three witnesses still stands. Apostles are not self-appointed but are called of God and recognized by other ascension gift ministers. This recognition often comes after prayer and revelation from God to independent leaders who know the person's lifestyle and character. Most often prophets sound the calling to the apostolic. It is important to note the second time of waiting on God in the passage above. After they had heard God's call, they waited on Him for specifics in how to go about releasing these men to their apostolic calling.

The New Testament pattern seems to be that those who were called as attendants of the bride into "Doma" gift responsibilities knew they had been called to that specific space of ministry. They were clear about their calling by Jesus and others around them were clear about it as well. This clarity allowed them to be faithful to their calling but also propelled them to more success as people honored them and thereby received the rewards of their calling. Those who refused to acknowledge Paul's apostolic calling did not receive his grace and ministry in their own lives. The New Testament ascension gift minister should be clear about his or her call and those around them should also sanction and receive it. We do ascension gift ministers a disservice when we don't recognize them and we lose out when we do not bring them honor, which is the primary vehicle of inheritance. We receive an inheritance from those we choose to honor, but we will receive nothing from those we dishonor.

Some who believe in ascension ministry today, assert that we cannot state emphatically what ascension gift we have. Some say that even if we are aware of our ascension gifting our view will not be universally shared and therefore should not be universally declared. To re-enforce this theory, they practice poor exegesis from the scripture in 1 Corinthians 9 taking it out of its context and have made an entire doctrine out of it. This is motivated by true desires in not wanting to draw attention to ones-self and avoiding selfish ambition which is rife among many ministers. Unfortunately, it does not reflect the scriptural pattern however well-intended. Paul's statement regarding the fact that some Judaizers were claiming that he was not a real apostle, is immediately followed by his own assertion that he is an apostle and that the Corinthians of all people should recognize it.

1 Corinthians 9:1 Am I not free? Am I not an apostle? Have I not seen Jesus our Lord? Are you not the result of my work in the Lord? 2 Even though I may not be an apostle to others, surely I am to you! For you are the seal of my apostleship in the Lord. 3 This is my defense to those who sit in judgment on me.

On 15 separate declarations in the New Testament, Paul is emphatic about both recognizing and declaring his apostleship. For the sake of brevity, I have abbreviated the word apostle or apostles to "A" in the following references. These show that Paul was exceptionally clear about his calling as an apostle. He says he was called to be an "A" (Rom 1:1, 1 Cor 1:1), "A" to the gentiles (Rom 11:13, Gal 2:8), Am I not an "A" (1 Cor 9:1), Least of all the "A" (1 Cor 15:9), "A" by the will of God (2 Cor 1:1), Not the least inferior to the super "A" (2 Cor 12:12), An "A" sent not from men nor by man, but by Jesus Christ (Gal 1:1), "A" by the will of God (Eph 1:1, Col 1:1, 2 Tim 1:1), "A" by the command of

God (1 Tim 1:1), "A" and a herald (1 Tim 2:7) "A" and a teacher (2 Tim 1:11).

Was this merely a Pauline idiosyncrasy? No, a clear recognition and declaration of apostleship is consistently demonstrated throughout the New Testament. Peter declares himself an apostle in the books he authored, An "A" of Jesus (1 Pet 1:1), A servant and an "A" (2 Pet 1:1). Barnabus is clearly recognized as one, "...some sided with the Jews, others with the "A" (Acts 14:4); When the "A" Barnabus and Paul heard this (Acts 14:14). Silas and Timothy likewise are so recognized, Paul, Silas and Timothy, (1 Th 1:1) As "A" of Christ we could have been a burden to you, (1 Th 2:6). The list continues with an unashamed recognition afforded to many as apostles. Greet Andronicus and Junias - outstanding among the "A", (Rom 16:7), I saw none of the other "A" --only James, the Lord's brother (Gal 1:19). Apollos is mentioned as an equal to Paul and Peter.

1 Corinthians 1:12 What I mean is this: One of you says, "I follow Paul"; another, "I follow Apollos"; another, "I follow Cephas "; and 1 Corinthians 4:6 Now, brothers, I have applied these things to myself and Apollos for your benefit,

Other Ephesians 4 ministers are also recognized for their gifts and are sent by the apostolic team of Jerusalem because of them. John the Baptist was recognized as a prophet, (Mat 14:5) they considered him a "P". (Mat 11:9) A "P"? Yes, I tell you, (Mat 21:26) for they all hold that John was a "P"." Agabus is honored for his prophetic role. "P" came down from Jerusalem to Antioch. One of them, named Agabus, (Acts 11:27-28), a "P" named Agabus came down from Judea. (Acts 21:10). Judas and Silas were recognized as prophets and sent because of this gifting to convey by word of mouth the Jerusalem counsel's decision in collaboration with the Holy Spirit. Judas and Silas, who themselves were "P" (Acts 15:32). Antioch recognized a team of prophets and teachers. In the church at Antioch there were prophets and teachers: Barnabas, Simeon called Niger, Lucius of Cyrene, Manaen (who had been brought up with Herod the tetrarch) and Saul. (Acts 13:1). Phillip is celebrated as an evangelist while his daughters are recognized as having a prophetic gift. "and stayed at the house of Philip the evangelist, one of the Seven. He had four unmarried daughters who prophesied." (Acts 21:8-9)

3. THEY BUILD TEAMS OF MINISTERS WHO HELP THEIR APOSTOLIC MANDATE

Acts 20:4 (Paul) He was accompanied by Sopater son of Pyrrhus from Berea, Aristarchus and Secundus from Thessalonica, Gaius from Derbe, Timothy also, and Tychicus and Trophimus from the province of Asia.

2 Corinthians 2:12 Now when I went to Troas to preach the gospel of Christ and found that the Lord had opened a door for me, 13 I still had no peace of mind, because I did not find my brother Titus there. So I said good-by to them and went on to Macedonia.

Jesus sent out His apostles in two's so that they would serve in team and as the scripture above demonstrates, Paul walked away from a God-opened door because he was not supported by at least one other team member.

The lone hero is not God's pattern. If a man cannot build loving and lasting relationships where other recognized Christian leaders support him, then he has not yet learnt enough about the Spirit of Jesus and His kingdom. An apostle needs to be able to point to the friends he has in team.

When a person's gifting is elevated beyond their character we often find damage wrought in the body of Christ. In our bodies, any cell that rebels against the others is more typical of a cancer than anything healthy. Ministers who cannot and do not regularly build up the body and bring unity and health to it, need to be questioned. True apostles build and work in team. They create and maintain deep and loving relationships in their ministries. As the scriptures below will illustrate, Paul loved deeply and from the heart those with whom he ministered and the churches he ministered into. The first few scriptures deal with Onesimus, Timothy, Titus and even John Mark who wasat one time, the cause of great contention between Paul and Barnabus, who it seems was reunited with Paul and useful to him in the latter part of his ministry.

*Philemon 1:11 Formerly he was useless to you, but now he has become useful both to you and to me. 12 I am sending him—**who is my very heart**—back to you. 13 I would have liked to keep him with me so that he could take your place in helping me while I am in chains for the gospel.*

*1 Timothy 1: 1 Paul, an apostle of Christ Jesus by the command of God our Savior and of Christ Jesus our hope, 2 To Timothy **my true son** in the faith: Grace, mercy and peace from God the Father and Christ Jesus our Lord.*

*Philippians 2: 22 But you know that Timothy has proved himself, because **as a son with his father** he has served with me in the work of the gospel.*

*Titus 1:1 Paul, a servant of God and an apostle of Jesus Christ . . .   4 To Titus, **my true son in our common faith**: Grace and peace from God the Father and Christ Jesus our Savior.*

2 Timothy 4:11 Only Luke is with me. Get Mark and bring him with you, because he is helpful to me in my ministry.

Paul also wrote to the churches with great affection. We must not be misled into thinking that apostles merely minister truth and do not share their lives with God's people. Their ministry is not selfishly based, nor is their first consideration personal comfort or gain. They give themselves and their hearts to the churches they minister into. They are marked by the healthy relationships they constantly form. Additionally we should expect the body of Christ to have a testimony in their hearts that these ministers are God-given. Both the ministers and the body will then show the love that is supposed to be the primary validation of believers. Notice the relationship that exists between ascension gift ministers and the churches they ministered into in the following scriptures.

*Romans 1:10 in my prayers at all times; and I pray that now at last by God's will the way may be opened for me to come to you. 11 **I long to see you** so that I may impart to* *you some spiritual gift to make you strong— 12 that is, that you and I may be mutually encouraged by each other's faith.*

1 Thessalonians 2:7 But we proved to be gentle among you, as a nursing mother tenderly cares for her own children. 8 Having so fond an affection for you, we were well-pleased to impart to you not only the gospel of God but also our own lives, because you had become very dear to us.(NASB)

Philippians 4:1 Therefore, my brothers, you whom I love and long for, my joy and crown, that is how you should stand firm in the Lord, dear friends!

4. THEY PRODUCE MATURE CHURCHES

The fruit of their ministry is well established churches. When someone plants a church, that accomplishment does not necessarily make them an apostle. Repeated success in planting churches, in conjunction with the other signs are good indicators. It is not necessarily the amount of time they spend with a church, which in Paul and Barnabus' case was often cut short, but the fruit of their ministry. If the fruit is churches set in Biblical order with people's eyes on Jesus, the Holy Spirit evident in their hearts, and perseverance despite opposition, these are a good signs. Ultimately, the apostle should be able to point to the lives of the people he has ministered to, which serve as demonstrable fruit. Their grounding in God is the seal of his apostleship. Listen to Paul's defense of his apostleship with the Corinthians, as he points to the fruit of his ministry in their lives.

1 Corinthians 9:2 Even though I may not be an apostle to others, surely I am to you! For you are the seal of my apostleship in the Lord. 1 Cor 9:3 This is my defense to those who sit in judgment on me.

2 Corinthians 3:1 Are we beginning to commend ourselves again? Or do we need, like some people, letters of recommendation to you or from you? 2 You yourselves are our letter, written on our hearts, known and read by everybody. 3 You show that you are a letter from Christ, the result of our ministry, written not with ink but with the Spirit of the living God, not on tablets of stone but on tablets of human hearts.

Again, let me state that their ministry is not the result of specific gifting experienced over one weekend or in one service, but rather the result of the impact of their lives, gifts, ministry, example and the power God demonstrates through them.

5. THEY SACRIFICE MORE, SERVE MORE, ENDURE MORE AND FACE MORE RESISTANCE

Apostles lay their lives down for the church. Their ministry is akin to the drink offering, joyfully being spent before the Lord. Apostles should be afforded the highest honor for they are called to the greatest servant role. They sacrifice their lives for the body of Christ.

1 Corinthians 4:9 For I think that God has displayed us, the apostles, last, as men condemned to death; for we have been made a spectacle to the world, both to angels and to men. 10 We are fools for Christ's sake, but you are wise in Christ! We are weak, but you are strong! You are distinguished, but we are dishonored! 11 To the present hour we both hunger and thirst, and we are poorly clothed, and beaten, and homeless. 12 And we labor, working with our own hands. Being reviled, we bless; being persecuted, we endure; 13 being defamed, we entreat. We have been made as the filth of the world, the offscouring of all things until now. (NKJV)

2 Corinthians 6:4 Rather, as servants of God we commend ourselves in every way: in great endurance; in troubles, hardships and distresses; 5 in beatings, imprisonments and riots; in hard work, sleepless nights and hunger; 6 in purity, understanding, patience and kindness; in the Holy Spirit and in sincere love; 7 in truthful speech and in the power of God; with weapons of righteousness in the right hand and in the left; 8 through glory and dishonor, bad report and good report; genuine, yet regarded as impostors; 9 known, yet regarded as unknown; dying, and yet we live on; beaten, and yet not killed; 10 sorrowful, yet always rejoicing; poor, yet making many rich; having nothing, and yet possessing everything.

2 Corinthians 4:11 For we who live are always delivered to death for Jesus' sake, that the life of Jesus also may be manifested in our mortal flesh. 12 So then death is working in us, but life in you. (NKJV)

2 Corinthians 12:7 To keep me from becoming conceited because of these surpassingly great revelations, there was given me a thorn in my flesh, a messenger of Satan, to torment me.

The apostolic ministry, more than the other ascension gifts, faces the enemy head on. As a kingdom envoy, the apostle breaks into the enemy's strongholds and goes to war. For this reason, they face severe opposition. History records that all the apostles of the lamb were martyred. Apostles deserve our respect, prayer, and support that comes through sending mature leaders with them and financial contributions because of their work in the Lord. Their ministry produces a deeper level of the Father's heart in our churches and stirs us to fulfill this great commission to go into the world and make disciples of every nation.

PROPHETS

*J*ust as ascension gifts add to the body, prophets add depth of insight into the church. In the last days, recognition of prophets and prophetic ministry will be the precursor to a greater celebration and recognition of all the other ascension gift ministries through the prophetic ministers. As with all the other ascension gifts, prophets come into their office when they have fulfilled the following criteria.

First, they must have a personal sense of calling along with a desire for the office. Second, they have a proven track record of faithful and helpful service in a local church. Their being faithful with the little has enabled them to be released to more. Third, they are recognized and released by the Lord through a local eldership or a trans-local presbytery usually with prayer and fasting. They are the gateway gift to the rest of the ascension gifts, just as tongues are to manifestation gifts and leadership is to grace gifts. When we recognize and bring forth prophets they will recognize and highlight the rest of the ascension gifts.

Acts 13:1 In the church at Antioch there were prophets and teachers: Barnabas, Simeon called Niger, Lucius of Cyrene, Manaen (who had been brought up with Herod the tetrarch) and Saul. Acts 13:2 While they were worshiping the Lord and fasting, the Holy Spirit said, "Set apart for me Barnabas and Saul for the work to which I have called them."

The Greek work in the New Testament is the word "prophetes" meaning "to speak before" or "to speak for," or "an inspired speaker." We will come back specifically to ascension gift prophets but we need to recognize that prophesying is the

139

only gift that is an ascension gift, a grace gifting and a manifestation gift. We will look at the manifestation gift and then the grace gift before we focus on the ascension gift of prophetic ministry.

EVERYONE CAN PROPHESY - MANIFESTATION

Prophecy in the New Testament differs from the Old Testament prophecy in that in the Old Testament, the Holy Spirit was only given to the few anointed positions of prophets, priests or kings. This exclusivity has been disbanded because God has promised the gift of His Spirit to all and consequently all have the potential to prophesy. Whatever a person's role in the church, they have all been given one Spirit and are therefore encouraged to desire prophesy above all other manifestation gifts. This desire to see all of God's people prophesying was first expressed by Moses when it was discovered that elders were also prophesying. It was then translated into a promise through Joel the prophet that a day would come when all of God's people would prophesy. Then Paul again reminds believers that we have all been given one Spirit to drink.

Numbers 11:27 And a young man ran and told Moses, and said, "Eldad and Medad are prophesying in the camp." 28 So Joshua the son of Nun, Moses' assistant, one of his choice men, answered and said, "Moses my lord, forbid them!" 29 Then Moses said to him, "Are you zealous for my sake? Oh, that all the Lord's people were prophets and that the Lord would put His Spirit upon them!" (NKJV)

Acts 2:16 No, this is what was spoken by the prophet Joel: 17 "'In the last days, God says, I will pour out my Spirit on all people. Your sons and daughters will prophesy, your young men will see visions; your old men will dream dreams. 18 Even on my servants, both men and women, I will pour out my Spirit in those days, and they will prophesy.

1 Corinthians 12:13 For we were all baptized by one Spirit into one body--whether Jews or Greeks, slave or free--and we were all given the one Spirit to drink.

We are all offered to drink of one Spirit and we can all prophesy. Paul exhorts God's people to eagerly desire these things.

*1 Corinthians 14:31 For **you can all** prophesy in turn so that everyone may be instructed and encouraged. . . . 1 Corinthians 14:1 Follow the way of love and eagerly desire spiritual gifts, especially the gift of prophecy. . . . 1 Corinthians 14:5 I would like **every one of you** to speak in tongues, but I would rather have you prophesy. He who prophesies is greater than one who speaks in tongues, unless he interprets, so that the church may be edified.*

The manifestation of prophecy is part of the 1 Corinthians 12 groupings of gifts called the manifestations of the Spirit. They are the overflow of the Holy Spirit in believer's lives. Those who desire to be used in this way will find themselves with a prophetic ability. This manifested ability is not the "doma" gift mentioned in Ephesians 4 regarding ascension gifting. This ability to manifest the Holy Spirit through prophecy is subject to a number of boundaries set up by Paul primarily in 1 Corinthians as rules for orderly worship. The heart of the matter is that this manifestation ought to be directed to strengthening, encouraging and comforting the body. This gift is not for the correction, rebuke or direction of its recipients. The manifestation should be administered considerately in keeping with the basic guidelines Paul outlines for all manifestation gifts (see chapter 17). The entire body of believers, along with overseers, should measure this manifestation gift of prophecy. Care and effort should be added to ensure the prophecy's meaning is plain.

*1 Corinthians 14:3 But everyone who prophesies speaks to men for their **strengthening, encouragement** and **comfort**. . . 1 Corinthians 14:29 Two or three prophets should speak, and the others should weigh carefully what is said. 30 And if a revelation comes to someone who is* *sitting down, the first speaker should stop. 31 For you can all prophesy in turn so that everyone may be **instructed** and **encouraged**. 32 The spirits of prophets are subject to the control of prophets. 33 For God is not a God of disorder but of peace. As in all the congregations of the saints . . . 1 Corinthians 14:7 Even in the case of lifeless things that make sounds, such as the flute or harp, how will anyone know what tune is being played unless there is a distinction in the notes? 8 Again, if the trumpet does not sound a clear call, who will get ready for battle? 9 So it is with you. Unless you speak intelligible words with your tongue, how will anyone know what you are saying? You will just be speaking into the air. . . . 1 Corinthians 14:18 I thank God that I speak in tongues more than all of you. 19 But in the church I would rather speak five intelligible words to instruct others than ten thousand words in a tongue.*

We will cover this in more detail in the chapter on the basic principles of manifestation gifts.

SOME ARE GRACED TO PROPHESY

The grace gift of prophesying is found in those people graced by the Father to speak out truth. They tend to be intuitive or perceptive in the Spirit, often they will see pictures or sense impressions from God. They can easily turn these 'natural' abilities of their spirits into a powerful ministry of encouragement. These are the people who sense when God is doing something specific in a person's life. They are exhorted by scripture not to prophesy beyond their faith. That is to say they should only prophesy what they truly believe is true, thereby avoiding the desire to manufacture kind or good things God is not saying. When we prophesy beyond our faith, we make a contribution to expectations most likely to be unfulfilled and thereby cause confusion and a diminishment of faith.

Romans 12:5 so in Christ we, though many, form one body, and each member belongs to all the others. 6 We have different gifts, according to the grace given to each of us. If your gift is prophesying, then prophesy in accordance with your faith;

SOME ARE PROPHETS - THE ROLE OF ASCENSION PROPHETS

EQUIP THE SAINTS TO SERVE (PREPARE GOD'S PEOPLE)

Ephesians 4:11 some to be prophets . . . 12 to prepare God's people for works of service, so that the body of Christ may be built up

Ascension prophets have a specific function, common to all ascension gift ministries, that separates them from those manifesting prophecy and operating in a grace to prophesy. They are to equip the saints for service. This forms the basis of their ministerial focus. Their prophetic ministry prepares people to be more effective in the calling on their lives. Part of this equipping is to bring clear and distinct prophesy so that the specific race God has marked out for individuals is confirmed to them in prophecy. This kind of prophecy encourages the body to hear God's voice, and to prophesy themselves. Part of this equipping is the demonstration and encouragement to the rest of the body on how to hear God's voice, perceive His intent and to prophesy. This is a profound and pivotal role that all believers need equipping in.

PRODUCE MATURITY AND THE FULLNESS OF CHRIST

Ephesians 4:13 until we all reach unity in the faith and in the knowledge of the Son of God and become mature attaining to the whole measure of the fullness of Christ.

Their ministry has more of a directional, fathering aspect to it because its goal is the development of maturity. This leads to more encouragement, exhortation but also admonishment. They share the call to the training up of the body, equipping, directing and bringing release to the members of the body. Different from the manifestation gift and the grace gifts of prophecy, ascension prophets have a much more declarative aspect to their calling. They declare seasons in the Spirit, and often times speak out direction. They are called on to correct people with the lowest form of discipline necessary, to see them turn back to God and His ways. They speak definitive words over key leaders in the body as Agabus, the New Testament prophet mentioned in Acts, did with Paul.

BUILD SUPERNATURAL FOUNDATIONS IN THE CHURCH

Ascension prophets have a unique position to build the kingdom of God as their Old Testament counterparts had unique authority to build the kingdom of Israel. They are set high in authority in the church behind apostles.

1 Corinthians 12:28 And in the church God has appointed first of all apostles, second prophets, third teachers, then workers of miracles, also those having gifts of healing, those able to help others, those with gifts of administration, and those speaking in different kinds of tongues.

Together, with the apostles, they labor at a foundational level in the church. They create the revelation, culture and community within the church. The kingdom of God is not established on any reasoning of men; it is holy and set apart and descends from heaven. It is not founded on earth which is why Jesus said His kingdom was not of this world. The foundational revelations and understanding of the kingdom must come through revelation. On this rock of the revelation of Jesus, the church is built. Prophets are a key part in establishing these fundamental presuppositions in order for kingdom lifestyle to be established in people's lives.

Prophets also supply the sense of God's favor and presence. They cultivate excitement and freedom in the church. They give the leadership of the church a supernatural and visionary edge.

Ephesians 3:4 In reading this, then, you will be able to understand my insight into the mystery of Christ, 5 which was not made known to men in other generations as it has now been revealed by the Spirit to God's holy apostles and prophets.

Eph 2:19 So then you are no longer strangers and aliens, but you are fellow citizens with the [a]saints, and are of God's household, 20 having been built on the foundation of the apostles and prophets, Christ Jesus Himself being the corner stone, (NASB)

Prophets also carry a unique ability to strengthen and encourage both churches and individual members.

Acts 15:32 Judas and Silas, also being prophets themselves, [a]encouraged and strengthened the brethren with a lengthy message. 33 After they had spent time there, they were sent away from the brethren in peace to those who had sent them out. (NASB)

THE BLESSING OFFICE PROPHETS BRING

Let's discuss some practical contributions that they make to the body. Some of these compare to the contributions of the Old Testament prophets. When this is the case, we will look at scriptures from both Testaments. New Testament prophets demonstrate a stark difference with their Old Testament counterparts in one area. Old Testament prophets partnered with the Law to prophesy. New Testament prophets partner with grace. The law and the prophets were co laborers under the old but in these last days God speaks by His Son who is full of grace and truth. New Testament prophets no longer focus on judgment because it has been removed by Jesus blood. They now focus on grace, peace, reconciliation with God and glory revealed.

THEY SPEAK FOR GOD

Jeremiah 15:19. . . if you utter worthy, not worthless, words, you will be my spokesman.

2 Peter 1:21 for prophecy never came by the will of man, but holy men of God spoke as they were moved by the Holy Spirit. (NKJV)

145

Acts 13:2 While they were worshiping the Lord and fasting, the Holy Spirit said,

THE LORD CONFIDES IN THEM

Amos 3:7 Surely the Sovereign LORD does nothing without revealing his plan to his servants the prophets.

Acts 21:10 After we had been there a number of days, a prophet named Agabus came down from Judea. Acts 21:11 Coming over to us, he took Paul's belt, tied his own hands and feet with it and said, "The Holy Spirit says, 'In this way the Jews of Jerusalem will bind the owner of this belt and will hand him over to the Gentiles.'"

THEY ADD PROPHETIC DIRECTION

Hosea 12:13 The LORD used a prophet to bring Israel up from Egypt, by a prophet he cared for him.

Acts 11:27 And in these days prophets came from Jerusalem to Antioch. 28 Then one of them, named Agabus, stood up and showed by the Spirit that there was going to be a great famine throughout all the world, which also happened in the days of Claudius Caesar. 29 Then the disciples, each according to his ability, determined to send relief to the brethren dwelling in Judea. 30 This they also did, and sent it to the elders by the hands of Barnabas and Saul. (NKJV)

THEY RECOGNIZE AND IMPART GIFTING

This is perhaps their most needed ministry in the modern church. So many leaders and leadership positions in the church are being filled by the mechanisms of man without reference to direct revelation and the recognition of the Holy Spirit. It is an extraordinary arrogance for people to assume that the supernatural organism of the body of Jesus Christ, the living building of God, the bride of Christ, can be led or managed by people not submitted to the Holy Spirit's leading. God's leaders must be appointed under revelation by the Holy Spirit. Sadly, this is often not how they are appointed but rather they appointed by consensus, a vote, or out of a desire to encourage their faithfulness. The Holy Spirit knows each person's heart and the gifts He has given them. He is the person who calls leaders forward in His church. Prophets are usually, but not exclusively, at the forefront of this recognition process. It is for this reason that much of the church languishes in confusion regarding leadership and recognition of giftings, because we have not yet learned to acclaim and receive ascension gift prophets. In the New Testament, prophets declared the word of the Holy Spirit in releasing Paul and Barnabus to their apostolic ministries.

1 Samuel 10:1 Then Samuel took a flask of oil and poured it on Saul's head and kissed him, saying, "Has not the LORD anointed you leader over his inheritance?

1 Samuel 16:13 So Samuel took the horn of oil and anointed him in the presence of his brothers, and from that day on the Spirit of the LORD came upon David in power.

1 Timothy 4:14 Do not neglect your gift, which was given you through a prophetic message when the body of elders laid their hands on you.

THEY WITNESS AND POINT TO THE LORD

One of the great hallmarks of ascension prophets is the picture of Jesus they leave in the hearts those they minister to. When the body has been under the ministry of a prophet, they should all be enriched by the greatness of their God as it is revealed through the message of the prophet. It is not necessary to receive a word from God directly from a prophet to receive a vision of the nature of God through the prophet's ministry. I have been in meetings where a prophet has ministered and I have been blessed as God spoke through the prophet to others and I caught a glimpse again of His amazing kindness and love. God's person was revealed, a revelation of foundational value to the church. Prophets who lift themselves up are to be avoided and the church should run screaming from them. Those who lift Jesus up ought to be honored and received.

Isaiah 53: 5 But he was pierced for our transgressions, he was crushed for our iniquities; the punishment that brought us peace was on him, and by his wounds we are healed.

Acts 10:43 All the prophets testify about him that everyone who believes in him receives forgiveness of sins through his name."

Revelation 19:10 . . . Worship God! For the testimony of Jesus is the spirit of prophecy."

Beyond and superseding the prediction, announcements of blessings and admonitions, symbolic actions, receiving and delivering of visions, these prophets give themselves to glorifying God and to testifying to His goodness.

THEY PROVIDE SUPERNATURAL CLARITY ON GOVERNMENTAL DECISIONS

Prophets should be released not only to prophesy, but also to illuminate teachings and engage in explanations, bringing their supernatural insight and ability to outline truth by revelation to the body. This is clearly seen at the Jerusalem council when, after they announced what seemed right to the Holy Spirit and to them, the first thing they did was to give their decision to two prophets and charge them to communicate it to the church. Paul and Barnabus were included in the team as apostles to relay the truth to Antioch where the dispute had erupted. It was the prophets who were tasked with making plain the truth understood at Jerusalem.

*Acts 15:22 Then the apostles and elders, with the whole church, decided to choose some of their own men and send them to Antioch with Paul and Barnabas. They chose **Judas** (called Barsabbas) and **Silas**, men who were leaders among the believers. 23 With them they sent the following letter: The apostles and elders, your brothers, To the Gentile believers in Antioch, Syria and Cilicia: Greetings. 24 We have heard that some went out from us without our authorization and disturbed you, troubling*

148

*your minds by what they said. 25 So we all agreed to choose some men and send them to you with our dear friends Barnabas and Paul— 26 men who have risked their lives for the name of our Lord Jesus Christ. 27 Therefore we are sending Judas and Silas to confirm by word of mouth what we are writing. 28 It seemed good to the Holy Spirit and to us not to burden you with anything beyond the following requirements: 29 You are to abstain from food sacrificed to idols, from blood, from the meat of strangled animals and from sexual immorality. You will do well to avoid these things. Farewell. 30 So the men were sent off and went down to Antioch, where they gathered the church together and delivered the letter. 31 The people read it and were glad for its encouraging message. 32 **Judas and Silas, who themselves were prophets**, said much to encourage and strengthen the believers. 33 After spending some time there, they were sent off by the believers with the blessing of peace to return to those who had sent them.*

WHO MUST THEY SUBMIT TO?

They must submit to the word of God always. They must submit to the apostles when in team, to the local eldership when functioning governmentally in a local church, and to the entire body when prophesying. Those who will not be in submission ought not to be listened to. In the scriptures, Paul demanded orderly, Christ-honoring, encouraging prophecy which submits to apostolic authority. Prophets are not without restraint .

1 John 4:1 Dear friends, do not believe every spirit, but test the spirits to see whether they are from God, because many false prophets have gone out into the world.

1 Corinthians 14:37 If anyone thinks he is a prophet or spiritual, let him recognize that the things which I write to you are the Lord's commandment. 38 But if anyone does not recognize this, he is not recognized.(NASB)

RECOGNIZE AND HONOR THEM TO RECEIVE THE MOST FROM THEM

Prophets who serve well are worthy of honor and respect because they have paid a price for the calling on their lives. Jesus has taught them how to hear His voice and they have learned obedience oftentimes through what they have suffered. When we receive them with gratitude and celebration for their gifting we receive the reward of their ministry. Prophets who are recognized as prophets will achieve the most fruitful ministry. When people viewed Jesus with disdain and were offended at him in Nazareth it hampered His ministry He remarked that it was a lack of honor which was the problem. Lack of recognition robs God's people of their inheritance in Christ and they remain in ignorance and suffer desolate inheritances.

Matthew 13:54 Coming to his hometown, he began teaching the people in their synagogue, and they were amazed. "Where did this man get this wisdom and these miraculous powers?" they asked. 55 "Isn't this the carpenter's son? Isn't his mother's name Mary, and aren't his brothers James, Joseph, Simon and Judas? 56 Aren't all his sisters with us? Where then did this man get all these things?" 57 And they took offense at him. But Jesus said to them, "A prophet is not without honor except in his own town and in his own home." 58 And he did not do many miracles there because of their lack of faith.

To receive the most from Prophets, we set our hearts to work in team with them. We celebrate and respect ascension prophets because of their role in the body of Christ. This respect and honor does not supersede our responsibility to hold them to godly standards. We do not venerate them unduly, nor do we pretend that they are not unique in gifting and calling. We love them and co labor with them in God's house.

Apostles, Prophets and Teachers

Apostles and prophets, prophets and teachers are most closely modeled in the book of Acts for us. Their unique gift mixes create tremendous results. Apostles and prophets build foundations into the churches as the scriptures above have shown. Prophets and teachers create a pattern of godly living as is the case in Antioch where the church was led by a coalition of prophets and teachers and where the believers were first called Christians or "like Christ". The discipling nature of this combination is a potent elixir for the church.

When apostles and prophets minister together they experience a multiplied synergy. The apostles create safe boundaries for ministry, and the prophets experience the security of these boundaries. This "safety net" environment is helpful for the prophet and provides a covering for the body. In this partnership, prophets are able to minister freely, trusting in the wisdom and guidance of the apostolic leadership. Apostles have greatly enhanced vision and insight when the prophets are around. It gives the apostles boldness to know what the Lord is saying with greater accuracy. Apostles find clarity when they partner with prophets. The prophet speaks about the things to come, and spurs the apostle on in courage and confidence. Apostles discover that those elements formerly unclear or at the edge of their spiritual sight, snap into sharp focus when they are around the prophets anointing and ministry. The prophets ability to bring into clarity what is yet afar off helps the apostle know what is out there, much like sharp headlamps are an aid on a dark night allowing for greater confidence and speed in the darkness.

Similarly, prophets aid teachers in showing them clear answers and biblical truth. Often all a teacher needs is this "truth destination" declared by the prophet and scriptures line up in their hearts. They see and understand truth in a new and clearer way. They are then able to bring the body into that revelation step by step.

EVANGELISTS

*E*vangelists are given to the church to enthuse and train the body toward evangelization. Although we do not have many examples in the book of Acts, it does single out Phillip who it specifically names as an evangelist. He was one of the deacons established in the first church. The writers of the gospels are also called evangelists.

Acts 21:8 Leaving the next day, we reached Caesarea and stayed at the house of Philip the evangelist, one of the Seven.

EVERYONE SHOULD EVANGELIZE

The Great commission is the mandate shared by all who believe in Jesus. The Scriptures show that the entire church shared in spreading the gospel around the world.

Acts 8:3 But Saul began to destroy the church. Going from house to house, he dragged off men and women and put them in prison. Acts 8:4 Those who had been scattered preached the word wherever they went.

These people were to spread the gospel and were promised that Jesus' presence would always be with them. They were also assured that certain signs would accompany them in their belief.

Matthew 28:19 Go therefore and make disciples of all the nations, baptizing them in the name of the Father and the Son and the Holy Spirit, 20 teaching them to observe all that I commanded you; and lo, I am with you always, even to the end of the age." (NASB)

Mark 16:15 He said to them, "Go into all the world and preach the good news to all creation. 16 Whoever believes and is baptized will be saved, but whoever does not believe will be condemned. 17 And these signs will accompany those who believe: In my name they will drive out demons; they will speak in new tongues; 18 they will pick up snakes with their hands; and when they drink deadly poison, it will not hurt them at all; they will place their hands on sick people, and they will get well."

These are amazing blessings promised to those who shoulder this mandate. Understanding that we all share in this commission, let's consider the specific role of the ascension evangelist.

THE ROLE OF EVANGELISTS

EQUIP THE SAINTS TO SERVE (PREPARE GOD'S PEOPLE)

Ephesians 4:11 some to be evangelists . . . 12 to prepare God's people for works of service, so that the body of Christ may be built up

Evangelists' most significant contribution is to equip God's people to evangelize. They have the grace to impart God's heart for the lost and have a unique ability to present the gospel clearly to all men. Their ministry enthuses us to the task of spreading the good news and leading people to faith in Jesus. Their heart for those not yet saved is transmitted through the grace of God on their lives. They build up the body by preparing them to spread the gospel all around the world. They also provoke us to greater levels of faith in expecting the Lord to work with us in the process of evangelism.

Mark 16:20 And they went out and preached everywhere, the Lord working with them and confirming the word through the accompanying signs. Amen.(NKJV)

The provocative nature of their ministry mobilizes believers for soul winning. As in all other areas of life, people are emboldened when they see success. Ascension evangelists make soul-winning immanently accessible and thereby help the church get beyond their personal fears.

WIN THE LOST

Evangelists are the publishers of glad tidings. They spread the gospel especially to areas where it does not have wide acceptance. They do not have the ability of the apostle to lay comprehensive foundations in a church, which is demonstrated in the response of the apostles in Acts 8, (they sent apostles to oversee the converts). Nor do they have the Pastor's shepherding gifts to care for the flock in an ongoing manner. However they can illicit salvations and responses to the gospel in areas where the church has not. They are prone to gathering large crowds because of the gifting on their lives.

Acts 8:5 Philip went down to a city in Samaria and proclaimed the Christ there. 6 When the crowds heard Philip and saw the miraculous signs he did, they all paid close attention to what he said. . . 14 When the apostles in Jerusalem heard that Samaria had accepted the word of God, they sent Peter and John to them. 15 When they arrived, they prayed for them that they might receive the Holy Spirit,

THE BLESSINGS EVANGELISTS BRING

THEY TRAVEL EXTENSIVELY

Evangelists travel extensively, appearing to spend less time in a single place than any of the other ascension-gift ministers. They find their most productive ministry under the direct commission of the Holy Spirit. Although they are itinerant, they can be based in a local church.

Acts 8:5 Philip went down to a city in Samaria and proclaimed the Christ there

Acts 8:26 Now an angel of the Lord said to Philip, "Go south to the road--the desert road--that goes down from Jerusalem to Gaza." . . . 29 The Spirit told Philip, "Go to that chariot and stay near it." 30 Then Philip ran up to the chariot and heard the man reading . . . 39 When they came up out of the water, the Spirit of the Lord suddenly took Philip away, and the eunuch did not see him again, but went on his way rejoicing. 40 Philip, however, appeared at Azotus and traveled about, preaching the gospel in all the towns until he reached Caesarea.

THEY OFTEN DEMONSTRATE EXTRAORDINARY POWER, SIGNS AND WONDERS

Evangelists tend to demonstrate the supernatural power of God through their ministry. Evangelists and Apostles see more of this than the other ascension gift ministers. This goes hand-in-hand with the ability to gather crowds and win the lost.

Acts 8:5 Then Philip went down to the[a] city of Samaria and preached Christ to them. 6 And the multitudes with one accord heeded the things spoken by Philip, hearing and seeing the miracles which he did. 7 For unclean spirits, crying with a loud voice, came out of many who were possessed; and many who were paralyzed and lame were healed. 8 And there was great joy in that city. (NKJV)

Acts 8:39 When they came up out of the water, the Spirit of the Lord suddenly took Philip away, and the eunuch did not see him again, but went on his way rejoicing

OTHER ASCENSION GIFTS EVANGELIZING?

In Scripture, when Evangelists were not around, other ministers would assume their role besides equipping and building the church. This was the charge that Paul gave to his son in the faith, Timothy.

2 Timothy 4:5 But you, keep your head in all situations, endure hardship, do the work of an evangelist, discharge all the duties of your ministry.

The word to evangelize is recorded in various places of the apostles as well.

Acts 8:25 When they had testified and proclaimed the word of the Lord, Peter and John returned to Jerusalem, preaching the gospel in many Samaritan villages.

Acts 14:3 So Paul and Barnabas spent considerable time there, speaking boldly for the Lord, who confirmed the message of his grace by enabling them to do miraculous signs and wonders. . . 6 But they found out about it and fled to the Lycaonian cities of Lystra and Derbe and to the surrounding country, 7 where they continued to preach the good news.

Our submission to this gift will stir up and equip us to complete the great commission God gave His church. Whenever the church loses its way and wanders off the heart of God's love for the world, the evangelist's ministry will help us find the path again. When in the busyness of our church programs we no longer are moved by the plight of the lost, it is the evangelists who remind us why Jesus came. Their ache to see the salvation of all is an indispensable gift to the body.

PASTORS, BISHOPS AND SHEPHERDS

The word Pastor is only directly mentioned in Ephesians 4. The duties of this office are mentioned throughout the New Testament, however. Before we look into these, we need to first clarify semantic differences.

ONE OFFICE - TWO FUNCTIONS

Elders are called to pastor (shepherd) and oversee (bishop) the flock. The words Pastor, Bishop and Shepherd are essentially speaking of one office in its various roles. The ascension gift translated Pastor in English, comes from the Greek word "poimen" meaning a shepherd. When shepherding, the pastor is "poimaino". A quick study of each specific Greek word used help us.

Poimaino - to tend as a shepherd, supervisor, feed, rule.

Episkopos - a superintendent, i.e. an officer in general charge of a church, a bishop, an overseer.

Presbuteros - as noun, a senior; Sanhedrist (also fig. Member of the celestial council) or "presbyter" - elder

These three words are used interchangeably when describing elders. Here are some examples:

Acts 20:17 From Miletus, Paul sent to Ephesus for the elders (Presbuteros - elders) of the church. 18 When they arrived, he said to them: . . . 28 Keep watch over yourselves and all the flock of which the Holy Spirit has made you overseers (Episkopos - bishop or oversee). Be shepherds

(Poimaino - shepherd or tend) of the church of God, which he bought with his own blood.

1 Peter 5:1 To the elders (Presbuteros - elders) among you, I appeal as a fellow elder (Presbuteros - elder), a witness of Christ's sufferings and one who also will share in the glory to be revealed: 2 Be shepherds (Poimaino - shepeherd or tend) of God's flock that is under your care, serving as overseers (Episkopeo - bishop or oversee) --not because you must, but because you are willing, as God wants you to be; not greedy for money, but eager to serve; 13 not lording it over those entrusted to you, but being examples to the flock

Some people have separated these roles and created a hierarchy of leadership that I believe Scripture does not intend. We like to think that a shepherd looks after a few sheep and elders watch over them, the Pastor oversees the elders and a Bishop oversees the Pastors. As common as this is in churches, it simply isn't supported scripturally as is proven above. Elders lead churches and are called on to shepherd them (shepherd/ pastor) and oversee them (bishop). So much validation has gone into establishing hierarchy in the church that it is widely accepted as the way things should be. This hierarchy of authority, which can support a domineering and "lording" authority where leaders do not hold themselves in check, is more suited to the executive office than a church. Unfortunately, we seem to have adopted the exercise of leadership authority which is not encouraged in the scriptures and shows the deficiency of mere leadership.

Let's take a closer look at the roles of elders presented in Scripture. The New Testament encourages those who seek to be elders to be honorable and trustworthy. The scriptures call the office noble, and those who seek it are positioned as people of noble desires. People with that desire are encouraged to live and prove the standards all Christians should attain. As elders will be leaders, their lives should model the outworking of God's glorious grace. It is not as though elders have one set of standards and the rest of the body is free to pursue lesser standards. For example its not as if elder must "not be given to much wine" but the people of God can be, or elders should "avoid conceit" but the body can embrace it. The list in Timothy and Titus below is merely stating that if someone desires the office of elder, they must maintain the lifestyle worthy of it, to which all Christians have been called. It ensures that those we are called to honor and respect, live honorably and respectably. It demands that those who are examples to the flock fulfill that role. Here are the scriptures that speak directly to the qualifications for elders.

1 Timothy 3:1 Here is a trustworthy saying: Whoever aspires to be an overseer desires a noble task. 2 Now the overseer is to be above reproach, faithful to his wife, temperate, self-controlled, respectable, hospitable, able to teach, 3 not given to drunkenness, not violent but gentle, not quarrelsome, not a lover of money. 4 He must manage his own family well and see that his children obey him, and he must do so in a manner worthy of full respect. 5 (If anyone does not know how to manage his own family, how can he take care of God's church?) 6 He must not be a recent convert, or he may become conceited and fall under the same judgment as the devil. 7 He must also have a good reputation with outsiders, so that he will not fall into disgrace and into the devil's trap.(NIV11)

Titus 1:5 The reason I left you in Crete was that you might put in order what was left unfinished and appoint elders in every town, as I directed you. 6 An elder must be blameless, faithful to his wife, a man whose children believe and are not open to the charge of being wild and disobedient. 7 Since an overseer manages God's household, he must be blameless—not overbearing, not quick-tempered, not given to drunkenness, not violent, not pursuing dishonest gain. 8 Rather, he must be hospitable, one who loves what is good, who is self-controlled, upright, holy and disciplined. 9 He must hold firmly to the trustworthy message as it has been taught, so that he can encourage others by sound doctrine and refute those who oppose it.

THE ROLE OF ASCENSION PASTORS

Lets investigate what the role of elders are. What do the scriptures say?

A team of elders function together to oversee the sheep God has entrusted to them. They understand that it is their responsibility to shepherd and watch those sheep. They must maintain strong relationships with ascension gift ministers so that they can call on them to come and minister and impart their gifting, heart and passion to the sheep. A beautiful balance exists in these relationships as the shepherds of the flock invite those whose gifts are necessary to bless, equip and provide nutrients to their flock. James, who is believed to be the lead elder in Jerusalem, as his name is usually mentioned before all the elders, was very involved with the apostles. After his arrest, Peter makes sure that James is kept up to date with decisions and communications from the apostles. At the Jerusalem council, Peter talks and Paul and Barnabus add their perspectives, yet it is James who closes the meeting and suggests the conclusion. Here are some scriptures to show the deliberate relational ties between the apostles and the elder team leader in Jerusalem.

Acts 15:2 This brought Paul and Barnabas into sharp dispute and debate with them. So Paul and Barnabas were appointed, along with some other believers, to go up to Jerusalem to see the apostles and elders about this question. . . . 13 When they finished, James spoke up: "Brothers, listen to me. . . . 19 "It is my judgment, therefore, that we should not make it difficult for the Gentiles who are turning to God.

Acts 12:17 Peter motioned with his hand for them to be quiet and described how the Lord had brought him out of prison. "Tell James and the brothers about this," he said, and then he left for another place.

Acts 21:18 The next day Paul and the rest of us went to see James, and all the elders were present.

GOVERN THE CHURCH

Elders provide vision, direction, and a specific culture and discipline in the church. The Scripture expects those who govern to have spent time hearing the voice of God before stepping out in their role. Elders are given authority and responsibility to lead according to the voice of God.

There are 3 words used in scripture for "governing" or "ruling" in the context of leading the church.

PROISTEMI

The first word means to stand in front of, stand at the head of, or to lead. The Greek word is proistemi- to stand before, (in rank) to preside, or (by impl.) to practice:--maintain, be over, rule. This word is used as follows in the context of elders:

1 Timothy 5:17 17 The elders who direct (proistemi) the affairs of the church well are worthy of double honor, especially those whose work is preaching and teaching.

1 Timothy 3:4 He must manage (proistemi) his own family well and see that his children obey him, and he must do so in a manner worthy of full respect. 5 (If anyone does not know how to manage his own family, how can he take care of God's church?)

1 Thessalonians 5:12 Now we ask you, brothers and sisters, to acknowledge those who work hard among you, who care (proistemi) for you in the Lord and who admonish you.

The word is most often used regarding a father and his family but is also used for a spiritual father relationship as Paul said he "was as a father" to Timothy (1Tim1:2, 2 Tim 2:1), to Titus (Titus 1:4), to Onesimus in Philemon 10 and even regarding churches in 1 Thess 2:11-12 and 1 Cor 4:15.

HEGEOMAI

This word denotes commanding and leading. It is hegeomai - to lead, command (with official authority), to deem, consider:--account, (be) chief, count, esteem, governor, judge, have the rule over, suppose, think.)

Hebrews 13:17 Have confidence in your leaders and submit to their authority (hegeomai), because they keep watch over you as those who must give an account. Do this so that their work will be a joy, not a burden, for that would be of no benefit to you . . . 24 Greet all your leaders and all the Lord's people (NIV11)

God's people are to trust and submit to those called to lead or command them. This word is often used of shepherds who led out their flocks and of a general leading out his army.

POIMAINO

The third word about the leadership and oversight of elders means to shepherd, feed and supervise. The Greek word is poimaino and means to tend as a shepherd, supervise, feedand rule. This is especially used of Jesus, the chief shepherd, and then of those under-shepherds who look to the lives of those God has entrusted to them.

1 Peter 5:2 Be shepherds of God's flock that is under your care, watching over them—not because you must, but because you are willing, as God wants you to be; not pursuing dishonest gain, but eager to serve; 3 not lording it over those entrusted to you, but being examples to the flock. 4 And when the Chief Shepherd appears, you will receive the crown of glory that will never fade away.

Ephesians 4:11 So Christ himself gave the apostles, the prophets, the evangelists, the pastors and teachers,

1 Peter 2:25 For "you were like sheep going astray," but now you have returned to the Shepherd and Overseer of your souls.

John 10: 11 "I am the good shepherd. The good shepherd lays down his life for the sheep. 12 The hired hand is not the shepherd and does not own the sheep. So when he sees

162

the wolf coming, he abandons the sheep and runs away. Then the wolf attacks the flock and scatters it. 13 The man runs away because he is a hired hand and cares nothing for the sheep. 14 "I am the good shepherd; I know my sheep and my sheep know me— 15 just as the Father knows me and I know the Father—and I lay down my life for the sheep. 16 I have other sheep that are not of this sheep pen. I must bring them also. They too will listen to my voice, and there shall be one flock and one shepherd."

GUARD THE CHURCH

Like shepherds who keep away the wolves and lead the sheep to safe pastures, the ascension pastor watches to keep away false teachers, false prophets, false apostles, unbiblical teachings, selfish ambitions and those who want to draw people away from wholehearted devotion to Jesus. They ensure correct doctrine, proper focus and point to safe environments. To do this, they must develop a backbone with enough fortitude to confront error and to speak up when wolves threaten their sheep. Shepherds who cannot confront cannot do a good job of watching over God's sheep. Predators need to be resisted as do those who sow to their fleshly lusts.

There needs to be a hands-on approach to their ministry, in other words they must connect with the sheep and live among them. In this way, they become aware of the mood of the sheep and attend to their diet and safety. Sheep are susceptible to the people nearby, who appear kind. It is amazing, that one visit from a shepherd to a distressed family can have such a calming and refocusing effect. Sheep need shepherds, because this is the way Jesus set it up in His church. Shepherds who approach this as a job, will more likely be the hirelings who out of self-preservation allow God's sheep to be hurt. People with God's heart for the sheep are a profound blessing. The Greek word "prosecho" means to hold the mind towards, pay attention to, be cautious about, apply oneself to, attend unto, beware, be given to, give (take) heed to, have regard. It is this word that Paul exhorts the Ephesians elders to accomplish for one another and for all the flock under their care.

Acts 20:28 Keep watch (prosecho) over yourselves and all the flock of which the Holy Spirit has made you overseers. Be shepherds of the church of God, which he bought with his own blood. Acts 20:29 I know that after I leave, savage wolves will come in among you and will not spare the flock. Acts 20:30 Even from your own number men will arise and distort the truth in order to draw away disciples after them. Acts 20:31 So be on your guard!

1 Timothy 4:16 Watch (prosecho) your life and doctrine closely. Persevere in them, because if you do, you will save both yourself and your hearers.

James 5:14 Is any one of you sick? He should call the elders of the church to pray over him and anoint him with oil in the name of the Lord. James 5:15 And the prayer offered in faith will make the sick person well; the Lord will raise him up. If he has sinned, he will be forgiven.

Titus 2:15 These, then, are the things you should teach. Encourage and rebuke with all authority.

GUIDE THE CHURCH

This means that they not only guard but they counsel and teach their people, suggesting, provoking, demonstrating and equipping them for the call of God on their lives. Again, the Greek word used of elders in various scriptures is didaskalia, meaning instruction, doctrine, learning, teaching. This presupposes that they know what they are teaching and have a certain moral authority to speak on that subject. The implications are that they be examples as a part of their teaching and guiding role. They are to disciple the church to become like Jesus and offer themselves as examples.

1 Peter 5:2 Be shepherds of God's flock that is under your care, serving as overseers--not because you must, but because you are willing, as God wants you to be; not greedy for money, but eager to serve; 3 not lording it over those entrusted to you, but being examples to the flock.

1 Timothy 5:17 17 The elders who rule well are to be considered worthy of double honor, especially those who work hard at preaching and teaching. (NASB)

1 Timothy 3:2 Now the overseer must be . . . able to teach,

Ephesians 4:11 It was he who gave some to be . . . pastors and teachers, Eph 4:12 to prepare God's people for works of service, so that the body of Christ may be built up

2 Timothy 4:2 2 Preach the word! Be ready in season and out of season. Convince, rebuke, exhort, with all long suffering and teaching. (NKJV)

In this role of guiding people into sound doctrine and correct ideas, pastors should take a great deal of effort to ensure that they are teaching the pure gospel. There are many fine sounding but un-researched options available these days for the ill prepared pastor. Ideas, quotes and sermon outlines abound. Pastors who for various reason did not prepare well can provide a variety of spiritual fast food, which may taste good and win the approval of their people but fail in the long run to provide healthy sustenance.

PASTORS, BISHOPS AND SHEPHERDS
CONTINUED

GOVERNMENT OF LOCAL CONGREGATIONS

While we know that Jesus is both the head of His church universal and of every local congregation, He cooperates with His appointed leaders to see His kingdom administered in a local setting. In Revelation-, He addresses each church with an individual message. For now, let's examine some examples of local eldership teams leading in response to Jesus.

Each congregation was locally governed. They did not report to a central denomination and no congregation had control over another. Each was under the sovereignty of Christ's lordship. Each congregation was accountable to Him. The angel (messenger or servant) of the Church delivered messages to them. The imagery in this book mirrors the times, as John compares heavenly worship to the earthly worship of the Emperor. Domitian was the Roman Emperor in the day of John, and he would be ushered into the games by twenty-four elders dressed in white who would throw down their crowns and worship him. Domitian would then bring in the satraps, governors or rulers of each province, He would say," I like this that you are doing but I have this against you. If you don't do what I say then I will . . . but if you do this you will receive this reward. . ." Early believers would have read this and understood that it is in this way that Jesus requires His appointed leaders to give an account for their area of responsibility.

The Biblical pattern shows that these local congregations

were each led by a group of elders. It is noteworthy that we never hear of an elder (singular) leading a church by himself but that there was plurality of elders. These elders related in deep and sincere relationships with Apostles and other ascension-gift ministries. It was the strength of their loving relationships that formed the structure and boundaries of the church. Here are some New Testament case studies;

THE CHURCH IN JERUSALEM

It was founded by Jesus and the Apostles aided by the one-hundred and twenty who had come out of the upper room full of the Holy Spirit. The Church was initially led by "the 12" and thus conforms to plurality of leadership.

Acts 2:14 Then Peter stood up with the Eleven, raised his voice and addressed the crowd

Acts 6:2 So the Twelve gathered all the disciples together and said

The scripture speaks later of an eldership at Jerusalem distinct from the apostles

Acts 15:6 The apostles and elders met to consider this question.

Acts 21:17 When we arrived at Jerusalem, the brothers received us warmly. Acts 21:18 The next day Paul and the rest of us went to see James, and all the elders were present.

We see that there were also other ascension-gift ministers recognized among the Jerusalem believers

Acts 11:27 During this time some prophets came down from Jerusalem to Antioch.

THE CHURCH IN ANTIOCH

The Biblical account of the church's beginnings as follows;

Acts 11:19 Now those who were scattered after the persecution that arose over Stephen traveled as far as Phoenicia, Cyprus, and Antioch, preaching the word to no one but the Jews only. 20 But some of them were men from Cyprus and Cyrene, who, when they had come to Antioch, spoke to the Hellenists, preaching the Lord Jesus. 21 And the hand of the Lord was with them, and a great number believed and turned to the Lord. 22 Then news of these things came to the ears of the church in Jerusalem, and they sent out Barnabas to go as far as Antioch. 23 When he came and had seen the grace of God, he was glad, and encouraged them all that with purpose of heart they should continue with the Lord. (NKJV)

The Church in Jerusalem sent Barnabus to Antioch (at that time recognized as a prophet) to strengthen the work of evangelism that had gave rise to the Church. Later in Acts, we see more prophets and teachers ministering within a pluralistic leadership model.

Acts 13:1 In the church at Antioch there were prophets and teachers: Barnabas, Simeon called Niger, Lucius of Cyrene, Manaen (who had been brought up with Herod the tetrarch) and Saul.

It was from here that Paul and Barnabus went out on their apostolic journeys. Their general modus operandi was to establish a Church and on their return voyage, appoint elders by prayer, fasting and the laying on of hands.

Acts 14:21 They preached the good news in that city and won a large number of disciples. Then they returned to Lystra, Iconium and Antioch, 14:22 strengthening the

168

disciples and encouraging them to remain true to the faith...... Acts 14:23 Paul and Barnabas appointed elders for them in each church and, with prayer and fasting, committed them to the Lord, in whom they had put their trust.

THE CHURCH IN EPHESUS

Paul stopped in Ephesus at the end of his second apostolic journey. It was at this time that the Ephesian church was founded. He left Priscilla and Aquila there and returned to Antioch (Acts 18:18-21). Apollos preached in Ephesus soon thereafter and met Priscilla and Aquila who "explained to him the way of God more adequately" (18:26). Paul, on his third journey, spent more than two years in Ephesus teaching and preaching in the synagogue and in the hall of Tyrannus. The Church was governed by elders who related to Paul as an apostle.

Acts 20:17 From Miletus, Paul sent to Ephesus for the elders of the church. Acts 20:18 When they arrived, he said to them.

The Church also welcomed other apostolic ministry and team members

1 Timothy 1:3 As I urged you when I went into Macedonia, stay there in Ephesus so that you may command certain men not to teach false doctrines any longer

2 Timothy 4:12 I sent Tychicus to Ephesus.

PRACTICAL RESPONSIBILITIES OF ELDERS

1. HEARING FROM GOD

As elders are appointed by the Holy Spirit, they must develop a habit of hearing from Him. Without a clear sense of His direction, the church is in danger of throwing off restraint.

The best kinds of elders are those who have trained themselves to tremble at God's word. If the elders cannot answer the question "What has God said to us?" then the church vision will be decided by the most vocal leaders or the sheep, which will more likely lead to personal quests than God's kingdom coming.

Proverbs 29:18 Where there is no revelation, people cast off restraint; but blessed is the one who heeds wisdom's instruction. (NIV 11)

Isaiah 66:2 "These are the ones I look on with favor: those who are humble and contrite in spirit, and who tremble at my word. (NIV 11)

2. Administering that word (Trembling)

The second important function of elders is to see that God's spoken word is incorporated practically into the vision and daily operation of the church. This may take a while to implement, because it involves discussion, teaching, explanation and strategic planning. What good is it if we hear God, but do not execute what He has said? The tiniest action is better than the greatest intention. This was why the Lord said that Moses could not lead the people into their inheritance, because Moses did not tremble at God's word and hold Him up to be Holy in the eyes of the people.

Numbers 20:12 But the LORD said to Moses and Aaron, "Because you did not trust in me enough to honor me as holy in the sight of the Israelites, you will not bring this community into the land I give them." (NIV 11)

3. Being an example to the flock

As the old saying goes, "you can't teach what you don't know and you can't lead where you won't go." Elders must model the life they are calling their members to lead. Our members are told to emulate our faith and way of life. The implications of this are that if it is good for an elder to be doing something then it is good for the sheep to emulate them. Our faith, love, hope, personal attitudes towards finances, family life, marriage, parenting skills and our friendships are all on display and are the credentials for our service as elders. Systemic failure in these areas is grounds for disqualification as an elder.

Hebrews 13:7 Remember those who rule over you, who have spoken the word of God to you, whose faith follow, considering the outcome of their conduct.(NKJV)

1 Peter 5:2 Be shepherds of God's flock that is under your care, . . 3 not lording it over those entrusted to you, but being examples to the flock. (NIV 11)

1 Timothy 3 1 Whoever aspires to be an overseer desires a noble task. 2 Now the overseer is to be . . faithful to his wife, . . .4 He must manage his own family well and see that his children obey him, and he must do so in a manner worthy of full respect. 5 (If anyone does not know how to manage his own family, how can he take care of God's church?) (NIV 11)

4. LEADING (GOVERNING)

We have already discussed elders' responsibility to govern the church. To do this, they should equip themselves with as much leadership development as they can. If you are an elder, since God's sheep are under your leadership, please ensure that it is good leadership. Elders will have to think about strategic planning and decisions which relate to the following areas. They are to lead the Community of the church. This is the sense of love and fellowship and belonging that is the hallmark of believers who love one another deeply from the heart. They should attend to the Calling of the Church. This is the mission that Jesus has specifically emphasized to that church, as He did in Revelations, beyond His general commission to disciple the nations. They are to oversee the Corporate side of the church, which is how they relate to the financial and legal entity that will differ depending on the legal requirements of the country you are in. That a church pays appropriate taxes, bills, manages staffing requirements and payroll expenses well is an important issue for a church. Some churches have sunk their callings and sense of community by not attending to the corporate side of the church.

People who are naïve in church government will find it distasteful that churches must deal with these things but they are even more crucial for churches than other entities.

5. WATCHING OVER THE SHEEP (GUARDING)

The shepherding of sheep involves awareness of their hurts, aspirations and dreams. Additionally, being aware of current attitudes, theological trends and dangerous accusations are important. Mark those who won't listen, repent, take advice or get involved. They are the people most likely to draw people after themselves.

6. FEEDING THE SHEEP (GUIDING)

Elders must pay attention to the theology that comes from the pulpit. This is no small issue. What we tell people to expect and what we hold up to be true has a profound ability to bring our people to freedom or into bondage. In Jesus' day, this explanation of the Law by Rabbi's was called binding or loosing. When a Rabbi said;"This is what the Law says and this is its application to your life. You may do this and you may not do that!" he was binding the people from doing some things and loosing them to do others. This is what was meant by the phrase binding and loosing. This process is repeated weekly from pulpits as elders bind and loose behaviors and expectations in their churches.

We watch over the sheep to give an account, the Bible says. We will not give an account for their personal decisions or actions but we will give an account for what we taught them about the Lord and the example we led before them. Besides Sunday teachings, elders can provide other good resources to teach and encourage the sheep.

7. RECOGNIZING ASCENSION GIFTS

Elders must make a habit of developing relationships with trans-local ascension gifts. When elders notice a deficit in the flock's diet, perhaps prophetic input or evangelistic heart, they should invite those ascension gifts to impart and equip the sheep under their care. While those gifts are ministering, the

172

elders remain as the oversight for the sheep they will have to massage in the ministry they received from that ascension gift long after that person has left. They should also take note of who is growing in faithful service at the local base and showing signs that they are emerging into ascension gift callings.

8. MANAGING STRATEGIC RELATIONSHIPS

God will call all the parts of His body to demonstrate their debt of love to one another. This co laboring with other ministries will take place at a local, national and international level. Elders should give attention to the development and maintenance of these relationships.

THE ORDINATION OF ELDERS

General guidelines in eldership appointments are inferred from the following scriptures.

A. ELDERS ARE APPOINTED BY APOSTLES OR THEIR REPRESENTATIVES

Paul to Titus 1:5 The reason I left you in Crete was that you might straighten out what was left unfinished and appoint elders in every town, as I directed you.

There is no indication in the New Testament that elders were ever appointed outside of the ministry of apostles, and the laying on of apostolic hands to release the necessary authority and grace for the task.

B. PRAYER AND FASTING WERE ESSENTIAL ELEMENTS IN THEIR APPOINTMENT

Acts 14:23 Paul and Barnabas appointed elders for them in each church and, with prayer and fasting, committed them to the Lord, in whom they had put their trust. (NIV 11)

The Holy Spirit knows those leaders He wants to work with in each local congregation and therefore the appointment of elders outside of His revelation is not wise. For this reason the apostles wait on Him until they hear His appointments. Their hands laid on those chosen is an acknowledgement that they are Spirit appointed.

C. ELDERS WERE CHOSEN FROM THE CONGREGATION MEMBERS

It appears that Apostles who essentially had an itinerant ministry could also serve as elders when they were at their home church. Peter operated like this in Jerusalem (1 Pet 5:1 To the elders among you, I appeal as a fellow elder,) yet they did not seem to exert superior authority in this position. See Acts 15:1-30.

The health of the sheep is not dependent on just one of the functions of the shepherd. A shepherd may feed his flock well but if he does not protect them from wolves he has merely fattened them for the slaughter. The shepherd who does not pick the parasites from his sheep will suffer the loss of some to sickness. An essential mix of feeding, directing, counseling, correcting and protecting produces safe, happy and growing sheep.

Teachers

The language of Ephesians 4 has led some people to say that the roles of Pastor and Teacher are the same. I think that the weight of other New Testament scriptures disprove this. Teachers are mentioned in many places as having a vital role in the church.

> *1 Corinthians 12:28 And in the church God has appointed first of all apostles, second prophets, third teachers, then workers of miracles,*

> *Acts 13:1 In the church at Antioch there were prophets and teachers:*

After the apostle and prophet, teachers carry authority in the church because of the vital role they fulfill.

The Role of Teachers

Teachers have the following vital role to play in the church;

Equip the church

Teachers equip the church with certain perspectives that form the members' kingdom world-view. They establish solid theological ground that provides a safe place in which people can grow in their faith. They equip the saints to understand the word of God and to gain insights into His character. They must aid in the maturing of the saints until we all reach unity in the faith and in the knowledge of the Son of God.

Those who teach must take care what they teach. It is of no use that we perfect our style of delivery without knowing what it is that we are to say. The content is way more important than the delivery. One of the informal fallacies in logic is called "Style over substance" which shows that the way in which the argument is presented often causes it to be believed while marginalizing the content of the argument. I heard a story about an acquaintance of mine who saw a preachers notes and periodically in his margins he had written in bold letters the word "SHAW". Inquiring of the preacher what the word was for, the preacher said with a wry smile, it stands for "Shout here argument weak!" Perhaps you have sat under those kinds of teachings. For this reason, Scripture describes clear expectations for those who are to teach the word. Their work is to pray, read and search out revelation truth that will set God's people free.

Acts 18:24 Meanwhile a Jew named Apollos, a native of Alexandria, came to Ephesus. He was a learned man, with a thorough knowledge of the Scriptures. Acts 18:25 He had been instructed in the way of the Lord, and he spoke with great fervor and taught about Jesus accurately, though he knew only the baptism of John. Acts 18:26 He began to speak boldly in the synagogue. When Priscilla and Aquila heard him, they invited him to their home and explained to him the way of God more adequately.

1 Timothy 1:7 They want to be teachers of the law, but they do not know what they are talking about or what they so confidently affirm.

2 Timothy 2:15 Be diligent to present yourself approved to God, a worker who does not need to be ashamed, rightly dividing the word of truth. (NKJV)

SHARE REVELATION

Teachers are to bring insights about God and make them plain to us. They often establish foundational principles that become a foundation for many lives. The teacher's gift usually helps us capture moments of truth in God that stay with us and aid in the renewing of our minds. The work of the cross happens instantaneously when we believe on Jesus Christ. The way of the cross is the path we walk every day from then onward, as we grow in our faith and in the grace of God that is ours. This process of growth and discovery is accelerated if we accept the grace of the teacher. The gift of the teacher is that through revelation teaching, he can propel God's people in the renewal of their minds to every good thing that is theirs. It was this ascension gift ministry that Paul operated in before he received his apostolic call. It was also the first time believers were called "Christians" as they sat under Paul's teaching anointing.

> *Acts 11:25 Then Barnabas went to Tarsus to look for Saul, 26 and when he found him, he brought him to Antioch. So for a whole year Barnabas and Saul met with the church and taught great numbers of people. The disciples were called Christians first at Antioch.*

ESTABLISH SOUND DOCTRINE

Along with the rest of the ascension giftings, the teacher has the responsibility to establish God's people in sound doctrinal practices. If we are to teach sound doctrine in our churches, there will be a few adversaries. First the scripture makes it plain that there will be many false teachers.

> *2 Peter 2:1 But there were also false prophets among the people, just as there will be false teachers among you. They will secretly introduce destructive heresies, even denying the sovereign Lord who bought them—bringing swift destruction on themselves.*

> *2 Peter 2:3 In their greed these teachers will exploit you with stories they have made up. Their condemnation has long been hanging over them, and their destruction has not been sleeping.*

Then we will come to a time in history when sound doctrine is no longer accepted but rather scorned by society.

2 Timothy 4:3 For the time will come when men will not put up with sound doctrine. Instead, to suit their own desires, they will gather around them a great number of teachers to say what their itching ears want to hear.

Third there will always be some people eager to hear new doctrine but who do not make any effort to apply it to their lives.

Acts 17:21 21 For all the Athenians and the foreigners who were there spent their time in nothing else but either to tell or to hear some new thing. (NKJV)

God has established teachers as the primary force against false teaching. This is why those who teach ought to take great care with what they teach. Teachers ought not to take this role on themselves as it bears tremendous spiritual importance and consequences.

James 3:1 Not many of you should presume to be teachers, my brothers, because you know that we who teach will be judged more strictly.

1 Timothy 1:3 As I urged you when I went into Macedonia, stay there in Ephesus so that you may command certain men not to teach false doctrines any longer

CREATE SPACIOUS PLACES FOR GOD'S PEOPLE

All good theology leads to worship. It has its focus on God and brings revelation, awe and worship. The nature of legalism is that it traps people in small cages. The nature of licentiousness is that it proclaims that there are no absolutes. True and sound doctrine sets God's people free and causes them to be focused on Jesus. Sound doctrine proclaims that we are free from the law of sin and death and are bond slaves to the Lord Jesus. God's truth brings freedom to people and His grace teaches us to say no to ungodliness. The teacher brings freedom and creates space for people to love the Lord. The teacher's gift adds grace to people to grow up in their faith and equips them for service.

The nature of True and False Teachers

The following guidelines may be helpful;

False teachers deny Jesus' deity, True teachers celebrate it

1 John 2:22 Who is the liar? It is the man who denies that Jesus is the Christ. Such a man is the antichrist—he denies the Father and the Son.

False teachers are secretive, disrespecting authority, True teachers speak openly respecting established authority

Jude 1:4 For certain men whose condemnation was written about long ago have secretly slipped in among you.

2 Peter 2:1 But there were also false prophets among the people, just as there will be false teachers among you. They will secretly introduce destructive heresies

False teachers add to the message of Jesus, True teachers stick to Jesus as close as possible

2 John 1:9 Anyone who runs ahead and does not continue in the teaching of Christ does not have God; whoever continues in the teaching has both the Father and the Son.

False teachers change God's grace into license, True teachers establish everyone in true liberty

Jude 1:4 For certain men have crept in unnoticed, who long ago were marked out for this condemnation, ungodly men, who turn the grace of our God into lewdness and deny the only Lord God and our Lord Jesus Christ. (NKJV)

FALSE TEACHERS TEND TO BE HARSH AND STRANGE, TRUE
TEACHERS ARE GRACIOUS AND BIBLICAL

*Col 2:23 These things indeed have an appearance of
wisdom in self-imposed religion, false humility, and
neglect of the body, but are of no value against the
indulgence of the flesh. (NKJV)*

Section 3.2

MANIFESTATION GIFTS

Manifestation Gifts

*O*ne of the primary three lists of gifts in the New Testament is found in 1 Corinthians 12:7–11. A further two lists are found in the same chapter but they contain references to these manifestations of the Holy Spirit as well as to ascension gifts and grace gifts. This then is the scripture relating to manifestations of the Holy Spirit.

1 Corinthians 12:7 Now to each one the manifestation of the Spirit is given for the common good. 8 To one there is given through the Spirit the message of wisdom, to another the message of knowledge by means of the same Spirit, 9 to another faith by the same Spirit, to another gifts of healing by that one Spirit, 10 to another miraculous powers, to another prophecy, to another distinguishing between spirits, to another speaking in different kinds of tongues, and to still another the interpretation of tongues. 11 All these are the work of one and the same Spirit, and he gives them to each one, just as he determines.

Phanerosis

The word used here for manifesting is phanerosis and it means to exhibit or express, bestow or manifest. When the Holy Spirit uses people to make Himself manifest in a meeting He usually manifests in one of these gifts. These gifts are given to make the Holy Spirit's presence apparent as they are exhibited through willing participants in supernatural ways.

They are usually categorized in the following ways; The "speaking" gifts – tongues, interpretation of tongues and prophecy. The "knowing" gifts – word of wisdom, word of knowledge and discerning of spirits. The "power" gifts – healings, faith and miracles.

Before we look into each of these gifts specifically, we need to lay some foundations.

TWO REASONS FOR ERROR

Jesus pointed out two reasons for the Sadducees straying from truth.

Matthew 22:29 Jesus replied, "You are in error because you do not know the Scriptures or the power of God.

We need to know the scriptures and additionally be familiar with the power of God, so that we can avoid error because it finds its way into Christians lives through a deficit in either of these issues. Some people have an extensive yet sterile theology and no experience with the visible power demonstrations of the Holy Spirit. Some people have experienced diverse supernatural manifestations of the Holy Spirit and yet they demonstrate poor theology and questionable biblical interpretation. Neither of these options is appropriate and both should be avoided because they lead to divergence from truth. The two ought to be in balance, the scriptures being wielded by the Spirit of God to become the sword of the Spirit. We should press into our own personal growth in both of these areas to avoid the dangers of error.

ARE THESE GIFTS SUPPOSED TO OPERATE TODAY?

Didn't these all peter out with Peter? No they did not, but there is a large portion of the church universal that teach that these gifts were given until the church was established and the scriptures had finally been written. They say that now that we have the scriptures, these manifestations have fallen away. This thesis is founded mostly on the passage in 1 Corinthians 13:8 which they mistakenly believe speaks to the fact. A good example of this teaching is found in the commentary by Jamieson, Fausset and Brown who say "A primary fulfillment of Paul's statement took place when the Church attained its maturity;

183

then "tongues" entirely "ceased," and "prophesyings" and "knowledge," so far as they were supernatural gifts of the Spirit, were superseded as no longer required. When the ordinary preaching of the word, and the Scriptures of the New Testament collected together, had become established institutions."

While this belief is widely held it is not consistent with what the scriptures say. Biblical truth, as the context of 1 Corinthians 13 shows, is that these things will cease at a specific time. Here is the passage;

1 Corinthians 13:8 Love never fails. But where there are prophecies, they will cease; where there are tongues, they will be stilled; where there is knowledge, it will pass away. 9 For we know in part and we prophesy in part, 10 but when perfection comes, the imperfect disappears. . . 12 Now we see but a poor reflection as in a mirror; then we shall see face to face. Now I know in part; then I shall know fully, even as I am fully known.

The context places the ceasing of tongues and prophecies at the same time as; "when perfection comes" (v10) the imperfect disappears. "when we see Him face to face" (v12) as opposed to now seeing but a poor reflection and "when we know fully even as we are fully known" (v12) and opposed to our current knowing in part.

There is not one passage that speaks about the scriptures superseding or putting an end to tongues or prophesying. There are many scriptures teaching to the subject of these manifestations and showing their use as a normal part of the life of the church. In many churches today, anyone demonstrating any of the gifts found in 1 Corinthians 12 or 14 would be considered "fringe" if not bordering on heretical, while those boldly proclaiming the love preached in 1 Corinthians 13 are hailed as true saints. Thus the process of relegating large portions of the New Testament to the "currently irrelevant" bin is their ongoing and difficult proposition. Those who take this stand must deliberately speak against the clear scriptural injunctions in 1 Cor 12:31 and 1 Cor 14:1 to eagerly desire these spiritual gifts or to not treat prophecies with contempt in 1 Th

5:20 or to not forbid tongues and to encourage prophecy as in 1 Cor 14:39. Combine this with the fact that millions of believers worldwide still experience the wonderful manifestations of the Holy Spirit in these ways, this cessationist position is very flimsy.

The harsh reality is that many who believe that the Holy Spirit still works signs and wonders today, tend to act in excess that is unhelpful. They seem to assume that the louder and more extreme the practices, the more extravagant the message and delivery, the more spiritual the moment. Many times the leadership or direction of a meeting is surrendered to anything that seems supernatural or flamboyant. I understand that the Lord often breaks into His church in ways we did not anticipate and I love those moments. The point I'm making here is that it does not follow that if something is unexpected or abnormal it must be God.

People who believe that the Holy Spirit still does today what He did in the early church tend to experience far more "supernatural" events. Those who expect spiritual gifts, manifestations, and fruit to be a regular part of church life see them often. These churches tend to enjoy a greater degree of the free expression of emotion, yet at the same time, these demonstrations can also tend to the dramatic and silly when not checked. In this context, spiritual leaders who create security in the body by encouraging people to step out in spiritual gifts while at the same time not allowing excess or error to take the lead, are particularly important. Many Christians choose to walk within a church whose theology does not embrace these gifts not because they don't believe in them but because those churches are a safer spiritual environment. The lack of spiritual oversight when the gifts are exercised create harmful meetings.

We must aim to manifest the gifts of the Holy Spirit in a mature fashion, helpful to those who experience them. Here are a few foundational truths about manifesting His gifts.

NINE FOUNDATIONAL TRUTHS TO MANIFESTING THESE GIFTS

1. THE GIFTS DO NOT SPEAK TO THE MATURITY OF THE PERSON MANIFESTING THEM.

Paul addresses the Corinthians as mere babes in Christ needing baby milk and still unable to digest true food or depth. In this very epistle he answers their questions regarding spiritual gifts. If someone manifests a gift of the Holy Spirit, it is a testimony to their availability and willingness, not to their maturity in Christ.

1 Corinthians 3:1 Brothers, I could not address you as spiritual but as worldly--mere infants in Christ. 2 I gave you milk, not solid food, for you were not yet ready for it. Indeed, you are still not ready. . . . 12:1 Now about the gifts of the Spirit, brothers and sisters, I do not want you to be uninformed.

2. GOD USES THE FURNISHINGS OF OUR MINDS WHEN HE SPEAKS TO AND THROUGH US.

Many times God uses pictures, elements and images that are already within our lifeworld to communicate eternal truths to us. These constitute the first part of manifesting a spiritual gift. Once we understand the message we can then manifest the gift. Most people do this in the way they prefer. Jesus, who functioned in these areas all the time, manifested the Holy Spirit without drawing attention to Himself. He seemed to be naturally supernatural, and so should we.

Peter went up on the roof to pray. (Acts 10:10) He became hungry and wanted something to eat, and while the meal was being prepared, he fell into a trance. God used the furnishings of Peter's mind as a Jew and the hunger of his body to deliver a word from heaven for him.

Acts 10:11 He saw heaven opened and something like a large sheet being let down to earth by its four corners. 12 It contained all kinds of four-footed animals, as well as reptiles of the earth and birds of the air. 13 Then a voice told him, "Get up, Peter. Kill and eat." 14 "Surely not, Lord!" Peter replied. "I have never eaten anything impure or unclean."

186

3. The Gifts Must Be Eagerly Desired

The first lesson of the great mystery of Godliness is that God appeared in flesh (see 1 Tim 3:16). The mystery of God's glory being made manifest in human flesh. He still wants to display this great mystery by manifesting the Holy Spirit through His bride. She must work with Him and cooperate with Him. Her eager desire to be used demonstrates to Him that she is ready. Jesus longs to manifest and spread His grace to His body when we come together and waits eagerly for those who will cooperate with His Spirit during these times. Desire is a strong trait in those who manifest His gifts. Seldom do disinterested or antagonistic people taste any of this manifestation. The Holy Spirit works most through those who eagerly partner with Him. The Holy Spirit works with those with surrendered hearts and who desire His gifts.

1 Corinthians 12:31 But eagerly desire the greater gifts. . . 1 Corinthians 14:1 Follow the way of love and eagerly desire spiritual gifts, especially the gift of prophecy. . . . 1 Corinthians 14:39 Therefore, my brothers, be eager to prophesy, and do not forbid speaking in tongues.

4. They Are Given For The Benefit Of All

We must get beyond the idea that these manifestations are primarily for the individual bringing them. Their purpose is always for the common good. The context of 1 Corinthians 12 through 14, shows that the unity of the body is of paramount importance. These manifestations have in their basic design a purpose for common good, and when used correctly, foster unity and blessing across the whole body. Manifestations not focused on the common good of the church, are off base. Personal benefit and blessing are subject to the whole body being blessed. The only manifestation for private use is tongues for personal edification. (see 1 Cor 14:4, Jude 1:20)

1 Corinthians 12:7 Now to each one the manifestation of the Spirit is given for the common good.

1 Corinthians 14:5 I wish you all spoke with tongues, but even more that you prophesied; for he who prophesies is greater than he who speaks with tongues, unless indeed he interprets, that the church may receive edification. (NKJV)

1 Corinthians 14:12 So it is with you. Since you are eager to have spiritual gifts, try to excel in gifts that build up the church.

5. IGNORANCE AND IMMATURITY IN THEIR USE CAN DO MORE HARM THAN GOOD

The fact that these gifts originate with God does not imply that their use is always beneficial. Like the rest of God's creation, people can mismanage them. Ignorance in these issues can do damage and put people off. Immaturity can lead to the practice of unbiblical standards. For this reason, the manifestation gifts are subject to standards and oversight of leaders and mature believers or else they do more harm than good.

1 Corinthians 12:1 Now about spiritual gifts, brothers, I do not want you to be ignorant . . . . 1 Corinthians 11:17 In the following directives I have no praise for you, for your meetings do more harm than good.

6. CLARITY AND SIMPLICITY ARE THE MOST EFFECTIVE

Clarity is vital. Everyone needs to understand this and leaders are to ensure it. It is better to wait until there is a clear sense of what the Holy Spirit wants, than to bring something that is confusing and disorderly. Without a clear sense of God's purpose, people are left perplexed or fearful, which is never God's intent. Peter, on the day of Pentecost, had to get up and present an explanation to those present because until that time the crowd was "confused", "amazed" and "perplexed" see Acts 2:14 - Acts 2:16. Vague or weird manifestations do not serve this purpose.

1 Corinthians 14:6 But now, brethren, if I come to you speaking with tongues, what shall I profit you unless I speak to you either by revelation, by knowledge, by prophesying, or by teaching? 7 Even things without life, whether flute or harp, when they make a sound, unless they make a distinction in the sounds, how will it be known what is piped or played? 8 For if the trumpet makes an uncertain sound, who will prepare for battle? 9 So likewise you, unless you utter by the tongue words easy to understand, how will it be known what is spoken? For you will be speaking into the air. 10 There are, it may be, so many kinds of languages in the world, and none of them is without significance. 11 Therefore, if I do not know the meaning of the language, I shall be a foreigner to him who speaks, and he who speaks will be a foreigner to me. 12 Even so you, since you are zealous for spiritual gifts, let it be for the edification of the church that you seek to excel. 13 Therefore let him who speaks in a tongue pray that he may interpret. (NKJV)

7. THEY ARE TO BE JUDGED BY THE CONGREGATION AND LEADERS

No one is going to get it right all the time because we live in the age when we see and prophesy only in part. Therefore, believers are told to judge these things, discarding the wrong yet maintaining respect for the grace God gives. This means that no one ought to take offense when they are corrected by leaders or other members of the church. The first act of spiritual maturity is to acknowledge truth and be subject to the rest of the body of Christ.

1 Corinthians 13:9 For we know in part and we prophesy in part,

1 Thessalonians 5:21 Test everything. Hold on to the good. 1 Th 5:22 Avoid every kind of evil. . . . 1 Th 5:19 Do not put out the Spirit's fire; 1 Th 5:20 do not treat prophecies with contempt.

1 Corinthians 14:37 If anybody thinks he is a prophet or spiritually gifted, let him acknowledge that what I am writing to you is the Lord's command. 38 If he ignores this, he himself will be ignored.

8. THEIR TIMING AND STYLE CAN BE CONTROLLED

Personal control is necessary to facilitate an orderly environment for all to hear and experience the purposes of God. The person manifesting the Holy Spirit is in control of themselves. If they can no longer function normally, someone else needs to bring explanation. I have no problem with the idea that someone can be overcome by God's glory and power, but if that is the case they are not the best candidates to be leading the meeting or bringing clarity to it.

1 Corinthians 14:29 Let two or three prophets speak, and let the others pass judgment. 30 But if a revelation is made to another who is seated, the first one must keep silent.31 For you can all prophesy one by one, so that all may learn and all may be exhorted; 32 and the spirits of prophets are subject to prophets; 33 for God is not a God of confusion but of peace, as in all the churches of the)saints.(NASB)

9. THEY SHOULD BE USED WITH REGARD TO THE LOST

These gifts cannot be used without regard to the lost that are in our meetings. We must have regard for those who do not know the Lord and who may find these manifestations weird. The proper use of the gifts, with clarity and maturity, will bring them to a place of evident faith, saying, "Wow, God is in this place!"

1 Corinthians 14:23 So if the whole church comes together and everyone speaks in tongues, and some who do not understand or some unbelievers come in, will they not say that you are out of your mind? . . . . . 24 But if an unbeliever or someone who does not understand comes in while everybody is prophesying, he will be convinced by all that he is a sinner and will be judged by all, 25 and the secrets of his heart will be laid bare. So he will fall down and worship God, exclaiming, "God is really among you!"

So we see that these gifts given by the Holy Spirit can bring great excitement and blessing to the body. Like any other gift from God, if poorly managed, these gifts can bring frustration and damage. Good church leaders will labor to create a safe environment where these manifestation gifts can function. This will open up tremendous sources of the life of God to flow into the churches they lead. Lets take a closer look at each of these manifestation gifts.

THE MESSAGE OF WISDOM

*T*his is the first gift mentioned as a manifestation gift of the Holy Spirit. It is given to make an aspect of God's wisdom known to His people. It is given by the Holy Spirit supernaturally and as such is not the same as human wisdom that is gained through hard work and life experience. This gift is unearned and free from the Holy Spirit.

A word of wisdom often accompanies the word of knowledge. When the Lord speaks about an issue or event that is to come He often gives with that knowledge, a godly answer for His people.

OLD TESTAMENT EXAMPLES OF THIS GIFT

Joseph shows us the most obvious demonstration of God-given wisdom. Joseph's gift of wisdom led Pharaoh to elevate him to a position of authority.

> *Genesis 41:37 Now the proposal seemed good to Pharaoh and to all his servants. Joseph Is Made a Ruler of Egypt 38 Then Pharaoh said to his servants, "Can we find a man like this, in whom is a divine spirit?" 39 So Pharaoh said to Joseph, "Since God has informed you of all this, there is no one so discerning and wise as you are. 40" You shall be over my house, and according to your command all my people shall do homage; only in the throne I will be greater than you."(NASB)*

Daniel, another political leader and prophet, functioned in this gift when Nebuchadnezzar had a dream.

Daniel 2:30 As for me, this mystery has been revealed to me, not because I have greater wisdom than anyone else alive, but so that Your Majesty may know the interpretation and that you may understand what went through your mind. . . 46 Then King Nebuchadnezzar fell prostrate before Daniel and paid him honor and ordered that an offering and incense be presented to him. 47 The king said to Daniel, "Surely your God is the God of gods and the Lord of kings and a revealer of mysteries, for you were able to reveal this mystery."

Other Old Testament examples include Noah, to whom was given the knowledge of a coming flood along with the details to construct an ark. David was given wisdom for the plans of the great temple that Solomon built. Elijah was shown where to go during the famine to find provision. Just about anyone who sought the Lord earnestly was guided by supernatural wisdom from the Holy Spirit. This pattern continues in the New Testament with the great reality that all believers are now indwelt by God's Spirit and therefore have direct access to His wisdom.

NEW TESTAMENT EXAMPLES

Agabus, who is recognized as an ascension-gift prophet, functioned in a word of knowledge when he predicted a famine to come. The disciples, functioning under a word of wisdom, decided to send money with Paul and Barnabas.

Acts 11:28 One of them, named Agabus, stood up and through the Spirit predicted that a severe famine would spread over the entire Roman world. (This happened during the reign of Claudius.) 29 The disciples, as each one was able, decided to provide help for the brothers and sisters living in Judea. 30 This they did, sending their gift to the elders by Barnabas and Saul.

Jesus promised that believers would be given this gift when they are persecuted and especially when they are called on to give testimony before governing authorities. His promise is soon demonstrated with Stephen, as he gives a defense of the gospel.

Matthew 10:19 But when they arrest you, do not worry about what to say or how to say it. At that time you will be given what to say, 20 for it will not be you speaking, but the Spirit of your Father speaking through you.

Acts 6:8 Now Stephen, a man full of God's grace and power, performed great wonders and signs among the people. 9 Opposition arose, however, from members of the Synagogue of the Freedmen (as it was called)—Jews of Cyrene and Alexandria as well as the provinces of Cilicia and Asia—who began to argue with Stephen. 10 But they could not stand up against the wisdom the Spirit gave him as he spoke.

The gift of wisdom is promised to us in the New Covenant. James tells us that God is a generous giver of wisdom without regarding our faults. It is amazing that we, who have so little, can ask for an abundance of wisdom from our Father who gives freely, without finding fault. It remains then for us only to ask in faith, believing He will give to us generously.

James 1:5 If any of you lacks wisdom, you should ask God, who gives generously to all without finding fault, and it will be given to you.

Paul teaches us in the book of Ephesians that it is God's intent to demonstrate the many facets of His Divine wisdom through His body, the church. God wants to rub the devil's nose in it. He wants to show the world that He has the answers to all of our problems.

Ephesians 3:8 Although I am less than the least of all the Lord's people, this grace was given me: to preach to the Gentiles the boundless riches of Christ, 9 and to make plain to everyone the administration of this mystery, which for ages past was kept hidden in God, who created all things. 10 His intent was that now, through the church, the manifold wisdom of God should be made known to the rulers and authorities in the heavenly realms, 11 according to his eternal purpose that he accomplished in Christ Jesus our Lord.

Why does the Holy Spirit give this gift?

To win the lost

The word of wisdom enables Christians to present the gospel clearly to unbelievers. The apostles, throughout the book of Acts, present the gospel in a different manner each time they preach. Sometimes bold and public, other times gentle and private. Sometimes, they preached within a Jewish framework and at other times with Greek philosophy in a lecture hall. This gift is also used when opponents of the gospel need to be silenced or refuted. As with Stephen, the Holy Spirit manifests in wisdom to make the gospel compelling and clear.

When God's people are in difficulty

God loves to give wisdom when we most need it. When life is bleak and difficult, He provides perfect wisdom. God's wisdom can make difficult and seemingly immovable situations turn to peace and success. Often, it will be extremely practical in its application. James exhorts us that when we are in trouble, we should seek God in prayer.

James 5:13 Is anyone among you in trouble? Let them pray. (NIV11)

To demonstrate God's priorities and perspectives

We are called to the renewing of our minds and to fix our minds in heavenly places. It is easy for those who are not watchful to lose sight of the kingdom and to fill their minds with worldly thoughts. This is the mistake Peter made when he rebuked Jesus for talking about the sufferings He was about to go through. Jesus called Peter "Satan" because he did not have in mind the things of God but the things of man. God will give a word of wisdom to His people to help them renew their minds and catch a glimpse of His priorities. A mind once opened by this kind of wisdom does not easily go back to earthly thoughts. James again warns us of this kind of poor thinking and extols the wisdom of God as the answer.

James 3: 13 Who is wise and understanding among you? Let them show it by their good life, by deeds done in the humility that comes from wisdom. 14 But if you harbor bitter envy and selfish ambition in your hearts, do not boast about it or deny the truth. 15 Such "wisdom" does not come down from heaven but is earthly, unspiritual, demonic. 16 For where you have envy and selfish ambition, there you find disorder and every evil practice. 17 But the wisdom that comes from heaven is first of all pure; then peace-loving, considerate, submissive, full of mercy and good fruit, impartial and sincere.

Paul constantly prayed that our hearts would be open to God's wisdom, so that we might realize all the blessing that is ours in Jesus.

Ephesians 1:17 I keep asking that the God of our Lord Jesus Christ, the glorious Father, may give you the Spirit of wisdom and revelation, so that you may know him better. 18 I pray that the eyes of your heart may be enlightened in order that you may know the hope to which he has called you, the riches of his glorious inheritance in his holy people, 19 and his incomparably great power for us who believe.

God's wisdom given supernaturally by the Holy Spirit, changes lives. It is a gift to be sought after, along with all the other manifestation gifts, but is a precious commodity for anyone seeking to grow in their walk with God.

THE WORD OF KNOWLEDGE

*A*lthough many Old and New Testament examples of this gift exist, it is only mentioned once by name in the New Testament. It is a harbinger of faith and has the power to stir people's sense of God's Presence.

1 Corinthians 12:7 But to each one is given the manifestation of the Spirit for the common good. 8 For to one is given the word of wisdom through the Spirit, and to another the word of knowledge according to the same Spirit; (NASB)

WHAT IS A WORD OF KNOWLEDGE?

A word of knowledge is the gift of the Holy Spirit to make His will, nature, and presence manifest. He does this by revealing a piece of what He knows to one of His people, for a specific reason. It is the supernatural revelation of certain facts. These facts concern something previously unknown through normal human process. The Holy Spirit shares some of His "supernatural" knowledge because He wants to further His purposes and demonstrate His heart.

Manifestation of this gift does not mean that we share God's omniscience. It is merely the revelation of a small portion of God's endless knowledge. If someone receives a word of knowledge, it does not mean that they have a perfect or divine character. Old Testament prophets, like Elijah, were still fallible even thought they received many words of knowledge.

2 Kings 4:25 So she went and came to the man of God to Mount Carmel. When the man of God saw her at a distance, he said to Gehazi his servant, "Behold, there is the Shunammite. 26 "Please run now to meet her and say to her, 'Is it well with you? Is it well with your husband? Is it well with the child?'" And she answered, "It is well." 27 When she came to the man of God to the hill, she caught hold of his feet. And Gehazi came near to push her away; but the man of God said, "Let her alone, for her soul is troubled within her; and the LORD has hidden it from me and has not told me." (NASB)

Similar examples are found with the prophet Elisha.

2 Kings 6:8 Now the king of Aram was at war with Israel. After conferring with his officers, he said, "I will set up my camp in such and such a place."9 The man of God sent word to the king of Israel: "Beware of passing that place, because the Arameans are going down there." 10 So the king of Israel checked on the place indicated by the man of God. Time and again Elisha warned the king, so that he was on his guard in such places. 211 This enraged the king of Aram. He summoned his officers and demanded of them, "Will you not tell me which of us is on the side of the king of Israel?" 12 "None of us, my lord the king," said one of his officers, "but Elisha, the prophet who is in Israel, tells the king of Israel the very words you speak in your bedroom."

A word of knowledge that is found in 1 Corinthians 12 is distinct from other forms of naturally occurring or human induced knowledge. It is not the outcome of education or the gathering of learned teaching. People who do not have the Holy Spirit cannot manifest this gift.

A word of knowledge is not fortune telling or even predictive in its emphasis. It does not come through the working of our minds or the exercise of our imaginations and it shouldn't be guesswork. God speaks to our spirits by His Spirit, bypassing our minds and depositing the knowledge directly into our spirits, which then presents the knowledge to our minds, complete as given.

Although it functions within the boundaries of good theology, hemmed in by the scriptures and character of God, it is not merely the product of these. In other words, it is not simply knowledge about God. It should function together with good teaching and mature expression.

HOW DOES THE GIFT COME TO US?

The Holy Spirit can bring these words of knowledge to us in a number of ways. Sometimes He will use general knowledge to start or provoke our thought processes. Whatever way He chooses to reveal this knowledge, we are left with a definite conviction, an impression, or a sudden knowing in our spirits. Scriptural examples that demonstrate these words of knowledge can sometimes comes through a Scripture that is quickened to us.

Daniel 9:2 in the first year of his reign, I, Daniel, understood from the Scriptures, according to the word of the LORD given to Jeremiah the prophet, that the desolation of Jerusalem would last seventy years.

Sometimes it occurs like an insight, a perception or understanding of circumstances. It is as though someone whispered certain facts in your ear at a level too low to be audible to others, except that no audible whisper occurs. The knowledge is not there in one moment and it is the next. You end up knowing something, perceiving it in your spirit without normal mechanisms of communication.

Mark 2:7 "Why does this fellow talk like that? He's blaspheming! Who can forgive sins but God alone?" Mark 2:8 Immediately Jesus knew in his spirit that this was what they were thinking in their hearts, and he said to them, "Why are you thinking these things?

To some, God chooses to deliver this gift through dreams, visions, and mental pictures. This is probably one of the most common ways the Holy Spirit gives these words. In these cases, the Lord often adds a great amount of detail.

Acts 9:10 Now there was a disciple at Damascus named Ananias; and the Lord said to him in a vision, "Ananias." And he said, "Here I am, Lord." 11 And the Lord said to him, "Get up and go to the street called Straight, and inquire at the house of Judas for a man from Tarsus named Saul, for he is praying, 12 and he has seen in a vision a man named Ananias come in and lay his hands on him, so that he might regain his sight." (NASB)

Sometimes words of knowledge come through angelic visitation or audible voice. I do not know why God uses such different ways to give us these words of knowledge. The variety of delivery mechanisms is part of His infinite creativity.

Luke 24:5 In their fright the women bowed down with their faces to the ground, but the men said to them, "Why do you look for the living among the dead? Luke 24:6 He is not here; he has risen! Remember how he told you, while he was still with you in Galilee:

Acts 8:26 Now an angel of the Lord said to Philip, "Go south to the road--the desert road--that goes down from Jerusalem to Gaza."

Often these words come as a simple deep impression left in our spirit. They form convictions that are certain.

Acts 20:22 "And now, behold, bound by the Spirit, I am on my way to Jerusalem, not knowing what will happen to me there, 23 except that the Holy Spirit solemnly testifies to me in every city, saying that bonds and afflictions await me. (NASB)

WHY DOES THE GIFT COME TO US?

As we said in the beginning of this section, the Holy Spirit wants to demonstrate and make God manifest. When He gives a person a word of knowledge, it is given to accomplish His

200

purpose and requires that the person cooperates with Him. Here are a few reasons why He gives this particular gift.

1. FOR EVANGELISM

Jesus used this gift to make the presence and love of God manifest to a Samaritan woman whose testimony led to many to Christ. She was astounded that He knew details of her life and afforded Him prophet status. She told everyone in the city that He knew everything about her.

> *John 4:15 The woman said to Him, "Sir, give me this water, that I may not thirst, nor come here to draw." 16 Jesus said to her, "Go, call your husband, and come here." 17 The woman answered and said, "I have no husband." Jesus said to her, "You have well said, 'I have no husband,' 18 for you have had five husbands, and the one whom you now have is not your husband; in that you spoke truly."19 The woman said to Him, "Sir, I perceive that You are a prophet. . . . . John 4:28 The woman then left her waterpot, went her way into the city, and said to the men, 29 "Come, see a Man who told me all things that I ever did. Could this be the Christ?" 30 Then they went out of the city and came to Him. . . . . John 4:39 And many of the Samaritans of that city believed in Him because of the word of the woman who testified, "He told me all that I ever did." 40 So when the Samaritans had come to Him, they urged Him to stay with them; and He stayed there two days. (NKJV)*

2. FOR COLLABORATION WITH THE OTHER GIFTS

A. TO STIR FAITH FOR HEALING OR OTHER MINISTRY

A specific piece of knowledge makes the love of God, His intimate knowledge of the person, and His imminent care for the person, manifest to them and stirs their faith to believe that He will heal or minister to them. It pierces through the carefully laid lies of the enemy that God is distant and unconcerned with the person's life and details. Once their heart is open and faith is stirred, they are ready to receive the gifts of healing or a prophetic word of encouragement etc.

B. TO IDENTIFY AND ENCOURAGE SPECIFIC PEOPLE, PLACES, PROBLEMS OR PERSPECTIVES

This authenticates prophetic words, words of wisdom, calls for ministry, words of encouragement and is a bulwark against the enemy's standard temptation of "Did God really say . . .? " It allows for a specific and confirming sense of the will of the Lord. People are greatly encouraged by an accurate word of knowledge.

3. TO EXPOSE REBELLION OR UN-REPENTED SIN

James teaches that we all stumble in many ways (James 3:2) and yet there are some who determine to sin in a deliberate sense, a form of rebellion to the will, word and purposes of God. These hardened hearts can bring great destruction to the kingdom and its people and this gift can be used to expose this kind of sin. This gift is most often used in this manner by people who are in spiritual authority in the church. That is to say that it is used by elders or apostles who are authorized to bring this kind of correction.

Acts 5:1 Now a man named Ananias, together with his wife Sapphira, also sold a piece of property. Acts 5:2 With his wife's full knowledge he kept back part of the money for himself, but brought the rest and put it at the apostles' feet. Acts 5:3 Then Peter said, "Ananias, how is it that Satan has so filled your heart that you have lied to the Holy Spirit and have kept for yourself some of the money you received for the land? . . . Acts 5:9 Peter said to her, "How could you agree to test the Spirit of the Lord? Look! The feet of the men who buried your husband are at the door, and they will carry you out also." Acts 5:10 At that moment she fell down at his feet and died. Then the young men came in and, finding her dead, carried her out and buried her beside her husband. Acts 5:11 Great fear seized the whole church and all who heard about these events.

Joshua 7:10 The LORD said to Joshua, "Stand up! What are you doing down on your face? Josh 7:11 Israel has sinned; they have violated my covenant, which I commanded them to keep. They have taken some of the devoted things; they have stolen, they have lied, they have put them with their own possessions.

4. TO REVEAL GOD'S WILL AND PURPOSE

At the right time, God reveals a portion of knowledge to direct His people. This is common in the New Testament and should be expected by church leaders today. Here are a few Scriptural examples.

Acts 8:29 The Spirit told Philip, "Go to that chariot and stay near it." Acts 8:30 Then Philip ran up to the chariot and heard the man reading Isaiah the prophet. "Do you understand what you are reading?" Philip asked.

Acts 10:19 While Peter was still thinking about the vision, the Spirit said to him, "Simon, three men are looking for you. Acts 10:20 So get up and go downstairs. Do not hesitate to go with them, for I have sent them."

Acts 16:9 During the night Paul had a vision of a man of Macedonia standing and begging him, "Come over to Macedonia and help us." Acts 16:10 After Paul had seen the vision, we got ready at once to leave for Macedonia, concluding that God had called us to preach the gospel to them.

5. TO HELP PEOPLE WHO NEED TO SPECIFIC KNOWLEDGE

A. SPIRITUAL ISSUES

It may highlight the cause of a problem or give someone clear direction. Again here are Old and New Testament examples.

1 Samuel 9:15 Now a day before Saul's coming, the LORD had revealed this to Samuel saying, 16 "About this time tomorrow I will send you a man from the land of Benjamin, and you shall anoint him to be prince over My people Israel; and he will deliver My people from the hand of the Philistines For I have regarded My people, because their cry has come to Me." 17 When Samuel saw Saul, the LORD said to him, "Behold, the man of whom I spoke to you! This one shall rule over My people." (NASB)

Matthew 28:5 The angel said to the women, "Do not be afraid, for I know that you are looking for Jesus, who was crucified. 6 He is not here; he has risen, just as he said. Come and see the place where he lay. 7 Then go quickly and tell his disciples: 'He has risen from the dead and is going ahead of you into Galilee. There you will see him.' Now I have told you."

B. COMMUNITY EVENTS

A word of knowledge can aid the church community in building relationships or highlighting problems.

1 Samuel 10:21 Finally Saul son of Kish was chosen. But when they looked for him, he was not to be found. 22 So they inquired further of the LORD, "Has the man come here yet?" And the LORD said, "Yes, he has hidden himself among the baggage."

C. LOST PROPERTY

Sometimes, this gift can help people find lost property.

1 Samuel 9:5 When they reached the district of Zuph, Saul said to the servant who was with him, "Come, let's go back, or my father will stop thinking about the donkeys and start worrying about us." 6 But the servant replied, "Look, in this town there is a man of God; he is highly respected, and everything he says comes true. Let's go there now. Perhaps he will tell us what way to take." . . . . 20 As for the donkeys you lost three days ago, do not worry about them; they have been found. And to whom is all the desire of Israel turned, if not to you and all your father's family?"

D. THOSE WHO NEED TO KNOW AND UNDERSTAND

This gift provides knowledge and unique heavenly perspectives of the conditions, nature, whereabouts or thoughts of a person or group of people or things. It gives us a glimpse into heavens perspective and knowledge of people's thoughts, heart, their nature and current struggles. God can reveal other peoples secrets and intentions.

HOW SHOULD WE RESPOND?

The gift of a word of knowledge, as with all the other "phanerosis" gifts, is given by the Holy Spirit as He determines for the common good. The best question to ask when the Lord brings revelation to us is, "What do You want me to do with it?" To simplify this, we can act on one of three things.

1. ACT ON IT PRIVATELY

PRAY

a. This word may be for a prayer burden. All the information the Lord chooses to share with us is not for immediate declaration. Often we must display discretion just as the Lord does towards us. Sometimes, when the Lord shares knowledge with us, it is for prayer only. When we pray, God can re-arrange hearts and minds, change circumstances, and re-align people so that potential hurts or threats are avoided..

SPEAK PRIVATELY IN LOVE

b. It may be a cautionary word that enables us to avoid pain or heartache. Words of warning should be heeded. If you feel you have this kind of word for someone, it is best to pray first. If, after prayer, you feel it is still right to share this word, do so in private and in love. Even encouraging words can bring embarrassment by what they disclose so take care to give thought about how to give them and if in doubt give them in person and in private.

c. A word of knowledge can sometimes be just between God and an individual. There will be some knowledge the Lord shares with us that is specific to our own personal walk with Him and He meant for it to remain between us. These kinds of words tend to educate and change us. Sometimes, however, it is possible to share this insight with others as we relate what the Lord has taught us. Once you have certain knowledge it affects the way you see things. You can't un -ring that bell. Words of knowledge given by the Lord for our training will change us for the better and these changes can be beneficial to others as well, if we feel it is right to share them.

2. ACT ON IT WITH A LIMITED GROUP

a. This allows for a small group to experience the manifestation of the Spirit in this way.

b. Often family groups or small collections of people can be really blessed if the word is spoken out. In this way, it can be a great encouragement to them but also an implied invitation to all of them to ask God to speak with them as well.

3. ACT PUBLICLY.

a. This helps, instructs, disciples and encourages the whole group or church. It allows for those who are not directly connected to the word or who do not have any knowledge of it personally to see God's care and love for the people involved. It speaks of the character of God and manifests an element of revelation about who He is to everyone who will take note.

b. It demonstrates the correct behavior or mature response to all, acting as an example. This is a key issue especially when recognized church leaders operate in this gift. The way we operate in this gift is an example to others.

The word of knowledge has a great power to make people aware of God's presence. It sends a message that God cares, communicates, and is involved in the details of our lives. As with all manifestation gifts, word of knowledge comes to those who eagerly desire it. It can engender faith and catalyze a meeting from ordinary to supernatural, by the obedience of someone courageous enough to say what God has told them. Be bold and ask God for this gift.

THE GIFT OF FAITH

*T*he gift of faith is another one of the manifestation gifts mentioned in 1 Corinthians 12:7-10.

1 Corinthians 12:7 Now to each one the manifestation of the Spirit is given for the common good. . . . 9 to another faith by the same Spirit,

Let me say again, these gifts are given to make the Holy Spirit's presence, nature and will apparent. In this regard, a supernatural gift of God's faith will bring demonstration to believers of God's power. This context is very important for us to grasp or else we will be drawn into the never-ending debate between Catholics, Calvinists and various Protestant denominations regarding the role of faith in salvation.

The gift of faith mentioned in Corinthians is a supernatural gift given by the Holy Spirit in a specific context. The passage above does not speak to the faith that all believers have, but rather speaks to the fact that "...to another was given faith by the same Spirit." It is given to those who are already believers in Jesus Christ. This faith gift is given to those whose faith has already caused them to be included in God's family. It is not saving faith but faith for specific issues and situations that life presents us with. This gift of faith is an apportionment of special faith to believers to manifest God's will in a specific moment.

LET'S TALK ABOUT FAITH

By definition, every Christian must have a measure of faith (Rom 12:3) because it is by grace, through faith, that we are saved (Eph 2:8). This kind of faith is a logical requirement for every Christian. It comes from your decision to believe through the influence of God's Holy Spirit in your heart. It can be strengthened (Acts 16:5, Rom 4:20, Col 2:7) by relationship with Jesus, and through hearing and responding to His word (Rom 10:17) or by observing the hand of God working either in your own life or someone else's life in some visible way e.g. a physical healing. Therefore, hearing other people's testimonies and carefully recording and remembering your own can be a great source of faith-building and encouragement.

The scriptures talk about what may be called assenting faith. This is the kind of faith that believes in the president or believes that Jesus is the Christ, but as James teaches, this kind of faith is not personal, incorporating faith that believes in and on Christ, but merely believes that He is. The demons have this kind of faith and it is strong enough to solicit a response from them.

James 2:19 You believe that God is one You do well; the demons also believe, and shudder. (NASB)

Saving faith is that faith which believes in Jesus Christ as the source of salvation. It is a personal, action-inducing faith that forsakes all other methods of salvation. The Philippian jailor came to Jesus in this way, as must we all. This kind of faith is what keeps us, shields us, and helps us persevere until Jesus returns. This faith is the commanded response to the gospel message. It is a verb. People are called on to believe in Jesus Christ. Believing in Him was the work Jesus said we should be engaged in.

Acts 16:30 He then brought them out and asked, "Sirs, what must I do to be saved?" Acts 16:31 They replied, "Believe in the Lord Jesus, and you will be saved--you and your household."

Romans 1:16 For I am not ashamed of the gospel, for it is the power of God for salvation to everyone who believes, to the Jew first and also to the Greek. (NASB)

Galatians 3:11 Clearly no one is justified before God by the law, because, "The righteous will live by faith."

In Jesus' ministry, He attributed many peoples' faith as the reason for their healing, e.g. the Centurion (Matt 8:13), the blind man (Matt 9:29), the Canaanite woman (Matt 14:28), the epileptic boy (Matt 17:20), The woman with perfume (Luke 7:50), and the lepers (Luke 17:19). Many people have used this to condemn believers for their lack of results. If we are going to believe God for the kingdom to break in and we are disappointed by the results, let's not blame others. Miraculous faith, or faith that believes God for definitive results in the present, is where some people become nervous. This is the gift of faith mentioned in 1 Corinthians 12.

Proponents of this kind of "miraculous" faith usually place a demand on the primacy of scripture over personal experience or tradition, believing that the scriptures alone are the basis for firm conviction. If a dismissal of any portion of scripture is accepted, we remove the basis for any belief in the concrete and fundamental inerrancy of God's word. It all then becomes subject to personal comfort levels and preferences while assuming responsibility for defining God and his lordship. When we will not believe all the word of God, we have become the arbiters of truth that we prefer. This is a very dangerous place and most often leads to error. This inevitably leads to a gospel defined by the wisdom of men that lacks any supernatural power.

Colossians 2:23 Such regulations indeed have an appearance of wisdom, with their self-imposed worship, their false humility and their harsh treatment of the body, but they lack any value in restraining sensual indulgence.

1 Corinthians 1:17 For Christ did not send me to baptize, but to preach the gospel--not with words of human wisdom, lest the cross of Christ be emptied of its power.

1 Corinthians 2:4 My message and my preaching were not with wise and persuasive words, but with a demonstration of the Spirit's power, 5 so that your faith might not rest on men's wisdom, but on God's power.

2 Timothy 3:5 having a form of godliness but denying its power. Have nothing to do with them.

Rather than being presumptuous as some assert, expectant faith honors God by taking Him at His word. It holds His words, promises and statements up as absolute truth and seeks to respond to them absolutely. God's word has a supernatural origin; it is eternal in its duration, unrivaled in value, endless in scope, incomparable in power, infallible in authority, universal in relevance, personal in application, and totally inspired. It should be read, memorized, studied, meditated on, quoted and believed. Our faith comes from hearing, believing and acting upon this word. It is the source of our faith and strengthens us daily.

THE GIFT OF FAITH

Various definitions apply to this wonderful gift. I list some of them below in the effort to fully define the manifestation.

1) The spiritual gift of faith is the supernatural manifestation of the Spirit of God that enables a believer to have no doubt or anxiety about a specific issue.

2) It is the supernatural ability to believe for the impossible or that which is not yet made manifest; the gift where God miraculously drops the assurance of the answer to one's prayers into one's heart.

3) The gift of faith is an unwavering conviction of the truth of God's word and God's promises concerning an event or situation, and an accompanying trust in Jesus Christ springing from that faith, to accomplish what He has promised at a given moment.

4) It is a supernatural ability to meet adverse circumstances with trust in God's word.

5) It is a portion of God's faith given to aid a believer in a specific set of circumstances.

Various examples of the gift

Old Testament examples

Elisha - Death in the pot

2 Kings 4:40 So they poured it out for the men to eat. And as they were eating of the stew, they cried out and said, "O man of God, there is death in the pot." And they were unable to eat. 41 But he said, "Now bring meal." He threw it into the pot and said, "Pour it out for the people that they may eat." Then there was no harm in the pot. (NASB)

The axehead

2 Kings 6:5 As one of them was cutting down a tree, the iron axhead fell into the water. "Oh, my lord," he cried out, "it was borrowed!" 2 Ki 6:6 The man of God asked, "Where did it fall?" When he showed him the place, Elisha cut a stick and threw it there, and made the iron float. 7 "Lift it out," he said. Then the man reached out his hand and took it.

In the ministry of Jesus

The fig tree

Matthew 21:18 Early in the morning, as he was on his way back to the city, he was hungry. 19 Seeing a fig tree by the road, he went up to it but found nothing on it except leaves. Then he said to it, "May you never bear fruit again!" Immediately the tree withered. 20 When the disciples saw this, they were amazed. "How did the fig tree wither so quickly?" they asked. 21 Jesus replied, "I tell you the truth, if you have faith and do not doubt, not only can you do what was done to the fig tree, but also you can say to this mountain, 'Go, throw yourself into the sea,' and it

212

will be done. 22 If you believe, you will receive whatever you ask for in prayer. "

THE STORM

Luke 8:24 The disciples went and woke him, saying, "Master, Master, we're going to drown!" He got up and rebuked the wind and the raging waters; the storm subsided, and all was calm. 25 "Where is your faith?" he asked his disciples.

Other examples include the dead girl,(Mark 5:39–42), and the dead boy (Luke 7:13-15).

OTHER NEW TESTAMENT EXAMPLES

PAUL

Acts 20:7 On the first day of the week we came together to break bread. Paul spoke to the people and, because he intended to leave the next day, kept on talking until midnight. Acts 20:8 There were many lamps in the upstairs room where we were meeting. 9 Seated in a window was a young man named Eutychus, who was sinking into a deep sleep as Paul talked on and on. When he was sound asleep, he fell to the ground from the third story and was picked up dead. 10 Paul went down, threw himself on the young man and put his arms around him. "Don't be alarmed," he said. "He's alive!" 11 Then he went upstairs again and broke bread and ate. After talking until daylight, he left.

PETER

Acts 9:39 Peter went with them, and when he arrived he was taken upstairs to the room. All the widows stood around him, crying and showing him the robes and other clothing that Dorcas had made while she was still with them. 40 Peter sent them all out of the room; then he got down on his knees and prayed. Turning toward the dead woman, he said, "Tabitha, get up." She opened her eyes, and seeing Peter she sat up. 41 He took her by the hand and helped her to her feet. Then he called the believers and the widows and presented her to them alive.

GUIDELINES

1. TIMING

All the manifestations of the Spirit are best executed when we are in step with the Spirit. This implies that this is not always the case which is why the Corinthian meetings where doing more harm than good. When we function in one of these gifts, we should care about how we present Him and how we accomplish His will. Not all miracles are instantaneous in their manifestation. In the same way, not each gift of faith demands public attention.

2. LOVE

Faith must always be balanced with love. Indeed, it works by love and finds its meaning when harnessed by love. Let love govern the use of this gift and the sense of invincibility it engenders. Imagine a gift of faith in a loveless heart. It will most likely not produce blessing and growth. Love, as faith's conduit, is explained a few places in the New Testament.

Galatians 5:6 For in Christ Jesus neither circumcision nor uncircumcision has any value. The only thing that counts is faith expressing itself through love.

1 Corinthians 13:2 if I have a faith that can move mountains, but have not love, I am nothing.

Many times, Jesus' faith was stirred by His compassionate love for people. His compassion for people ignited great faith and demonstrations of power in His life.

Matthew 14:14 When Jesus landed and saw a large crowd, he had compassion on them and healed their sick.

Matthew 15:3 And Jesus called His disciples to Him, and said, "I feel compassion for the people, because they have remained with Me now three days and have nothing to eat; and I do not want to send them away hungry, for they might faint on the way." (NASB)

Matthew 20:33 "Lord," they answered, "we want our sight." 34 Jesus had compassion on them and touched their eyes. Immediately they received their sight and followed him.

Mark 1:40 A man with leprosy came to him and begged him on his knees, "If you are willing, you can make me clean." 41 Filled with compassion, Jesus reached out his hand and touched the man. "I am willing," he said. "Be clean!"

3. WISDOM

Wisdom is a wonderful attribute to seek always and especially when manifesting one of the gifts of the Holy Spirit. All gifts are subject to discussion, testing, counsel and training so we may fully honor the Lord Jesus in all things. As always, we should make it our goal to please the Lord and to place no stumbling blocks in anyone's path. When someone is given a manifestation gift, they are not above accountability to Scripture or the body of Christ. This needs to be especially true when people manifest power gifts which tend to leave others in awe. The person who manifests a gift of faith, or any manifestation gift, does not necessarily possess moral character, spiritual maturity or emotional wholeness.

The gift of faith enables ordinary believers to take command of certain situations by faith. It enables them to see the will of God manifested in the circumstances around them. It is not hidden or refused to any who eagerly desire it.

The gifts of Healing

*I*t is very important that we know what God's will is in these matters or we will not cooperate with the Holy Spirit in the operation of these gifts. What is the will of God for the healing of mankind? Many and varied opinions are offered on the subject. If we do not believe that it is the will of God to heal people then we have no faith to pray for it. If we believe that He does heal, we approach with greater confidence to make our request. At the outset of this emotional topic we need to set our ground rule for the teaching. If we are to take the scriptures as the absolute rule for faith and conduct, then we will come to a very clear and specific conclusion. If we are going to embrace anecdotal stories of failure in addition to the scriptures, we might be tempted to revise our theology to fit our experience to date. This chapter seeks to focus on the word of God only and to exclude stories of both tragedy and great elation. This does not mean that multiple stories and experiences of God's Divine gifts of healing are not known to me nor that their omission here is a good thing. I believe in the keeping of testimonies as a God-given means of stirring our faith.

In studying this topic, two books have been immensely helpful to me personally. Besides being people who are recognized leaders in the areas of healing, they have provided credible arguments from the scriptures. I have leaned on their perspectives, and though not quoting much from them directly in this chapter their impact is seminal. They are "Healing the sick" by T. L. Osborn of Harrison House, Inc and "Power Healing" by John Wimber of Hodder and Stoughton. I recommend them to you as books written from the fires of the frontline, filled with great joys of thousands of people healed and fraught with the tears of those who have not yet seen all the church is called to see.

HEALING OVERVIEW

DOES GOD WANT TO HEAL?

We believe that it is God's will to heal all people just as it is His will to save people from their sin. I understand that this declaration may stir the hearts of many who have lost loved ones too early, or are currently suffering the ravages of sickness and infirmity; but let me outline why I have come to this firm conviction.

HE REVEALED HIMSELF AS THE GOD WHO HEALS

In the Old Covenant, God revealed Himself as the God who heals His covenant people. He told one of His redemptive covenantal names to Israel through Moses, which forms part of the progressive revelation God has given mankind about Himself. He calls Himself the God who heals.

Exodus 15:26 He said, "If you listen carefully to the LORD your God and do what is right in his eyes, if you pay attention to his commands and keep all his decrees, I will not bring on you any of the diseases I brought on the Egyptians, for I am the LORD, who heals you."

HEALING IS REVEALED AS A BLESSING

Healing is promoted as a blessing from the Lord, which was given through the servants of the Lord in demonstration of His glory while sickness is consistently shown to be part of a curse.

Deuteronomy 28:2 All these blessings will come upon you and accompany you if you obey the LORD your God: 4 The fruit of your womb will be blessed, and the crops of your land and the young of your livestock--the calves of your herds and the lambs of your flocks. . . . . 15 However, if you do not obey the LORD your God and do not carefully follow all his commands and decrees I am giving you today, all these curses will come upon you and overtake you: . . . 18 The fruit of your womb will be cursed, and the crops of your land, and the calves of your herds and the lambs of your flocks. . . . .21 The LORD will plague you with diseases until he has destroyed you from the land you are entering to possess. 22 The LORD will strike you with wasting disease, with fever and inflammation, with scorching heat and drought, with blight and mildew, which will plague you until you perish. . . . Hosea 6:1 "Come, let us return to the LORD. He has torn us to pieces but he will heal us; he has injured us but he will bind up our wounds.

THE ATONEMENT INCLUDES HEALING

The atonement speaks to the dual issue of salvation from sin and sickness. If we are going to embrace all that Jesus did on the cross, it not only includes the complete salvation of our soul s but makes provision for the complete healing of our bodies. Before anyone can say that the healing mentioned in Isaiah is for the sin malady of man, I have added the Matthew scripture that directly correlates physical healing with that passage in Isaiah.

Isaiah 53:4 4 Surely our griefs He Himself bore, And our sorrows He carried; Yet we ourselves esteemed Him stricken, Smitten of God, and afflicted. 5 But He was pierced through for our transgressions, He was crushed for our iniquities; The chastening for our well-being fell upon Him, And by His scourging we are healed. 6 All of us like sheep have gone astray, Each of us has turned to his own way; But the LORD has caused the iniquity of us all To fall on Him. (NASB)

Matthew 8:16 When evening came, many who were demon-possessed were brought to him, and he drove out the spirits with a word and healed all the sick. 17 This was to fulfill what was spoken through the prophet Isaiah: "He took up our infirmities and carried our diseases."

218

JESUS DEMONSTRATED GOD'S WILL

Jesus came as the perfect and exact representation of the will of God and He healed all who asked for healing. He is the same and does not change. When He was asked if He was willing to heal, He responded by saying yes and healing that person.

Matthew 4:24 The news about Him spread throughout all Syria; and they brought to Him all who were ill, those suffering with various diseases and pains, demoniacs, epileptics, paralytics; and He healed them. (NASB)

Matthew 8:16 When evening had come, they brought to Him many who were demon-possessed. And He cast out the spirits with a word, and healed all who were sick, (NKJV)

Matthew 12:15 Aware of this, Jesus withdrew from that place. Many followed him, and he healed all their sick.

Matthew 14:36 and they implored Him that they might just touch the fringe of His cloak; and as many as touched it were cured. (NASB)

Mark 6:56 And wherever he went--into villages, towns or countryside--they placed the sick in the marketplaces. They begged him to let them touch even the edge of his cloak, and all who touched him were healed.

Luke 4:40 When the sun was setting, the people brought to Jesus all who had various kinds of sickness, and laying his hands on each one, he healed them.

Hebrews 10:7 Then I said, 'Here I am--it is written about me in the scroll-- I have come to do your will, O God.'"

Hebrews 13:8 Jesus Christ is the same yesterday and today and forever.

Matthew 8:2 And a leper came to Him and bowed down before Him, and said, "Lord, if You are willing, You can make me clean." 3 Jesus stretched out His hand and touched him, saying, "I am willing; be cleansed." And immediately his leprosy was cleansed.(NASB)

JESUS COMMISSIONED HIS FOLLOWERS TO HEAL

THE TWELVE

Matthew 10:7 As you go, preach this message: 'The kingdom of heaven is near.' Mat 10:8 Heal the sick, raise the dead, cleanse those who have leprosy, drive out demons. Freely you have received, freely give.

Acts 5:15 to such an extent that they even carried the sick out into the streets and laid them on cots and pallets, so that when Peter came by at least his shadow might fall on any one of them. 16 Also the people from the cities in the vicinity of Jerusalem were coming together, bringing people who were sick or afflicted with unclean spirits, and they were all being healed. (NASB)

Acts 19:11 God did extraordinary miracles through Paul, 12 so that even handkerchiefs and aprons that had touched him were taken to the sick, and their illnesses were cured and the evil spirits left them.

THE SEVENTY

Luke 10:8 "When you enter a town and are welcomed, eat what is set before you. 9 Heal the sick who are there and tell them, 'The kingdom of God is near you.'

ALL WHO BELIEVE

Mark 16:17 And these signs will accompany those who believe: In my name they will drive out demons; they will speak in new tongues; 18 they will pick up snakes with their hands; and when they drink deadly poison, it will not hurt them at all; they will place their hands on sick people, and they will get well."

WE SHOULD PRAY FOR HEALING

We are told to pray for healing directly and as part of anything we ask in His name.

James 5:14 Is anyone among you sick? Then he must call for the elders of the church and they are to pray over him, anointing him with oil in the name of the Lord; 15 and the prayer offered in faith will restore the one who is sick, and the Lord will raise him up, and if he has committed sins, they will be forgiven him. 16 Therefore, confess your sins to one another, and pray for one another so that you may be healed. The effective prayer of a righteous man can accomplish much. (NASB)

John 14:13 Whatever you ask in My name, that will I do, so that the Father may be glorified in the Son. 14 If you ask Me anything in My name, I will do it.(NASB)

WE HAVE BEEN HEALED

New Testament theology speaks to the fact that provision for healing has already been made. Anyone who believes on the completed work of the cross has access to healing that was bought by that past event. We were healed by the wounds He received there.

1 Peter 2:24 He himself bore our sins in his body on the tree, so that we might die to sins and live for righteousness; by his wounds you have been healed.

SICKNESS IS OF THE DEVIL

Sickness is most often associated with the work of the Devil in the scriptures and Jesus came to destroy these and His Church is commissioned to do the same.

Matthew 8:16 When evening came, many who were demon-possessed were brought to him, and he drove out the spirits with a word and healed all the sick.

Luke 13:16 Then should not this woman, a daughter of Abraham, whom Satan has kept bound for eighteen long years, be set free on the Sabbath day from what bound her?"

Matthew 12:22 Then they brought him a demon-possessed man who was blind and mute, and Jesus healed him, so that he could both talk and see.

Matthew 9:32 As they went out, behold, they brought to Him a man, mute and demon-possessed. 33 And when the demon was cast out, the mute spoke. And the multitudes marveled, saying, "It was never seen like this in Israel!"(NKJV)

Mark 9:25 When Jesus saw that a crowd was running to the scene, he rebuked the evil spirit. "You deaf and mute spirit," he said, "I command you, come out of him and never enter him again."

Mark 1:23 Just then a man in their synagogue who was possessed by an evil spirit cried out,

1 John 3:8 The reason the Son of God appeared was to destroy the devil's work

FAITH IS NECESSARY

In the New Testament, a person's faith was a significant factor in their healing. At the risk of some abusing this truth and apportioning blame for the lack of a healing on people not having enough faith, it is still true that Jesus acknowledged faith as a participating factor in healing. Here follows a few examples of this.

BLIND MEN

Matthew 9:29 Then he touched their eyes and said, "According to your faith will it be done to you"; Mat 9:30 and their sight was restored.

(SYRO-PHOENECIAN WOMAN)

Matthew 15:28 Then Jesus answered, "Woman, you have great faith! Your request is granted." And her daughter was healed from that very hour.

(WOMAN WITH ISSUE OF BLOOD)

Mark 5:34, Luke 8:46 and Mat 9:22 He said to her, "Daughter, your faith has healed you. Go in peace and be freed from your suffering."

BARTIMAEUS

Mark 10:52 "Go," said Jesus, "your faith has healed you." Immediately he received his sight and followed Jesus along the road.

LAME MAN AND FRIENDS

Luke 5:20 When Jesus saw their faith, he said, "Friend, your sins are forgiven."

PROSTITUTE IN THE PHARISEE'S HOME

Luke 7:50 Jesus said to the woman, "Your faith has saved you; go in peace."

THE LEPER WHO RETURNED TO GIVE THANKS

Luke 17:19 Then he said to him, "Rise and go; your faith has made you well."

If we accept that faith is necessary for healing then we need to ask how we can build our faith. The disciples learned it from two sources. They developed faith by listening to Jesus' teachings and explanations. The second way they grew in faith was by witnessing the thousands of miraculous healings done at the hands of Jesus. In business, if we are starting a new venture, it is best to solicit the advice of people who are successful and positive. Those who are negative and unsuccessful will point out all the problems and difficulties in the market. Someone once quoted the proverb that the people who say that something cannot be done should not be allowed to interfere with the people doing it. In this issue of healing, it is best that we build up our faith by submerging ourselves in God's word and by listening to those who have seen or are seeing people getting healed in Jesus' name.

Romans 10:17 Consequently, faith comes from hearing the message, and the message is heard through the word of Christ.

John 21:25 Jesus did many other things as well. If every one of them were written down, I suppose that even the whole world would not have room for the books that would be written.

Lets be careful to soak ourselves in the truth about healing and hang around people who see it manifesting. The anointing to heal like all anointing, will rub off on those who are around it enough. Likewise if we sit in the counsel of the cynical, the offended and the unbelieving, we can tend to get discouraged and start believing a lie.

The Gifts of Healing and their
HINDRANCES

*T*he plural is used here (1 Cor 12:9) and is thought to mean that either some have a gift for the healing of a particular complaint or sickness or alternatively each healing is a separate gift in itself given by the Holy Spirit. This is the gift given by the Holy Spirit to make manifest God's will and character through the healing of a person whether physically, emotionally or spiritually. It is supernatural enablement to minister various kinds of healing and restoration to people by the instigation and power of the Holy Spirit.

Luke 5:17 One day as he was teaching, Pharisees and teachers of the law, who had come from every village of Galilee and from Judea and Jerusalem, were sitting there. And the power of the Lord was present for him to heal the sick.

Acts 3:6 Then Peter said, "Silver or gold I do not have, but what I have I give you. In the name of Jesus Christ of Nazareth, walk."

This gift, like the others mentioned in Corinthians, should be eagerly desired and exercised in order to bless the entire body. It will require boldness to step out and offer prayer for healing with all the attached inferences. The only specific pattern shown in scripture is the call for the elders to anoint sick people with oil. Otherwise, the scriptures show diverse practices that result from the outworking of this gift.

Sometime healing accompanied a word (Matt 8:8; Act 3:6), A touch (Matt 8:15), Laying on of hands (Mark 16:18; Act 28:8), Saliva and dust (John 9:6), A shadow (Act 5:15), Cloths (Act 19:11–12), An embrace (Act 20:10), Prayer (James 5:14–15), Anointing with oil (James 5:14–15)

As with the other gifts, it need not come with excessive baggage and fanfare. The perfect church environment is not necessary, nor are feelings of joy or ecstasy. What is necessary is the willingness to hear the Lord and the boldness to identify and pray for each person that requires healing.

A simple approach is to hear what the Lord is saying. Ask the person what they would like prayer for, and in faith, offer up prayer. The scriptures say that those who believe will lay hands on the sick and they will recover. Lay your hands gently and appropriately on the sick person and pray for healing or speak out healing over the person as the Lord directs you.

OBSTACLES TO HEALING

1. UNSURE OF THE WILL OF GOD.

What we get saved into is more important than what we get saved out of. There is no better demonstration of this fact than the issue of diving healing. Where did we get the idea that asking for healing may be an affront to God? Certainly not from the scriptures, which commissions us to heal the sick as we preach the gospel and to ask the elders to pray for us and to lay hands on the sick for their recovery. Yet a large portion of the church languishes in these doldrums, unsure and without faith when approaching God on this subject.

I believe that one of the greatest hindrances to healing is the absence of certainty about God's will on healing.

"There is lurking in most everyone, who has not properly studied God's word, a feeling that God may not be willing, that we have to persuade Him to heal us." "Healing from Heaven", Lillian B. Yeomans, MD as quoted in "Healing

the Sick" T. L. Osborn © Harrison House 1951 33rd edition

The best remedy for extreme teaching is not to counter it with the opposite extreme but with the truth. Most theology is developed in the manner of thesis, antithesis and synthesis. This reflects the backdrop of the times and cultural settings the theology is formed in. Much of modern theology was formed in a time of increasing cynicism and unbelief. Unfortunately those two imposters made inroads into what is preached in many places. It is time for the Church to study the scriptures to rediscover God's heart in healing and to settle in her heart His determined will to heal. That conviction will prove the key and coinage to do business in the kingdom of God.

Hebrews 3:12 See to it, brothers, that none of you has a sinful, unbelieving heart that turns away from the living God.

2. THE PERVASIVE INFLUENCE OF A SECULARIZED WESTERN WORLDVIEW

While sincerely believing in Christ, many Christians' thinking is tainted by secularism, especially materialism and rationalism. Materialism and rationalism are an intellectual grid through which we sift our experience. These two philosophies, which together form the cornerstone of modern secularism, can be traced to the 18th century French enlightenment. Over the past two hundred years they have taken deep root in Western minds.

"A materialistic worldview assumes that nothing exists except matter and its movements and modifications, that there is no supernatural reference point in this life. Rationalism proposes that for every human problem there is a rational solution and that one can rationally understand everything, that there is no room for Divine providence. Most Christians recognize the more obvious anti-Christian influences of secularism: materialistic lust and sexual promiscuity. Nevertheless they are affected by secularism in other ways. Many find it difficult to accept supernatural intervention, especially physical healing in the material universe. "

"Power Healing" – John Wimber, © Hodder and Stutton 1986 pg 28 para 4 and 29 para 1

3. THEOLOGICAL STREAMS AND TEACHINGS

3.1 DISPENSATIONALISM

Dispensationalism is an emphasis on different eras of God's moving in history. This teaching says that God did, at one stage, give these gifts but no longer does so. Therefore, to seek them now is dangerous and contrary to the will of God. The general consensus is that now that the word of God has been established for the church, the signs and wonders demonstrated by the early church are no longer necessary to validate their preaching. There is no scriptural reference to form a basis for this theology. This shows a limited view of the purpose of healing. While the authentication of the gospel and the establishing of the church were, and still are, part of the purpose for physical healing they are not the entire picture. Scripture shows many other reasons why Jesus healed.

Below, I have listed some hindrances mentioned in the New Testament to healing.

RESISTANCE / INDIGNATION / DISHONOR

In His home town Jesus was hindered from doing miracles and could only accomplish a few healings because the people took offense at Him.

Mark 6:3 And they took offense at him. Mark 6:5 He could not do any miracles there, except lay his hands on a few sick people and heal them.

CONCEALED OR CHERISHED SIN

Jesus has destroyed sin's power over the lives of believers. Not all believers understand this. Some need to have elders to declare it broken, especially when they have been secretly

228

cherishing a sin in their lives. When the power of that sin is destroyed by their faith and willingness to renounce it their healing flows easily.

James 5:15 If he has sinned, he will be forgiven. James 5:16 therefore confess your sins to each other and pray for each other so that you may be healed.

INCORRECTLY DISCERNING THE BODY OF CHRIST

Correctly discerning the body of Christ means that we are to understand that all of our brokenness, weaknesses, sins, shame, sicknesses, the punishment that secures our peace, were absorbed and destroyed in the body and blood of Jesus Christ. When we try to add anything to that perfect sacrifice we are guilty of not recognizing the work Jesus did.

1 Corinthians 11:29 For anyone who eats and drinks without recognizing the body of the Lord eats and drinks judgment on himself. 30 That is why many among you are weak and sick, and a number of you have fallen asleep.

OPENNESS TO OCCULT

Any collaboration or openness to occult sources invites the enemy's influence into our lives. It should be avoided and resisted by believers. The enemy is not close to being as powerful as Jesus so when we submit to Him and resist the devil he must run screaming from us.

James 4:7 Submit yourselves, then, to God. Resist the devil, and he will flee from you.

LACK OF WISDOM OR SELF CONTROL

Our bodies are fearfully and wonderfully made but even so with wrong foods in wrong quantities, poor hygiene and too little sleep we can cause a weakening in them or even abuse them. Common sense, a little knowledge and consideration can make significant differences.

Philemon 2:25 But I think it is necessary to send back to you Epaphroditus, my brother, fellow worker and fellow soldier, who is also your messenger, whom you sent to take care of my needs. 26 For he longs for all of you and is distressed because you heard he was ill. 27 Indeed he was ill, and almost died. 30 because he almost died for the work of Christ, risking his life to make up for the help you could not give me.

WHY JESUS HEALED

Authentication of the gospel and establishment of the church were not the only reasons for healing. Here are more reasons why Jesus healed. Was the only purpose of healing to authenticate the gospel and establish the church? Here are a few other obvious reasons why healing was manifested.

TO DEMONSTRATE HIS COMPASSION AND MERCY

Matthew 14:14 When Jesus landed and saw a large crowd, he had compassion on them and healed their sick. . . Matthew20:34 Jesus had compassion on them and touched their eyes. Immediately they received their sight and followed him... Mark 1:41 Filled with compassion, Jesus reached out his hand and touched the man. "I am willing," he said. "Be clean!"

TESTIFYING THAT HE WAS THE MESSIAH

Matthew 8:16 When evening came, many who were demon-possessed were brought to him, and he drove out the spirits with a word and healed all the sick. 17 This was to fulfill what was spoken through the prophet Isaiah: "He took up our infirmities and carried our diseases."

Luke 5:21 The Pharisees and the teachers of the law began thinking to themselves, "Who is this fellow who speaks blasphemy? Who can forgive sins but God alone?" 24 But that you may know that the Son of Man has authority on earth to forgive sins." He said to the paralyzed man, "I tell you, get up, take your mat and go home." .

230

Matthew 11:3 and said to Him, "Are You the Expected One, or shall we look for someone else?" 4 Jesus answered and said to them, "Go and report to John what you hear and see: 5the bind receive sight and the lame walk, the lepers are cleansed and the deaf hear, the dead are raised up, and the poor have the gospel preached to them. (NASB)

DEMONSTRATION THAT HIS KINGDOM IS AMONG US

Matthew 4:23 Jesus went throughout Galilee, teaching in their synagogues, preaching the good news of the kingdom, and healing every disease and sickness among the people.

TO BRING PEOPLE TO REPENTANCE

Luke 10:8 "When you enter a town and are welcomed, eat what is set before you. 9 Heal the sick who are there and tell them, 'The kingdom of God is near you.' 10 But when you enter a town and are not welcomed, go into its streets and say, 11 'Even the dust of your town that sticks to our feet we wipe off against you. Yet be sure of this: The kingdom of God is near.'

SHOWING THAT GENTILES WERE ALSO INCLUDED IN THE GOSPEL

Luke 7:9 When Jesus heard this, he was amazed at him, and turning to the crowd following him, he said, "I tell you, I have not found such great faith even in Israel." 10 Then the men who had been sent returned to the house and found the servant well.

3.2 THE THEOLOGY OF SUFFERING

This is a well documented teaching of scripture that some have annexed to make suffering and sickness synonymous. The Bible does not do this. Jesus bore our sin and our sickness through His substitutionary sacrifice for us. By His sacrifice our sins are removed and our sicknesses were borne. There are some things we must bear because it is an honor to share in His sufferings. He said that we should take up our cross and follow Him. The weight of the cross and sharing in His sufferings are what we are called to. There is a Greek word that is specific to suffering through sickness and each time Jesus met with this kind of suffering He destroyed it. Peter in his epistle makes this clear by showing us that suffering is attendant to God's call but forgiveness and healing are our gifts.

1 Peter 1:6 In this you greatly rejoice, though now for a little while you may have had to suffer grief in all kinds of trials.

1 Peter 1:13 Therefore, prepare your minds for action; be self-controlled;

1 Peter 4:1 Therefore, since Christ suffered in his body, arm yourselves also with the same attitude, because he who has suffered in his body is done with sin.

1 Peter 2:20 For what credit is it if, when you are beaten for your faults, you take it patiently? But when you do good and suffer, if you take it patiently, this is commendable before God. 21 For to this you were called, because Christ also suffered for us,[a] leaving us an example, that you should follow His steps: 22 "Who committed no sin, Nor was deceit found in His mouth"; 23 who, when He was reviled, did not revile in return; when He suffered, He did not threaten, but committed Himself to Him who judges righteously; 24 who Himself bore our sins in His own body on the tree, that we, having died to sins, might live for righteousness—by whose stripes you were healed. (NKJV)

The work that Jesus did on the cross was perfect and requires nothing more, especially not the feeble works of our flesh. Jesus took our place on the cross and completely bore our sin (Isa 53:4, 2 Cor 5:21), sickness (Isa 53:5, Matthew 8:17), curses (Gal 3:13), poverty (2 Cor 8:9), sorrow (Isa 53:4, Isa 61:3), and death (John 3:16, Isa 51:6, 2 Timothy 1:10).

We are called to suffer as Christ did, and we have no record that He was ever sick apart from the stripes He voluntarily took as our savior. We join in Jesus' suffering for righteousness sake (1 Peter 3:14), for the faith (1 Peter 4: 12-16), in the face of injustice, being accused falsely (Matt 5:11), for doing good. (1 Peter 3:17), and in being rejected (Luke 6:22).

Healing continued

3.3 Paul's thorn in the flesh

*S*ome people turn to Paul's thorn in the flesh, assuming it means a sickness as justification for believers being ill. Let's examine this more thoroughly.

2 Corinthians 12:7 To keep me from becoming conceited because of these surpassingly great revelations, there was given me a thorn in my flesh, a messenger of Satan, to torment me.8 Three times I pleaded with the Lord to take it away from me. 9 But he said to me, "My grace is sufficient for you, for my power is made perfect in weakness." Therefore I will boast all the more gladly about my weaknesses, so that Christ's power may rest on me.

He asked three times for it to be removed and was denied. The Lord said to him that His grace was sufficient for him. Many have taken this scripture and equated Paul's thorn with a sickness and therefore preach that Paul's request for healing was denied three times.

What was Paul's thorn?

The expression "thorn in the flesh" is used elsewhere in scripture, always speaking about a person or group of persons.

Numbers 33:55 "'But if you do not drive out the inhabitants of the land, those you allow to remain will become barbs in your eyes and thorns in your sides. They will give you trouble in the land where you will live.

Joshua 23:13 then you may be sure that the LORD your God will no longer drive out these nations before you. Instead, they will become snares and traps for you, whips on your backs and thorns in your eyes, until you perish from this good land, which the LORD your God has given you.

Judges 2:3 Now therefore I tell you that I will not drive them out before you; they will be thorns in your sides and their gods will be a snare to you."

Paul says it was a messenger from Satan. This is the word angelos which appears 188 times and is translated 181 times as angel and 7 times as messenger. In all 188 times it refers to a person and not a thing. In Matthew, Jesus shows that the devil has these angelos working for him.

Matthew 25:41 "Then he will say to those on his left, 'Depart from me, you who are cursed, into the eternal fire prepared for the devil and his angels. (angelos)

WHAT WAS THE PURPOSE OF PAUL'S THORN?

Paul's thorn was a constant buffeting from the enemy, a headwind of accusation, inciting angry resistance against him and fomenting of riots. Paul says this thorn was given to buffet him. This word is used in various contexts and always means blow after blow, like the disciples' ship being buffeted or Jesus being beaten. The thorn was the counterbalance to the surpassingly great revelations Paul had been given. The constant resistance served as Paul's reminder to remain humble and dependent on God. Below are listed some examples of this buffeting, starting with God's revealed purpose when He spoke with Ananias.

Acts 9:15 But the Lord said to Ananias, "Go! This man is my chosen instrument to carry my name before the Gentiles and their kings and before the people of Israel. Acts 9:16 I will show him how much he must suffer for my name."

JEWS TRIED TO KILL HIM AFTER HIS CONVERSION

Acts 9:23 After many days had gone by, the Jews conspired to kill him, Acts 9:24 but Saul learned of their plan. Day and night they kept close watch on the city gates in order to kill him. Acts 9:25 But his followers took him by night and lowered him in a basket through an opening in the wall. THE CHURCH DID NOT ACCEPT HIM

Acts 9:26 When he came to Jerusalem, he tried to join the disciples, but they were all afraid of him, not believing that he really was a disciple.

A SORCERER OPPOSED HIM

Acts 13:8 But Elymas the sorcerer (for that is what his name means) opposed them and tried to turn the proconsul from the faith.

MALIGNED AND DEFAMED

Acts 13:44 On the next Sabbath almost the whole city gathered to hear the word of the Lord. Acts 13:45 When the Jews saw the crowds, they were filled with jealousy and talked abusively against what Paul was saying.

THROWN OUT OF PISIDIAN ANTIOCH

Acts 13:14 From Perga they went on to Pisidian Antioch. . . . . Acts 13:44 On the next Sabbath almost the whole city gathered to hear the word of the Lord. . . . . Acts 13:50 But the Jews incited the God-fearing women of high standing and the leading men of the city. They stirred up persecution against Paul and Barnabas, and expelled them from their region.

PLOTTED AGAINST IN ICONIUM

Acts 14:1 In Iconium they entered the synagogue of the Jews together, and spoke in such a manner that a large number of people believed, both of Jews and of Greeks. 2

But the Jews who disbelieved stirred up the minds of the Gentiles and embittered them against the brethren. 3 Therefore they spent a long time there speaking boldly with reliance upon the Lord, who was testifying to the word of His grace, granting that signs and wonders be done by their hands. 4 But the people of the city were divided; and some sided with the Jews, and some with the apostles. 5 And when an attempt was made by both the Gentiles and the Jews with their rulers, to mistreat and to stone them, 6 they became aware of it and fled to the cities of Lycaonia, Lystra and Derbe, and the surrounding region; (NASB)

STONED IN LYSTRA

Acts 14:10 and called out, "Stand up on your feet!" At that, the man jumped up and began to walk. 11 When the crowd saw what Paul had done, they shouted in the Lycaonian language, "The gods have come down to us in human form!" 12 Barnabas they called Zeus, and Paul they called Hermes because he was the chief speaker. . . . . 18 Even with these words, they had difficulty keeping the crowd from sacrificing to them. 19 Then some Jews came from Antioch and Iconium and won the crowd over. They stoned Paul and dragged him outside the city, thinking he was dead. 20 But after the disciples had gathered around him, he got up and went back into the city. The next day he and Barnabas left for Derbe.

OFTEN IN DISPUTES

Acts 19:9 But some of them became obstinate; they refused to believe and publicly maligned the Way. So Paul left them. He took the disciples with him and had discussions daily in the lecture hall of Tyrannus.

BEATEN AND JAILED IN PHILLIPI

Acts 16:12 From there we traveled to Philippi, a Roman colony and the leading city of that district of Macedonia. And we stayed there several days. . . . Acts 16:22 The crowd joined in the attack against Paul and Silas, and the magistrates ordered them to be stripped and beaten. 23 After they had been severely flogged, they were

thrown into prison, and the jailer was commanded to guard them carefully. Acts 16:24 Upon receiving such orders, he put them in the inner cell and fastened their feet in the stocks.

MOBBED AND EXPELLED FROM THESSALONICA

Acts 17:1 When they had passed through Amphipolis and Apollonia, they came to Thessalonica, where there was a Jewish synagogue. . . . . 5 But the Jews were jealous; so they rounded up some bad characters from the marketplace, formed a mob and started a riot in the city. They rushed to Jason's house in search of Paul and Silas in order to bring them out to the crowd. . . . . 10 As soon as it was night, the brothers sent Paul and Silas away to Berea. On arriving there, they went to the Jewish synagogue.

MOBBED AND EXPELLED FROM BEREA

Acts 17:13 But when the Jews of Thessalonica found out that the word of God had been proclaimed by Paul in Berea also, they came there as well, agitating and stirring up the crowds. 14 Then immediately the brethren sent Paul out to go as far as the sea; and Silas and Timothy remained there. (NASB)

MOBBED AT CORINTH

Acts 18:1 After this, Paul left Athens and went to Corinth. . . . . Acts 18:12 While Gallio was proconsul of Achaia, the Jews made a united attack on Paul and brought him into court.

Mobbed at Ephesus

Acts 19:23 About that time there arose a great disturbance about the Way. . . . Acts 19:29 Soon the whole city was in an uproar. The people seized Gaius and Aristarchus, Paul's traveling companions from Macedonia, and rushed as one man into the theater. . . . Acts 19:30 Paul wanted to appear before the crowd, but the disciples would not let him. . . . Acts 20:1 When the uproar had ended, Paul sent for the disciples and, after encouraging them, said good-by and set out for Macedonia.

Plotted against in Macedonia

Acts 20:3 where he stayed three months. Because the Jews made a plot against him just as he was about to sail for Syria, he decided to go back through Macedonia.

Paul's ministry in his own words

2 Corinthians 6:4 Rather, as servants of God we commend ourselves in every way: in great endurance; in troubles, hardships and distresses; 5 in beatings, imprisonments and riots; in hard work, sleepless nights and hunger; . . 9 known, yet regarded as unknown; dying, and yet we live on; beaten, and yet not killed; 10 sorrowful, yet always rejoicing; poor, yet making many rich; having nothing, and yet possessing everything.

2 Corthians 11:23 Are they servants of Christ? (I am out of my mind to talk like this.) I am more. I have worked much harder, been in prison more frequently, been flogged more severely, and been exposed to death again and again. 24 Five times I received from the Jews the forty lashes minus one. 25 Three times I was beaten with rods, once I was stoned, three times I was shipwrecked, I spent a night and a day in the open sea, 26 I have been constantly on the move. I have been in danger from rivers, in danger from bandits, in danger from my own countrymen, in danger from Gentiles; in danger in the city, in danger in the country, in danger at sea; and in danger from false brothers. *27 I have labored and toiled and have often gone without sleep; I have known hunger and thirst and have often gone without food; I have been cold and naked. 28 Besides everything else, I face daily the pressure of my concern for all the churches.*

PAUL MENTIONS HIS SICKNESSES.

Paul did say that it was out of weakness or feebleness that he first preached to the Galatian church and also that he exulted in his weakness. The Greek word astheneia is used when he said that, and it means feebleness of body or mind, malady, moral frailty, infirmity, sickness or weakness. I think that after Paul was stoned at Lystra, he made his way through Galatia still bearing the bruises and battering from that experience. When he writes his letter to the churches he met during that time he speaks of how weak he was and how their heart to him was to help his "infirmity". The word astheneia is used in the following ways in their respective contexts.

1 Corinthians 2:3 I came to you in weakness (astheneia) and fear, and with much trembling. . . . 2 Corinthians 12:9 But he said to me, "My grace is sufficient for you, for my power is made perfect in weakness. (astheneia)" Therefore I will boast all the more gladly about my weaknesses (astheneia), so that Christ's power may rest on me. . . . 2 Corinthians 10:10 For some say, "His letters are weighty and forceful, but in person he is unimpressive (astheneia) and his speaking amounts to nothing."

Galatians 4:13 As you know, it was because of an illness (astheneia) that I first preached the gospel to you. Galatians 4:14 and that which was a trial to you in my bodily condition you did not despise or loathe, but you received me as an angel of God, as Christ Jesus Himself. 15 Where then is that sense of blessing you had? For I bear you witness that, if possible, you would have plucked out your eyes and given them to me. (NASB)

Acts 14:19 Then some Jews came from Antioch and Iconium and won the crowd over. They stoned Paul and

240

dragged him outside the city, thinking he was dead. 20 But after the disciples had gathered around him, he got up and went back into the city. The next day he and Barnabas left for Derbe.

Paul's apparent thorn did not hinder anyone from being healed. Everywhere he went, people were emboldened by his message to trust God for healing. If God gave Paul a thorn of infirmity why did He use him so extensively to preach and impart healing?

Healing continued

What actions can be taken during healing?

Laying on of hands

$\mathcal{L}$aying hands on the sick for the administration of healing grace is consistent with the laying on of hands to impart other graces as well. Jesus, the first apostles, and the early church did it and we are encouraged to do it.

(Matthew 8:2-4, 14-15; 9:29; 20:34, Mark 1:41; 7:32-33; 5:23; 6:4; 7:32-33; 8:23, 25; 16:18, Luke 13:13; 22:50-51, Acts 9:12,17; 28:8, James 5:14)

Anointing of oil by the elders

The scriptures speak to all believers about having the responsibility to preach and heal the sick. This is to demonstrate His kingdom come. Yet elders are especially exhorted to anoint with oil. Some people need elders to deal governmentally with sin issues in their lives and the authoritative declaration of the forgiveness of sins which these believers need to hear from someone they recognize in authority over them.

(Mark 6:13, James 5:14)

Prayer, Especially the prayer of agreement

We pray the kinds of prayers that acknowledge the finished work of the cross. We do not plead with God to do something that He has already done. James teaches that the prayer offered in faith will make the sick person well.

(Matthew 8:19, Matthew 21:22, Mark 11:24, James 5:15-16)

FASTING

Fasting is not a mechanism that moves God but one that focusses us on Him. Jesus spoke about a certain kind of sickness-inducing unclean spirit that comes out by prayer and fasting. It does not change the truth that God was already moved with compassion for our sin and sickness when He sent His beloved son to the cross.

(Mark 9:29, Acts 9:8-9, 17-19)

VARIOUS AND STRANGE ACTS OF OBEDIENCE

Jesus often required people to act. His obedience to His Father's voice led Jesus to do and ask some strange and seemingly unrelated actions. Here are a few illustrations. Mark 7:32, 3 (fingers put in ears of deaf), Mark 8:22 (spit put on eyes of blind), John 9:6-7, 11 (clay put on eyes of blind), Acts 19:11-12 (handkerchiefs taken from hands of Paul), Acts 3:7 (lame man lifted up by the hand)

SPEAKING IN FAITH

Sometimes healing came by a command from a faith-filled heart. These commands produced the intended results. Here are a few examples. Mark 11:23. Mark 5:41 ("Arise!"), Mark 7:34 ("Be opened."), Mark 9:25; Luke 4:39; 5:39 (Rebuked the sickness), Luke 5:13 ("Be thou clean."), Acts 9:33-34 ("Arise")

BELIEVING HIS WORD

Sometimes, Jesus merely required people to take Him at His word. Sometimes, He chose not to make a fuss or for it to take a long time, but sent people on their way with His assurance. (Matthew 8:8, Mark 10:52, Luke 17:19, John 4:50, Acts 3:16; 14:9)

AN INDIVIDUAL'S ACT OF FAITH.

When people heard testimonies about what Jesus was doing, it stirred their faith and motivated them to initiate action by faith. Jesus did not always command these actions but was pleased when He saw them.

Matthew 14:35, 36 (touching the edge of His garment), Luke 8:43-48

OBEDIENCE TO A SIMPLE COMMAND.

The actions that He commanded were not hard to do, that is to say they were not superhuman, but they did require faith. Luke 17:14 (commanded to show themselves to the priests), John 5:8, 9, etc. (told to pick up the bed and walk), John 9:7, 10-11 (told to wash in pool of Siloam), Acts 14:10 (told to stand up)

COMMON SENSE AND PRACTICAL ADVICE

We can be unwise in the way we treat our bodies by violating common sense. It is wisdom to get adequate sleep, rest, appropriate medication and nutrition. I Timothy 5:23 (wine for the stomach)

TAKING THE LORD'S SUPPER

Celebrating the death and resurrection of Jesus brings health to our bodies, souls and spirits. A constant reminder that all our sins and sickness were taken in His body on that tree is powerful. Jesus has absorbed all the wrath of God which was aimed at our former rebellion and sin. He has been cursed so that we no longer are, He was afflicted so that we won't be, and by His stripes we are healed.

(I Corinthians 1:18, 1 Cor 11:28 - 31)

ATTITUDES TO CULTIVATE

A SIMPLE FAITH

This is the object of divine healing: to be proof of the power of Jesus. It is a witness in the eyes of men, proclaiming His divine intervention, and attracting hearts to Him. Healing is not by our own power or holiness." We must insist on this

244

because many tend to believe otherwise. Those who have recovered their health in answer to "the prayer of faith" [James 5:15], "and the powerful and effective answers to prayer" (James 5:16), are often very impressed with the person involved in manifesting the gift. It is not by our own power or holiness that you function in these gifts, but by a childlike faith, which understands it has no power or holiness of its own, and which commits itself completely to Him who is faithful, and whose death has paid for our healing already. God's will is not wavering on this subject. Jesus already paid with His life to secure it for us. The Church needs to hear that it is because of her unbelief that she has lost these spiritual gifts of healing (I Corinthians 12: 9) and that the Lord restores to those who, with faith and obedience, have consecrated their lives to Him.

A LISTENING EAR

Faith comes from hearing the word of God. Sometimes while people listen, the revelation hits their spirit, faith explodes in them, and healing is made easy by their revelation and faith.

Acts 14:9 He listened to Paul as he was speaking. Paul looked directly at him, saw that he had faith to be healed

AN OBEDIENT HEART

It takes courage to move in these gifts. The "what if nothing happens?" question should be balanced by "What if something does?" We are going to need courage to operate in gifts of healing. This was the prayer of the early apostles and the church.

Acts 4:29 "And now, Lord, take note of their threats, and grant that Your bond-servants may speak Your word with all confidence, 30 while You extend Your hand to heal, and signs and wonders take place through the name of Your holy servant Jesus."(NASB)

What a joy is found in the healing of Jesus. We are promised as believers that when we lay our hands on sick people and offer up a faith-filled prayer they will be healed. It remains up to us to eagerly desire these gifts and to have the courage to see them operate by laying our hands on sick people and engaging our hearts to believe God.

The Gift of Miracles

Definition of Miracles

*B*efore we talk about the gift of miracles or miraculous powers we need to examine the topic of miracles and their history in scripture.

Easton's Bible Dictionary defines a miracle as "an event in the external world brought about by the immediate agency or the simple volition of God, operating without the use of means capable of being discerned by the senses, and designed to authenticate the divine commission of a religious teacher and the truth of his message (John 2:18; Matthew 12:38). It is an occurrence at once above nature and above man. It shows the intervention of a power that is not limited by the laws either of matter or of mind, a power interrupting the fixed laws which govern their movements; a supernatural power. "

Baker's Evangelical Dictionary of Biblical Theology says, "a miracle in the biblical concept is limited to those not explainable solely by natural processes but which require the direct causal agency of a supernatural being, usually God. These occur throughout all major eras of history but do appear with greater frequency at key periods of God's self-revelation".

In the Old Testament, two Hebrew words are most frequently used for the English word "miracle" and are often translated "sign"('oth) and "wonder" (mopheth). They mostly occur together in the same text (Ex. 7:3; Deut. 4:34; 6:22; 7:19; 13:1; 26:8; 28:46; 34:11; Neh. 9:10; Ps. 105:27; Isa. 8:18; Jer. 32:20; Dan. 6:27). Oth or Sign may be an object or daily activity as well as an unexpected divine action. It serves to point people to God. Mopheth or Wonder describes God's supernatural activity and the special manifestation of His power. Wonders often served as a sign of a future event.

In the New Testament, four Greek words are most frequently interpreted as defining miracles. **Semeion**, a "sign" an evidence of a divine authority or commission; the seal of a higher power, an attestation of a divine message. It is specifically translated as "miracle" in Luke 23:8 NIV; Acts 4:16,22 NASB, NIV. John used it as a major theme in his gospel showing Jesus was the Lord of nature by Turning water into wine in 2:1-11, Lord of life by healing the nobleman's son in 4:46-54, Lord over sickness by healing the paralyzed man in 5:1-15, Lord of provision by feeding the five thousand in 6:1-14, Lord of creation by walking on the sea in 6:15-21, Lord over sin by the healing of the man born blind in 9:1-41.

Teras or terata, "wonders;" from the Greek word from which the word terror comes, wonder-causing events; portents; producing astonishment in the beholder or causing the beholder to marvel. (Acts 2:19). a sign appeals to the understanding, Whereas a wonder appeals to the imagination. "Wonders" are most often God's activity (Acts 2:19; 4:30; 5:12; 6:8; 7:36; 14:3; 15:12), though sometimes they are counterfeited through the work of Satan in human instruments (Matt. 24:24; Mark 13:22; 2 Thess. 2:9; Rev. 13:11-13).

Dunameis, -"mighty works", inherent ability, works of superhuman power, activity of supernatural origin or character (Acts 2:22; Romans 15:19; 2th 2:9); of a new and higher power.

Erga, "works" employed in the New Testament in the sense of a miracle. John the Baptist heard of the "works" of Jesus while he was in prison (Matt. 11:2). The apostle John used the term frequently (5:20,36; 7:3; 10:38; 14:11,12; 15:24).

THE MIRACLES OF JESUS

Many teach that the sole reason for Jesus' display of miracles was to validate His person, message and ministry. This view negates the compassion Jesus had on people and the times He was moved by His love for His children. Jesus performed many acts of compassion by ministering to people's needs. If we fail to see these, it is easy to relegate God's miracles to purely academic discussions. Yet Jesus did use the miracles to authenticate His person and ministry.

John 5:18 For this reason therefore the Jews were seeking all the more to kill Him, because He not only was breaking the Sabbath, but also was calling God His own Father, making Himself equal with God.19 Therefore Jesus answered and was saying to them, "Truly, truly, I say to you, the Son can do nothing of Himself, unless it is something He sees the Father doing; for whatever the Father does, these things the Son also does in like manner. 20 For the Father loves the Son, and shows Him all things that He Himself is doing; and the Father will show Him greater works than these, so that you will marvel. (NASB)

John 10:24 Then the Jews surrounded Him and said to Him, "How long do You keep us in doubt? If You are the Christ, tell us plainly." 25 Jesus answered them, "I told you, and you do not believe. The works that I do in My Father's name, they bear witness of Me. 26 But you do not believe, because you are not of My sheep, as I said to you .... John 10:38 but if I do, though you do not believe Me, believe the works, that you may know and believe[a] that the Father is in Me, and I in Him."(NKJV)

The argument that says miracles cannot be expecting in church today, reasons that miracles were given only at specific times in the church's history and only to certain people. The argument suggests that in the New Testament, miracles were given to Jesus, His disciples, to the seventy, and to their acquaintances in the generation after He died. The premise is that miracles were given for the confirmation of their words until the scriptures were completed. If we equate miracles to the unique authority of Jesus and His twelve apostles, and assume that the only reason for miracles was to authenticate their teaching, it follows that the gift of miracles ceased with their departure from earth. This teaching does not take into account post ascension-gifting, nor does it take into account all other Scripture references on the subject.

One of the Manifesting gifts

The gift of miracles is mentioned along with the other "phanerosis" gifts (those that make manifest or exhibit Gods presence, person and nature) in 1 Corinthians 12.

1 Corinthians 12:7 Now to each one the manifestation of the Spirit is given for the common good. . . 10 to another miraculous powers,

Many people discount that miracles happen in our "modern days" and struggle to believe that they could occur on behalf of ordinary people, even if they did. Yet this scriptural context places them squarely in the same space as all the other "phanerosis" gifts and urges us to eagerly desire them along with all the others.

The miracles Jesus performed in the New Testament are never called "the gift of miracles." The Corinthian gift by that name is distinct from the miracles He performed. The Corinthian gift is given "to each one" just as the Holy Spirit determines. This passage, written near the end of what others call the apostolic age, does not say to each one is given the following gifts but only to the few are given healing and miracles. In fact in verse 28 the gift of apostle is clearly distinct from the "gifts of healings" and "miracles".

1 Corinthians 12:28 And in the church God has appointed first of all apostles, second prophets, third teachers, then workers of miracles, also those having gifts of healing, those able to help others, those with gifts of administration, and those speaking in different kinds of tongues.

The gift in Corinthians is given to each one by the Holy Spirit to make the presence, will and character of God manifest. They are not personal authentications of spiritual maturity and like all the other gifts mentioned in this context they are for common good and not personal acclaim. They speak to the grace of the Holy Spirit and not to the worthiness of the person through whom they come.

THEY ARE AVAILABLE TO ALL WHO BELIEVE

The Galatian church is admonished in a similar vein as Paul addresses the church where miracles are being done.

Galatians 3:1-5 You foolish Galatians! Who has bewitched you? Before your very eyes Jesus Christ was clearly portrayed as crucified. I would like to learn just one thing from you: Did you receive the Spirit by observing the law, or by believing what you heard? Are you so foolish? After beginning with the Spirit, are you now trying to attain your goal by human effort? Have you suffered so much for nothing--if it really was for nothing? Does God give you his Spirit and work miracles among you because you observe the law, or because you believe what you heard?

In these verses, Paul's intent was for the church members to experience miracles through their personal faith in Jesus. When they heard the gospel about Christ with all its freedoms they were emboldened to trust God for miracles they did not deserve. This is in accord with what Jesus said to His disciples about anyone who believed in Him.

John 14:11 Believe Me that I am in the Father and the Father in Me, or else believe Me for the sake of the works themselves.12 "Most assuredly, I say to you, he who believes in Me, the works that I do he will do also; and greater works than these he will do, because I go to My Father. 13 And whatever you ask in My name, that I will do, that the Father may be glorified in the Son. 14 If you ask[a] anything in My name, I will do it. (NKJV)

In Robertson's Word Pictures of the New Testament he says, "shall he do also (kakeinoß poihsei)" Emphatic pronoun ekeinoß, "that one also." Greater works than these (meizona toutwn). Comparative adjective neuter plural from megaß with ablative case toutwn. Not necessarily greater miracles and not greater spiritual works in quality, but greater in quantity. Cf. Peter at Pentecost and Paul's mission tours. "Because I go" (oti egw poreuornai). The reason for this expansion is made possible by the Holy Spirit as Paraclete (Exodus 16:7).

The emphatic "that one also" as mentioned above is talking about those who believe. This re-enforces the teaching that miracles will accompany believers. Miracles are not reserved only for particular people but rather for anyone who is eager to see them manifested for Jesus' glory. Jesus promised that miracles (signs) would accompany obedience to the great commission.

Mark 16:15-20 And He said to them, "Go into all the world and preach the gospel to every creature. 16 He who believes and is baptized will be saved; but he who does not believe will be condemned. 17 And these signs will follow those who believe: In My name they will cast out demons; they will speak with new tongues; 18 they will take up serpents; and if they drink anything deadly, it will by no means hurt them; they will lay hands on the sick, and they will recover."19 So then, after the Lord had spoken to them, He was received up into heaven, and sat down at the right hand of God. 20 And they went out and preached everywhere, the Lord working with them and confirming the word through the accompanying signs. Amen. (NKJV)

Jesus said that He would confirm the word of those who dared to go into all of the world and preach His gospel.He continued to rally those who heard Him, encouraging them to have faith, which would make everything possible, and nothing impossible for them.

Mark 9:22-23 "It has often thrown him into fire or water to kill him. But if you can do anything, take pity on us and help us." "'If you can'?" said Jesus. "Everything is possible for him who believes."

Mat 17:19-20 Then the disciples came to Jesus in private and asked, "Why couldn't we drive it out?" Mat He replied, "Because you have so little faith. I tell you the truth, if you have faith as small as a mustard seed, you can say to this mountain, 'Move from here to there' and it will move. Nothing will be impossible for you."

The scripture shows that more miracles seem to have been done by the apostles, prophets and evangelists than by others, yet they are a gift offered by the Holy Spirit to all who believe and eagerly desire them.

THE GIFT OF PROPHECY

WE CAN ALL PROPHESY

*T*he manifestation gift of prophecy is the gift that the scriptures tell us to desire more than any other. Prophesy has the power to build up the rest of the body.

1 Corinthians 14:1 Follow the way of love and eagerly desire spiritual gifts, especially the gift of prophecy.

1 Corinthians 14:4 He who speaks in a tongue edifies himself, but he who prophesies edifies the church.

1 Corinthians 14:12 So it is with you. Since you are eager to have spiritual gifts, try to excel in gifts that build up the church.

1 Corinthians 14:39 Therefore, my brothers, be eager to prophesy, and do not forbid speaking in tongues.

Every believer is urged to excel in this manifestation gift. It is available to any believer who desires it. Like all gifts given by God, these gifts are to be used wisely and within a framework that is clearly outlined in the scriptures. This gift can manifest through every believer and is different to the ascension gift of prophet who is a person,

1 Corinthians 14:5 I would like every one of you to speak in tongues, but I would rather have you prophesy . . . 29 Two or three prophets should speak, and the others should weigh carefully what is said. 30 And if a revelation comes

254

*to someone who is sitting down, the first speaker should
stop. 31 For you can all prophesy in turn so that everyone
may be instructed and encouraged.*

GUIDELINES FOR PROPHESYING
CONTEXT

There are 3 main reasons Jesus gives us a prophetic word
for others or the church. The first is that He wants to
communicate information to us that will shape our actions,
reactions or opinions regarding the situation. This is often a call
and opportunity to pray for the person or situation and to wait
on the Lord about whether to share the word with them. If we
feel not to share with them immediately, we should keep quiet in
the person's best interest. I have had the Lord warn me of an
intended temptation facing friends of mine in the ministry,
which has led me to pray for them in those areas for years while
not yet saying anything to them.

The second reason is that He wants to share with them an
encouragement or confirmation without revealing their hearts to
everyone in the room. For this reason, we must share privately
with the person. Prophecy has the power of revelation, and
therefore the deliveryand context in which we share the word
requires careful consideration. If I say out loud to someone who
is anxious "The Lord is going to help you with the deep seated
fear that has gripped you," it may ease their fear, but also make
them feel belittled. Worse yet, I could say "God is going to
deliver you of your cowardice," which seems to be
counterproductive and hardly encouraging. In sharing what the
Lord has given us, we must administer discretion, grace and
love. We must remember that it is the nature of love to cover,
while envy and pride seek to uncover.

*1 Corinthians 14:24 But if all prophesy, and an unbeliever
or an ungifted man enters, he is convicted by all, he is
called to account by all; 25 the secrets of his heart are
disclosed; and so he will fall on his face and worship God,
declaring that God is certainly among you. (NASB)*

Proverbs 10:12 Hatred stirs up dissension, but love covers over all wrongs.

1 Pet 4:8 Above all, love each other deeply, because love covers over a multitude of sins.

The third reason we are given prophetic words is so that we can share the Lord's heart publicly. These are words that edify and comfort all who hear them even if they are directed to one person. There are many reasons the Holy Spirit directs personal prophecy within a public meeting. I believe He wants others to learn His nature and understand what He is orchestrating.

Acts 21:10 As we were staying there for some days, a prophet named Agabus came down from Judea. 11 And coming to us, he took Paul's belt and bound his own feet and hands, and said, "This is what the Holy Spirit says: 'In this way the Jews at Jerusalem will bind the man who owns this belt and deliver him into the hands of the Gentiles.'" 12 When we had heard this, we as well as the local residents began begging him not to go up to Jerusalem. 13 Then Paul answered, "What are you doing, weeping and breaking my heart? For I am ready not only to be bound, but even to die at Jerusalem for the name of the Lord Jesus." (NASB)

Delivery

1. The aim is always edification, encouragement and comfort

Old Testament prophecy tended toward direction and judgment because it partnered with the Law. It was one of very few ways people could hear the word of the Lord. In the New Testament, we are all filled with the Holy Spirit, as Joel promised, with prophecy as the first sign.

Acts 2:17 "'In the last days, God says, I will pour out my Spirit on all people. Your sons and daughters will prophesy,

Now the New Testament manifestation gift of prophecy is for the specific purposes of strengthening, encouragement and comfort. There are examples of prophecy in the New Testament that additionally deal with direction, correction and commissioning, but these are done by prophets who have been called into the ascension gift. Manifestation gift prophecy is only for edification.

1 Cor 14:3 But he who prophesies speaks edification and exhortation and comfort to men. 4 He who speaks in a tongue edifies himself, but he who prophesies edifies the church. 5 I wish you all spoke with tongues, but even more that you prophesied; for he who prophesies is greater than he who speaks with tongues, unless indeed he interprets, that the church may receive edification. (NKJV)

2. PACKAGE THE PROPHETIC WORD IN LOVE

Once you have a sense of what the Lord is trying to communicate, ask Him how to best communicate it. Sometimes the Lord will have us say specific words in specific ways, and sometimes it will accompany specific actions. For the most part the "packaging" of the word, that is the tone, the exact words used or analogies offered, are up to the person delivering the word. Therefore, aim to say the word in the way it will most likely be positively received. Ask yourself "What is the most loving way to deliver this message?"

Ephesians 4:15 Instead, speaking the truth in love, we will in all things grow up into him who is the Head, that is, Christ. 16 From him the whole body, joined and held together by every supporting ligament, grows and builds itself up in love, as each part does its work.

3. PRESENTATION CAN BE IN THE FIRST OR THIRD PERSON

It is often better to preface it with "I believe the Lord is saying." or "I have a sense." which allows for judgment of the word. When a prophecy is spoken in the first person, as though it comes directly from the Lord, it is difficult for listeners to dispute. Leaving some room in the presentation allows people a little more space to assess the word on their own terms. The first person presentation of a prophetic word demands a response because we either accept it in its entirety as the word of the Lord, and we submit to it, or we must reject and confront it.

PROTOCOLS

Here are some suggestions on how to function in this manifestation gift.

1. ORDERLY PROPHECY

Fitting and orderly, are Paul's requirements on the most effective manner for the gifts of the Holy Spirit. This implies that before I start prophesying, I should recognize who is responsible for the meeting, person, or situation. This means that I don't speak out of turn, interrupting others or disrupting the flow of the meeting. I choose to submit the gift to the people God has set up in authority. If I have a word for a child I should see to it that I have their parent's authority or presence with me before I share it with that child. I suggest that spouses should be included in a word for their spouse. Shepherds of the flock should be present when a word is spoken over the flock. Anyone who consistently wants to prophesy to members of the opposite sex in private should be noted and discouraged. Essentially, anyone who is going to have to give an account of those under their care should be honored by the submission of the gift of prophecy. Prophesying without regard for authorities can be irresponsible. The guardians and shepherds of the flock should be able to assess the appropriateness of the word for their sheep before it is publicly stated. This idea of accountability is clearly demonstrated in the New Testament.

1 Corinthians 14:37 If anybody thinks he is a prophet or spiritually gifted, let him acknowledge that what I am writing to you is the Lord's command. 38 If he ignores this, he himself will be ignored. 39 Therefore, my brothers, be eager to prophesy, and do not forbid speaking in tongues. 40 But everything should be done in a fitting and orderly way.

2. CLARITY IS VITAL

Be as clear as you can be, even if the Lord shares something with you that does not seem to make sense. If this is the case, most times, it will make sense to the recipient of the word. Many times these kinds of prophecies will come with visions and pictures that are aids to communicate what the Lord is saying. If so, take care not to get lost in the details of the picture. Peter on the roof saw a sheet with unclean animals in it and heard the Lord say to eat, but he did not immediately understand what the Lord was saying. These pictures and visions will often require reflection to access their full meaning. After you believe you have heard what the Lord is saying, speak it out with as much clarity as you can. Try to remain as true to the meaning as you can without embellishments. Here is what Paul said about clarity.

1 Corinthians 14:6 But now, brethren, if I come to you speaking in tongues, what will I profit you unless I speak to you either by way of revelation or of knowledge or of prophecy or of teaching? 7 Yet even lifeless things, either flute or harp, in producing a sound, if they do not produce a distinction in the tones, how will it be known what is played on the flute or on the harp? 8 For if the bugle produces an indistinct sound, who will prepare himself for battle? 9 So also you, unless you utter by the tongue speech that is clear, how will it be known what is spoken? For you will be speaking into the air. (NASB)

3. WAIT FOR THE CORRECT TIMING

Prophecy is like any other communication that springs to mind. You can say it as it comes to mind, or make a mental note to say it when you see the person, or you can write it down. It does not have to be blurted out the moment it's received. Somehow, it has become an accepted belief that the moment we receive a prophetic word it is the time to bring it. This implies that the Holy Spirit pounces on people and overcomes them to the point that they must speak out a prophetic word and when He leaves them again they come back to their own senses. This could not be further from the truth. Paul says that the spirits of the prophets are subject to the prophets. That means that when

259

we receive a word from the Spirit we are able to think on it, mull it over, and speak it out under our own control. It is also true that we can wait our turn to speak and recognize and prefer others who also believe they have something from the Lord.

1 Corinthians 14:29 Let two or three prophets speak, and let the others judge. 30 But if anything is revealed to another who sits by, let the first keep silent. 31 For you can all prophesy one by one, that all may learn and all may be encouraged. 32 And the spirits of the prophets are subject to the prophets. 33 For God is not the author of confusion but of peace, as in all the churches of the saints. (NKJV)

4. ACCORDING TO YOUR FAITH

Never prophesy something you don't believe is from God. Sometimes we are tempted to encourage people with hopeful words or words we wish and hope God is saying to them. We should not speak out these kinds of words or to try to build the recipients up by sanctioning their desires. These are not helpful and can often miss the mark. These kinds of hopeful prophecies are dangerous because if people receive it as a word from God, it will cause disappointment and disillusionment when it does not come to pass or proves to be misguided. Stick with what God gives you in your spirit and if you are not clear or certain say, "I'm not sure" or "Perhaps this could be from God" and share with them what you have. Many times the Lord will use the smallest idea or phrase to confirm something inside of the person that will not have the same connection with you. Often, the more you say the more chance you have of muddying the waters. Just say what you believe the Lord has for you to say and stop there. People who function in this gift maturely have trained themselves in this discipline.

5. STOP IN TIME

It is such a joy when the Lord begins to use us and in that time, there is a very real temptation to say things that He did not originate. Understand that often God uses more than one person to reveal His word. So when you feel like you have said all you needed to say, stop there and be happy for the part you were able to contribute. The manifestation gift of prophesy acts as a choreographed dance as the Holy Spirit orchestrates different people to bring a piece of the collective revelation for that day. Just as in an orchestra, beauty is displayed as many instruments skillfully play under the direction of the same master.

1 Corinthians 14:30 And if a revelation comes to someone who is sitting down, the first speaker should stop. 31 For you can all prophesy in turn so that everyone may be instructed and encouraged

ACCOUNTABILITY

1. LET THE OVERSEERS GOVERN

Prophetic words about Government, discipline and direction should be routed through the elders who are responsible for these. People who consistently want to get to the sheep behind the backs of the shepherds are thieves.

John 10:1 "Truly, truly, I say to you, he who does not enter by the door into the fold of the sheep, but climbs up some other way, he is a thief and a robber. 2 But he who enters by the door is a shepherd of the sheep. (NASB)

John 10:7 Therefore Jesus said again, "I tell you the truth, I am the gate for the sheep.

2. BE EAGER TO LEARN AND RECEIVE INSTRUCTION

If we have clean hearts we will be eager to exhibit a more mature display of the gifts. This means that we are open to loving leaders who will point out areas of improvement. The congregation, and especially elders, are supposed to judge each word given to their church. They are sanctioned to keep alight each fire the Holy Spirit starts. Good leaders will draw people aside who need instruction so that they may produce more fruit the next time they minister.

1 Cor 13:9 For we know in part and we prophesy in part .

1 Corinthians 14:29 Two or three prophets should speak, and the others should weigh carefully what is said

3. BE EAGER TO GIVE TESTIMONY

We are far more interested in hearing the good blessings that emerge from this gift than in policing its mismanagement. Lives, destinies, churches and meetings have been radically altered by this gift. Let us spend more time celebrating prophetic ministry for the gift that Scripture says it is.

Galatians 6:6 Anyone who receives instruction in the word must share all good things with his instructor.

GUIDELINE FOR RECEIVING A PROPHETIC WORD

The gift of prophecy is always presented in the scripture as a gift with potential to bless and encourage. However, the scriptures never position it above careful scrutiny and judgment. We must weigh prophetic words carefully considering the following Biblical assertions.

THE GIFT OF PROPHECY IS SUBJECT TO WEAKNESS AND INCOMPLETE PERSPECTIVE.

1 Corinthians 13:9 For we know in part and we prophesy in part,

IT SHOULD ALWAYS BE GIVEN WITH THE UNDERSTANDING THAT IT WILL BE WEIGHED AND JUDGED.

1 Corinthians 14:29 Two or three prophets should speak, and the others should weigh carefully what is said.

1 Thessalonians 5:19 Do not put out the Spirit's fire; 20 do not treat prophecies with contempt. 21 Test everything. Hold on to the good.

IT SHOULD NOT BE DESPISED OR DERIDED.

1 Thessalonians 5:20 do not treat prophecies with contempt.

How to judge it for authenticity

Primary

Ask yourself the following questions concerning the prophetic word. If the answer to these questions is "no," there is some cause for concern or training.

1. Is it consistent with Scripture?

2. Is it consistent with the character of God revealed in the gospel?

3. Does it strengthen the centrality of Jesus i.e. Does it draw a sincere heart toward or away from Christ?

4. Does it bring strength and unity to the church? Sometimes however if people are in rebellion the word may seek to bring separation. Even Jesus said that His ministry would bring division sometimes.

5. Does it edify, encourage, and comfort?

6. Does it confirm what I believe God has been saying to me?

Secondary

Once these questions have been answered, consider the following questions.

Is it the correct tone?

If we embrace it, where does it lead?

What impression about God does it leave?

What fruit did / could it have?

Action steps

1. RECORD IT

Record it on tape, CD, or write it down for reflection and prayer. Many times when it is the Lord manifesting this gift through people, it is intensely emotional and exciting to the person receiving it. Often they will forget much of what was said and will regret that later. If they know it is being recorded, they can focus on assessing the word instead of memorizing every detail for later review. The recording of the word allows for a more accurate judging of it as the scriptures require. It is also a way to hold those who bring the gift accountable.

2. REVIEW IT

Look for a call to action. What does it call me to do? Be careful to follow the conditions. The Lord is giving someone a word for their edification and He will remain faithful even if they are faithless but He often invites people to share the adventure by giving them a part to play. If they are diligent and attend to it, they will prosper. Often the word requires or anticipates a response. Listen to what the Lord says and obey that. It is always exciting to see how the Lord establishes His plans.

3. PRAY OVER IT.

Both the person delivering the prophetic word and the person receiving it should shoulder the responsibility of prayer. Many times during prayer, the Lord will add details and understanding of His prophesied word. Ask Him about the things He has said to you.

4. FIGHT FOR IT

The places of greatest promise are the places of greatest battle. Those things that have been promised but not yet manifested are fertile ground for the enemy's lies. God's prophesies have creative power they are therefore the very ground the enemy tries to sow full of unbelief. This is why the Lord often gives us prophetic words to enlarge and encourage our faith. Faith comes by hearing God and we will do well if we fight in line with His prophesies over our lives.

1 Timothy 1:18 Timothy, my son, I give you this instruction in keeping with the prophecies once made about you, so that by following them you may fight the good fight,

The manifestation gift of prophecy has a great power to bless and encourage the church. When used well, it is unrivaled in its scope and elevating power. This gift is supposed to be the desire of every believer. Strive to hone this gift and it will be a fountain of blessing to you.

The discerning of spirits

$\mathcal{D}$iscernment of spirits is another of the manifestation gifts given to the church by the Holy Spirit.

1 Corinthians 12:7 Now to each one the manifestation of the Spirit is given for the common good. . . 10 to another distinguishing between spirits, 11 All these are the work of one and the same Spirit, and he gives them to each one, just as he determines.

Definition

Discerning of spirits is the supernatural ability to perceive the nature of a spirit exerting influence through a person, whether it is of human motivation, the Holy Spirit, or of demonic influence. It is the power of spiritual insight that enables us to see and understand the spiritual forces at work. It can also be the supernatural revelation of the plans and purposes of the enemy and his forces. It is a wonderful gift that protects and guards our Christian walk. Where a demonic spirit is at work, we have authority over it through the power of Jesus Christ and the authority of His name. They must run screaming from the life surrendered to Christ's Lordship. So we submit ourselves to God and resist the devil. Where we discern the Holy Spirit, we learn obedience and study to learn how best to cooperate with what He is doing. We need to learn to take His lead and respond with quick obedience. When we discern fleshly human motivation, we need to learn to be gracious and wise to bring them through to wholeness and wholehearted devotion to Jesus.

WHAT IS ITS PURPOSE?

This gift is both practical and purposeful in protecting our spiritual walk. Below are listed some practical reasons for this gift.

1. WARNING OF DECEPTION

We are warned to be on guard and alert because our enemy seeks to devour, mislead and tempt believers away from wholehearted devotion to Jesus. We understand that the enemy masquerades as an angel of light, as do his followers. Satan uses both deceptive teachings and influential people to lead believers away from a pure walk with Jesus. This gift is a supernatural weapon that warns us and shows us error. Therefore, not everything that sounds sweet, religious or wise can be taken at face value. It must be judged, discerned, and weighed to test its validity. This gift is given by the Holy Spirit to discern the spirit, to warn of "off the mark" teaching, and to confirm truth. This gift allows your spirit to testify when it encounters truth.

2 Corinthians 11:13 -15 For such men are false apostles, deceitful workmen, masquerading as apostles of Christ And no wonder, for Satan himself masquerades as an angel of light. It is not surprising, then, if his servants masquerade as servants of righteousness.

Colossians 2:4 I tell you this so that no one may deceive you by fine-sounding arguments.

Colossians 2:23 Such regulations indeed have an appearance of wisdom,

2. DELIVERANCE MINISTRY

When confronted with demonic forces the New Testament shows both Jesus and His disciples addressing the spirits while commanding them to leave. In the same way, this gift shows the kinds of spirits that are working in people today. Not every demonic manifestation displays the true nature of the demon. Jesus said that the enemy would masquerade as an angel of light. This gift helps us discover the true nature of the spiritual forces at work. Different words are used in the New Testament for the spiritual forces of evil that the church encountered. These include unclean spirits, deaf and dumb spirits, demonic spirits, oppressing spirits.

On the positive side, we can also perceive the Holy Spirit and His ministry. What joy is found when He speaks and ministers. Even when He is moving in ways that we don't understand, this gift of discernment allows us to be at peace.

Acts 16:16 It happened that as we were going to the place of prayer, a slave-girl having a spirit of divination met us, who was bringing her masters much profit by fortune-telling. 17 Following after Paul and us, she kept crying out, saying, "These men are bond-servants of the Most High God, who are proclaiming to you the way of salvation." 18 She continued doing this for many days. But Paul was greatly annoyed, and turned and said to the spirit, "I command you in the name of Jesus Christ to come out of her!" And it came out at that very moment. (NASB)

3. WITNESSING

When we know how a person thinks or is bound, influenced, or deceived, we have a very insightful witnessing tool. It allows us to pray specifically for the person.

Acts 13:7-12 . . . Sergius Paulus. The proconsul, an intelligent man, sent for Barnabas and Saul because he wanted to hear the word of God. But Elymas the sorcerer (for that is what his name means) opposed them and tried to turn the proconsul from the faith. Then Saul, who was also called Paul, filled with the Holy Spirit, looked straight at Elymas and said, "You are a child of the devil and an enemy of everything that is right! You are full of all kinds of deceit and trickery. Will you never stop perverting the right ways of the Lord? Now the hand of the Lord is against you. You are going to be blind, and for a time you will be unable to see the light of the sun."

Immediately mist and darkness came over him, and he groped about, seeking someone to lead him by the hand. When the proconsul saw what had happened, he believed, for he was amazed at the teaching about the Lord.

4. PERSONAL INSIGHT

Not everything we feel and experience is outside the realm of the enemy's attack. Sometimes, subtly, the enemy seeks to use everyday emotions to produce lies. This discernment gift is helpful in revealing the nature of the attack e.g. spirit of depression, suicide, hatred, perversion, lust, etc.

Acts 8:20 -24 Peter answered: "May your money perish with you, because you thought you could buy the gift of God with money! You have no part or share in this ministry, because your heart is not right before God. Repent of this wickedness and pray to the Lord. Perhaps he will forgive you for having such a thought in your heart. For I see that you are full of bitterness and captive to sin Then Simon answered, "Pray to the Lord for me so that nothing you have said may happen to me."

BASIC INSIGHT INTO THE SPIRITUAL WORLD

The bible teaches that God is Spirit. We know that there is an entire spiritual world full of spiritual beings. God exists without beginning or end but all of His creations had a beginning. We know that the angels sang and rejoiced while God was creating the physical universe. The spiritual world came first. Mankind was the first of God's creations born and designed to live in both the spiritual and the natural realms. For this, God has given us bodies, minds and spirits. We are three part beings.

1 Thessalonians 5:23 May God himself, the God of peace, sanctify you through and through. May your whole spirit, soul and body be kept blameless at the coming of our Lord Jesus Christ.

Hebrews 4:12 For the word of God is living and active. Sharper than any double-edged sword, it penetrates even to dividing soul and spirit, joints and marrow; it judges the thoughts and attitudes of the heart.

When we are born again, our spirits are made alive to God, everything is made new and we have the mind of Christ. We are called to the renewal of our minds through repentance and revelation, and are also called to grow in grace and in the knowledge of God. This means that although we have so much yet to learn and discover we are currently equipped with everything we need for victory.

1 Corinthians 6:17 But he who unites himself with the Lord is one with him in spirit.

John 4:24 God is spirit, and his worshipers must worship in spirit and in truth."

It is our spirit that is strengthened by God's grace and grows to know Him increasingly. Our bodies and minds, once dead to the spiritual realm, now learn to work with our spirit to perceive spiritual things. As we grow stronger in our walk with the Lord, our minds become renewed to the kingdom of God. From our spirits flows a steady stream of spiritual awareness.

1 Corinthians 2:11 For who among men knows the thoughts of a man except the man's spirit within him? In the same way no one knows the thoughts of God except the Spirit of God.

1 Corinthians 2:14 -15 The man without the Spirit does not accept the things that come from the Spirit of God, for they are foolishness to him, and he cannot understand them, because they are spiritually discerned. The spiritual man makes judgments about all things, but he himself is not subject to any man's judgment:

We can grow strong in spirit and develop our walk with the Lord. Jesus Himself grew strong in spirit and so did John the Baptist. We are encouraged to do the same.

Luke 1:80 And the child (John) grew and became strong in spirit; and he lived in the desert until he appeared publicly to Israel.

Luke 2:52 And Jesus grew in wisdom and stature, and in favor with God and men.

Jude 1:20 But you, dear friends, build yourselves up in your most holy faith and pray in the Holy Spirit.

CONDITIONS OF THE HUMAN SPIRIT

Scripture records many different conditions of the human spirit. We are told to purify ourselves from things that may contaminate our spirits. This is not speaking about demonic spirits having control but merely people's spirits being contaminated by the pressures and hardships of life here on sinful earth. Here is a list of scriptural examples of things that contaminate or enrich people's spirits;

2 Corinthians 7:1 Since we have these promises, dear friends, let us purify ourselves from everything that contaminates body and spirit, perfecting holiness out of reverence for God.

STUBBORNESS

Deuteronomy 2:30 But Sihon king of Heshbon refused to let us pass through. For the LORD your God had made his spirit stubborn and his heart obstinate in order to give him into your hands, as he has now done.

WISEDOM

Deuteronomy 34:9 Now Joshua son of Nun was filled with the spirit of wisdom because Moses had laid his hands on him. So the Israelites listened to him and did what the LORD had commanded Moses.

BITTERNESS

1 Samuel 30:6 David was greatly distressed because the men were talking of stoning him; each one was bitter in spirit because of his sons and daughters. But David found strength in the LORD his God.

Psalm 73:21 When my heart was grieved and my spirit embittered,

CRUSHED

Psalm 34:18 The LORD is close to the brokenhearted and saves those who are crushed in spirit.

Proverbs 18:14 A man's spirit sustains him in sickness, but a crushed spirit who can bear?

FAILING

Psalm 143:7 Answer me quickly, O LORD; my spirit fails. Do not hide your face from me or I will be like those who go down to the pit.

STEADFAST

Psalm 51:10 Create in me a pure heart, O God, and renew a steadfast spirit within me.

WILLING

Psalm 51:12 Restore to me the joy of your salvation and grant me a willing spirit, to sustain me.

BROKEN

Psalm 51:17 The sacrifices of God are a broken spirit; a broken and contrite heart, O God, you will not despise.

FAINT

Psalm 77:3 I remembered you, O God, and I groaned; I mused, and my spirit grew faint. Selah

Psalm 142:3 When my spirit grows faint within me, it is you who know my way. In the path where I walk men have hidden a snare for me.

INQUIRING

Psalm 77:6 I remembered my songs in the night. My heart mused and my spirit inquired:

HAUGHTY

Proverbs 16:18 Pride goes before destruction, a haughty spirit before a fall.

REFRESHED

Proverbs 25:13 Like the coolness of snow at harvest time is a trustworthy messenger to those who send him; he refreshes the spirit of his masters.

LONGING

2 Samuel 13:39 And the spirit of the king longed to go to Absalom, for he was consoled concerning Amnon's death.

FUNCTIONS OF THE HUMAN SPIRIT

I first heard this concept from the late David Griffith, one of my fathers in the faith. The basis of this idea is that just as we have physical bodies that are created with natural faculties, our spirits have abilities as well. With our bodies we can see, touch, taste, hear and smell. These abilities are assumed to be normal and healthy in all human beings. In like manner, the functions of the human spirit are normal and healthy. We are beings created to function in both the physical and spiritual worlds. These abilities are built, by design, in each human spirit. If we recognize them and develop strong spirits we will function in these areas effortlessly and see the kingdom of Jesus made manifest in our lives.

1. RECOGNIZE / DISCERN

Our spirits have a natural capacity to discern. This is not limited to the natural realm but is often supernatural in its focus. Our spirits discern evil and good. We can discern people's spirits as easily as evil spirits or angelic beings. When the Holy Spirit graces us with this gift He empowers this natural function of our spirits. With this gift, Many times we can walk into a room and sense the mood. Sometimes we sense the presence of evil or sense the presence of the Lord. These are demonstrations of the natural ability of our human spirit to discern things not revealed to our other senses. Sometimes, when talking with someone, we feel repelled by them as though something unclean is on them even though they may look perfectly respectable on the outside. Although this is not an infallible judge of character and should not be used to publicly accuse people, it is nevertheless often a first warning from our spirits that all is not well.

2. RECEIVE

People can receive great inheritance and blessing through their spirits. We can hear from God. Our Spirits are designed to receive messages, grace, refreshing, knowledge and wisdom. The Holy Spirit indwells us and we can receive His guidance at any stage. He downloads spiritual blessings into our spirits. Receiving from God is a natural, spiritual event. Many have received immense peace in testing times that defies the situation or logic. Often God can encourage us or stir our faith by a download into our spirits.

3. RELATE

Like lying down on a soft bed at the end of a long day, or sitting in a shady seat away from the heat, our spirits are designed to be refreshed as they commune with God. Our spirits have a wonderful capacity to fellowship and share a moment with God. The walks in the "cool of the evening" that Adam and Eve enjoyed are still available to us when we learn to fellowship with the Holy Spirit. Our spirits were created to connect and relate to God. Many years ago when the Soviet and American space stations sought to dock, it was discovered that they did not have the same space-docking mechanisms. A module was built that docked on the one side to the Soviet spacecraft and on the other it docked to the American spacecraft. Our spirits are like that docking station. They can relate to things in the heavenly realms and they can relate to the things our minds and bodies are saying in the physical realm. Do not believe the lie that you cannot connect with God. Your spirit was made to do just that.

4. SEE

Another function of our spirits in spiritual sight. This may take the form of a mental image that persists, growing in intensity to a trancelike state that Peter, Abraham, Adam, Isaiah, Ezekiel, Daniel and countless others have experienced. Some have even been caught away in a vision. The Scriptures say that no eye has seen what God has prepared for those who love Him, but God has revealed it by His Spirit. Paul prayed for the eyes of our heart to be enlightened. You were designed to see in the spirit.

5. PERCEIVE

Sometimes your spirit will perceive what people are thinking. Jesus often knew His audience's thoughts. Many times people who have eagerly desired manifestation gifts will perceive things that God is saying or doing in people's lives. This gift provides constant confirmation of the Spirit's heart and encourages all who notice. This is great for prayer purposes or when you desire to encourage others.

Colossians 2:5 For though I am absent from you in body, I am present with you in spirit and delight to see how orderly you are and how firm your faith in Christ is.

1 Corinthians 5:3 –4 Even though I am not physically present, I am with you in spirit. And I have already passed judgment on the one who did this, just as if I were present. When you are assembled in the name of our Lord Jesus and I am with you in spirit, and the power of our Lord Jesus is present,

RULE

Our spirits are designed to be strong and to have dominion over our minds and bodies. This governing ability of a strong spirit forms a monitor for our daily lives. A person with a strong spirit can lead his body and mind to do things that a person with a weak spirit cannot.

Proverbs 18:14 A man's spirit sustains him in sickness, but a crushed spirit who can bear?

Psalm 51:12 Restore to me the joy of your salvation and grant me a willing spirit, to sustain me.

What a great gift this is. It gives us clarity to know the difference between the Holy Spirit and other spirits while we seek the Lord for the wisdom to know what to do with each.

Tongues and Interpretation

The Gift of Tongues

*W*hile tongues are mentioned throughout the New Testament, the two major contexts include the day of Pentecost and a passage in 1 Corinthians. In 1 Corinthians, Paul is writing to the Corinthian church in response to a question about spiritual gifts. In this passage, Paul mentions that some tongues are unknown to man and require interpretation. This produces the following two theological terms;

Xenoglossia

This is the ability to spontaneously speak a foreign language without first having learned it, or even been exposed to it. This term is also derived from two Greek words: Xenos, which means "foreign" or "foreigner" and glõssai, which means "tongues" or "languages." An event in which an individual who knows only English, and who suddenly starts to speak in fluent French would be an example of Xenoglossia. There are some people who believe that the gift of tongues on the day of Pentecost was not recognizable tongues (xenoglossia) but that the miracle was that each person understood the tongues being spoken in their own language. I believe that they spoke in different recognizable languages.

Glossolalia

This is the most common meaning of "speaking in tongues." This term is derived from two Greek words: glõssai, which means "tongues" or "languages," and lalien which means, "to speak." The church world is divided on the topic of tongues.

Those who do not believe the manifestation gifts are available today, argue against tongues that are not recognized as a human language. Paul speaks to the reality of both tongues that are known by men and tongues that are spoken by angels. It seems the gift of tongues could source either of these groupings of tongues.

1 Corinthians 13:1 If I speak in the tongues of men and of angels, but have not love, I am only a resounding gong or a clanging cymbal.

If we believe that Paul was not merely trying to be poetic or creative with the phrase the "tongues of angels," then we should understand that if someone is given a gift of the tongue of angels, that it would not be recognizable to the human ear. If someone speaks in this kind of tongue, it will not benefit anyone else because its meaning will be hidden from them. Paul says that if this occurs, the speaker should concentrate this gift in a private capacity to build himself up, but refrain from its use in a corporate meeting unless an interpretation is brought. Read the following scriptures where Paul repeats that the kind of tongues being manifested at Corinth were unknown languages.

1 Corinthians 14:2 For anyone who speaks in a tongues does not speak to people but to God. Indeed, no one understands them; they utter mysteries by the Spirit.

1 Corinthians 14:5 I would like every one of you to speak in tongues, but I would rather have you prophesy. The one who prophesies is greater than the one who speaks in tongues, unless someone interprets, so that the church may be edified. 6 Now, brothers and sisters, if I come to you and speak in tongues, what good will I be to you, unless I bring you some revelation or knowledge or prophecy or word of instruction? 7 Even in the case of lifeless things that make sounds, such as the pipe or harp, how will anyone know what tune is being played unless there is a distinction in the notes? 8 Again, if the trumpet does not sound a clear call, who will get ready for battle? 9 So it is with you. Unless you speak intelligible words with your tongue, how will anyone know what you are saying? You will just be speaking into the air. 10 Undoubtedly there are all sorts of languages in the world, yet none of them is without meaning. 11 If then I do not grasp the meaning of what someone is saying, I am a foreigner to the speaker, and the speaker is a foreigner to me. . . . 16 Otherwise when you are praising God in the Spirit, how can someone else, who is now put in the position of an inquirer, say "Amen" to your thanksgiving, since they do not know what you are saying? 17 You are giving thanks well enough, but no one else is edified. 18 I thank God that I speak in tongues more than all of you. 19 But in the church I would rather speak five intelligible words to instruct others than ten thousand words in a tongue.

WHAT ARE TONGUES FOR?

AS A SIGN FROM GOD

We are given three important pictures of the gift of tongues at significant junctures in the life of the early church. These are the day of Pentecost, the first outreach to Gentiles, and the baptism of some followers of John the Baptist. In these instances, the gift is used as a sign of the moving of God.

I think if the Lord asked my advice on how to start His church on the earth, I would have suggested some significant miracles of healing and provision to cement His kindness in people's minds and then a clearly preached outline of the gospel by the most gifted orator. God chose to launch His church on the earth by a loud noise that sounded like a hurricane blowing through Jerusalem yet not a leaf was stirred and no wind was felt. While everyone was out in the streets wondering about this, a wild bunch of drunken looking disciples with flaming heads burst into the streets speaking in different tongues that everyone in the crowd could hear and understand. Even in that day, this gift of tongues, God's first step in demonstrating His church, was not celebrated by all as the mighty sign from God that it is. Various reactions are recorded in Acts chapter 2. In verse 5 a crowd came together in "bewilderment", verse 7 says they were "utterly amazed", verse 12 records their reaction as "amazed and perplexed", while verse 13 says that some "scoffed and made fun of them". Bewildered, amazed, perplexed and mocking are still the negative reactions to this great gift. For some, however it results in new revelation, salvation, and joy. Whatever we feel about tongues, God chose it as His first sign to a dying world that the church age had begun.

The second major New Testament event in which tongues are featured is the day that the Holy Spirit tells Peter that the Gentiles are to be included in the grace of Jesus Christ. Peter was coaxed into coming to Cornelius' home and while preaching, the Holy Spirit comes on those present with a great interruption of Peter's sermon. It is the demonstration of the gift of tongues that settles the matter for Peter and the Jews traveling with him. It is clear from the following passage that they equated the baptism in the Holy Spirit with the speaking in tongues.

Acts 10: 44 While Peter was still speaking these words, the Holy Spirit came on all who heard the message. 45 The circumcised believers who had come with Peter were astonished that the gift of the Holy Spirit had been poured out even on Gentiles. 46 For they heard them speaking in tongues and praising God. Then Peter said, 47 "Surely no one can stand in the way of their being baptized with water. They have received the Holy Spirit just as we have." 48 So he ordered that they be baptized in the name of Jesus Christ.

The third important event is Paul's time in Ephesus. Here, Paul talks to some believers about the baptism of the Holy Spirit and they speak in tongues. This opens up years of fruitful ministry for Paul in that city which leads to the spread of the gospel throughout the province.

Acts 19:1 And it happened, while Apollos was at Corinth, that Paul, having passed through the upper regions, came to Ephesus. And finding some disciples 2 he said to them, "Did you receive the Holy Spirit when you believed?" So they said to him, "We have not so much as heard whether there is a Holy Spirit." 3 And he said to them, "Into what then were you baptized?" So they said, "Into John's baptism." 4 Then Paul said, "John indeed baptized with a baptism of repentance, saying to the people that they should believe on Him who would come after him, that is, on Christ Jesus." 5 When they heard this, they were baptized in the name of the Lord Jesus. 6 And when Paul had laid hands on them, the Holy Spirit came upon them, and they spoke with tongues and prophesied. 7 Now the men were about twelve in all. (NKJV)

The early church and its leaders placed great importance on the gift of tongues as a sign of God's participation and sanction of an event.

TO MAKE MANIFEST THE HEART AND WILL OF GOD

Tongues are a sign, given to make the Holy Spirit's presence apparent, to exhibit His power. It is an immediate, external and most often initial sign of the Holy Spirit's presence. Large portions of the church, who speak in tongues, believe that tongues are the initial evidence of the baptism in the Holy Spirit. It is most often in scripture presented as the uniform evidence regardless of race, language or culture. It is not the only sign demonstrated nor is it presented as evidence every time it speaks of someone receiving the Baptism of the Holy Spirit.

1 Corinthians 12:7 Now to each one the manifestation of the Spirit is given for the common good. . . . 22 Tongues, then, are a sign, not for believers but for unbelievers;

TO EDIFY (BUILD UP) THE PERSON SPEAKING

It has power to build up the spirit of the person who speaks, prays or sings in a tongue. As Paul teaches, tongues are a pure form of communication with God by the Holy Spirit and as such, we utter mysteries from within our spirits to God. Paul boasted that he spoke in tongues privately more than all the Corinthians.

1 Corinthians 14:4 He who speaks in a tongue edifies himself, but he who prophesies edifies the church.

Jude 1:20 But you, dear friends, build yourselves up in your most holy faith and pray in the Holy Spirit.

1 Corinthians 14:18 I thank God that I speak in tongues more than all of you. 19 But in the church I would rather speak five intelligible words to instruct others than ten thousand words in a tongue.

Our edification and strengthening happens because our spirits have free reign to commune with God's Spirit Our spirit grows strong in this place of heavenly and uninterrupted communion. Speaking in tongues bypasses my mind for it is an activity of my spirit. This is why Paul says he will pray and sing in tongues and while he is doing so, to keep his mind engaged, he will also pray or sing praise in his mind. With this understanding, we can use this invaluable gift to intercede, give thanks and worship God. These actions can all be done while speaking in foreign tongue.

1 Corinthians 14:2 For anyone who speaks in a tongue does not speak to men but to God. Indeed, no one understands him; he utters mysteries with his spirit.

1 Corinthians 14:14 For if I pray in a tongue, my spirit prays, but my mind is unfruitful. 15 So what shall I do? I will pray with my spirit, but I will also pray with my understanding; I will sing with my spirit, but I will also sing with my understanding.

WITH INTERPRETATION IT REVEALS THE MIND OF GOD

This can be an exhortation or communication to the people hearing the tongue and interpretation. When directed as a message from God, it should follow the same rules as manifestation gift prophecy. That means it should be used to bless and edify people, not to judge and correct. It may be an expression of praise, worship or thanksgiving to the Lord

1 Corinthians 14:6 Now, brothers, if I come to you and speak in tongues, what good will I be to you, unless I bring you some revelation or knowledge or prophecy or word of instruction? . . . . 13 For this reason anyone who speaks in a tongue should pray that he may interpret what he says.

CAN ALL SPEAK IN TONGUES?

What about the question Paul asks regarding tongues and the statement he makes about the gifts being distributed as the Holy Spirit determines?

1 Corinthians 12:30 Do all have gifts of healing? Do all speak in tongues? Do all interpret? . . . . . 11 All these are the work of one and the same Spirit, and he gives them to each one, just as he determines

I believe that these statements are given in the context of Paul wanting to bring order to the services of the church in Corinth. Each person filled with the Holy Spirit is capable of speaking in tongues and are invited to do so. However, In each meeting there is not time, nor will orderly service allow for each person to function in all manifestation gifts. When we come together as a church, we should be eager to function in manifestation gifts under the orchestration of the Holy Spirit's prompting. This is how the Holy Spirit determines what each person should bring in each service. All gifts are available and worked in all believers who desire them. Paul makes it clear elsewhere in the same chapter that all can speak in tongues.

1 Corinthians 12:6 There are different kinds of working, but in all of them and in everyone it is the same God at work.

1 Corinthians 14:5 I would like every one of you to speak in tongues, but I would rather have you prophesy.

1 Corinthians 14:23 So if the whole church comes together and everyone speaks in tongues, and some who do not understand or some unbelievers come in, will they not say that you are out of your mind?

INTERPRETATION OF TONGUES

This is the gift whereby the person hearing the gift of tongues is empowered to bring an interpretation of the tongue. It is not the translation of the tongue; it is the interpretation of the tongue. This means that it is often the dynamic equivalent truth of what was spoken rather than the literal translation of the words. Exact repetition of what was said may lose the intent of the person in translation. The interpretation is rather the process of putting into words the intent of the message. I have been present in church when a tongue was spoken that was unknown to the speaker but was known to a visitor in the congregation. The visitor confirmed that the interpretation was congruent with what was spoken.

Interpretation of tongues is stirred when someone speaks in a tongue and someone catches the heart of what is being conveyed in their spirit and brings that interpretation.

In this way, it is very similar to the gift of prophecy. It gleans a word, or an instruction, or an encouragement from the Lord and sets it in words. As different languages differ in structure, tongues and interpretations into our own language differ. There can be a discrepancy between the length of the tongue and the interpretation. Putting the meaning into words may be concise or take a more wordy explanation.

One word can be understood differently according to the tone delivery of the person speaking. The interpretation of a tongue leaves the delivery to us and our spirits. The grace of the Holy Spirit in this gift enables people's spirits to understand what the Lord is communicating. In this arena, it is not uncommon for more than one person to bring an interpretation or prophetic word that highlights different facets of the same perspective.

Those who speak in tongues are told to seek this gift so that it may be used to build up the church as well as their own spirit.

1 Corinthians 14:13 For this reason anyone who speaks in a tongue should pray that he may interpret what he says.

All the manifestation gifts from the Lord, if used in unity and maturity, can bring great blessing and edification to the church body and its members.

Section 3.3

GRACE GIFTS

GRACE GIFTS.

DEFINITION

$\mathcal{T}$he gifts of grace are distributed to us by God and are often thought of as our 'strengths' or 'abilities'. They are gifts from God in line with the grace He places on each life. God gives us grace that enables us in specific areas. The grace on our lives as apportioned by God means that in the areas He has graced us, we have natural abilities. They are supernatural in origin but very often are only ever recognized as a particular person's aptitude or ability. Things in the arena where we are graced seem intuitive and easy to figure out. By example we all know we are asked to offer hospitality. People who are graced with hospitality will be able to host people in their homes with great ease Others who do not have this grace gift may try hard, but will not have the same ease in their hospitality.

Although we did nothing to deserve these grace gifts, we can develop them by exercising them faithfully. This is probably the most persistent message in the New Testament concerning these gifts. They work best when their recipients administer them faithfully in service to others. While they are different to the manifestation 'gifts' of the Holy Spirit, in that they do not specifically make the presence, will or character of God manifest, they are still God-given and can bless others around us. When used faithfully, they bless the body of Christ with supernatural grace. Some of these graces can even be seen in the lives of people who don't yet know Him.

The Greek word used for this group of gifts is "charisma" which means a divine gratuity, a spiritual endowment, religious qualification, miraculous faculty, or a free gift. Let's take a look at some of these lists where these gifts are mentioned in the New Testament. In some places, these gifts are mentioned in conjunction with other types of gifts and as such do not constitute a complete listing of all the different types of gifts mentioned in those passages.

Romans 12:6-8	I Peter 4:9-11	1 Cor 12:28
1. Prophesying	1. Hospitality	1. Helps
2. Serving	2. Serving	2. Administration
3. Teaching	3. Speaking	
4. Encouraging		1 Corinthians 7:7
5. Giving	Exodus 31:1-5	1. Celibacy
6. Leadership	1. Creative skills	
7. Mercy		

The two most comprehensive passages showing solely these Charisma gifts are found below.

Romans 12:6 We have different gifts, according to the grace given us. If a man's gift is prophesying, let him use it in proportion to his faith. Rom 12:7 If it is serving, let him serve; if it is teaching, let him teach; Rom 12:8 if it is encouraging, let him encourage; if it is contributing to the needs of others, let him give generously; if it is leadership, let him govern diligently; if it is showing mercy, let him do it cheerfully.

1 Peter 4:9 Be hospitable to one another without complaint. 10 As each one has received a special gift, employ it in serving one another as good stewards of the manifold grace of God. 11 Whoever speaks, is to do so as one who is speaking the utterances of God; whoever serves is to do so as one who is serving by the strength which God supplies; so that in all things God may be glorified through Jesus Christ, to whom belongs the glory and dominion forever and ever. Amen. (NASB)

COMMON PRINCIPLES

This set of gifts is subject to a few basic principles or directives established in scripture that will enable them to function as God intends.

EACH PERSON IS UNIQUELY GIFTED

Romans 12:6 says we have different gifts (charisma) according to the grace (Charis) – Greek word for grace God has given us. God has apportioned great grace to each of us and our gifts are in line with that grace.

GIFTS PURPOSE IS TO SERVE OTHERS

The passage in 1 Pet 4:10 shows that every person in the church should use their individual gifts to serve others. Our Father has gifted every person in the church with grace and grace gifts. Our service in the church should be according to the grace evident in our lives. People who have a great ability with children should serve with children. People with technical ability should serve in the sound or audio visual team. Each member of the body should be expected to serve practically in the church. When people serve in the arena that they have been graced in, greater joy and better results are produced. It is the responsibility of the church leadership to create an environment, an expectation and a structure that requires each person to faithfully administrate this grace on their lives.

1 Peter 4:10 speaks about grace in its various forms, which presents an opportunity for us to re-look at how we measure God's grace .God's infinite creativity will be reflected in the grace gifts He distributes among His children. Our role is to see that we do not inadvertently restrict or restrain people who have a particular grace because it is not one that we share or understand.

PRIMARY LAW OF THE BODY

These gifts of the graces of God, just like the others gifts mentioned in the scriptures, are always mentioned in the context of a body. Used selfishly, they are only for personal and temporary gain in this life. Used for the body, they are God's opportunity for each person to build, comfort, strengthen or establish the body of Christ. As with all the other spiritual gifts given by the Godhead, charisma gifts are given not primarily for the benefit of the person who exhibits them. The scriptures that set the context for charisma gifts are these;

Romans 12:4 Just as each of us has one body with many members, and these members do not all have the same function, 5 so in Christ we who are many form one body, and each member belongs to all the others.

God has arranged different functioning graces to produce fruit when we understand that only as a unified body will we experience all the grace He apportioned. Additionally, our faithful administration of these gifts will cause them to flow to the rest of the body. From God's perspective each part of the body belongs to the others. This means that the grace He apportions to one of the members is not intended to be hoarded for that member's benefit alone. That specific grace is centered in that one individual but will only bring forth the beauty and majesty of its full expression when given in service to the rest of the body.

AN INDIVIDUAL'S GRACE GIFT CANNOT BE A MEANS OF MEASUREMENT

In the areas of God's grace on our lives we experience ease, focus and clarity with little or no effort. This can easily lead to frustration with those who do not have this gift. The temptation of immature believers is to assume that their specific set of gifts is the most mature and that anyone who does not measure up to their specific set of gifts is less mature or gifted than they. Yet it is my observation that those who elevate themselves over others because of the grace on their lives, find it hard to see where the grace of God on other people's lives supersedes their own. We must resist the temptation to judge other people against the particular grace on our own lives. I do not want to be measured against someone else's set of gifts or judged by how I am running their race. I have my own set of gifts and my own race to run.

When God assigns grace to each one He also watches over the return. The one to whom much has been given, from him much will be demanded. Paul the apostle sums this up in 1 Corinthians.

1 Corinthians 4:6 Now these things, brethren, I have figuratively transferred to myself and Apollos for your sakes, that you may learn in us not to think beyond what is written, that none of you may be puffed up on behalf of one against the other. 7 For who makes you differ from another? And what do you have that you did not receive? Now if you did indeed receive it, why do you boast as if you had not received it? (NKJV)

God does not remove this grace from our lives

These graces are given without the threat of losing them if we turn from the Lord. They are gifts given by a generous God who does not remove them according to our fickle loyalties. We may use them as they were intended or we may use them for private and stingy gain. God gave us grace and He does not remove it from us. This is the promise of Romans.

Rom 11:29 for God's gifts and his call are irrevocable.

How do I administrate them?

Be faithful with them

Each member of the body is exhorted in 1 Peter 4:10 to see to the faithful application and use of their gift in service to other members of the body. How we can administer our gifts faithfully should have a high priority in the church and in our own hearts. As the old cliché goes "What you are is God's gift to you, what you become is your gift to God." This will involve thinking about the grace on our lives, investigating and discovering what we currently have and seeking to apply it in practical areas of service within our churches.

We already have observed from 1 Peter 4:10 that each person has grace gifts. When God knitted us together in our mother's womb He built into our wiring certain strengths and graces. God's intent for us in creation is mirrored in the grace He gives us. That purpose in creation is redeemed and empowered at rebirth. You are created in Christ Jesus for pre-envisioned works. You bear the fingerprints of Jesus who has re-formed you at salvation. When God's grace brings us to the free gift of salvation, His work is revealed as He creates and en-graces us do good works He planned and prepared in advance for us to do.

Ephesians 2:8 For it is by grace you have been saved, through faith—and this is not from yourselves, it is the gift of God— 9 not by works, so that no one can boast. 10 For we are God's handiwork, created in Christ Jesus to do good works, which God prepared in advance for us to do.

For example, when God created you He may have placed the grace of leadership on your life. Before your salvation it is likely that that gift was evident in your life but was obviously not used in service to the the body of Christ and therefore did not display all the glories God intended for your life. Often, before salvation, this gift will be demonstrated with all the negative aspects of unredeemed leadership. You were, in all likelihood opinionated, unwilling to follow others, constantly pulling away from where others were eager to go. When you came to salvation, God ignited that leadership gift and placed it within its intended context of a body of believers where it will enrich people and achieve eternal rewards. It flows best in your life when it is connected by a common faith and a commitment to serve others.

DON'T NEGLECT THEM

Paul exhorted Timothy not to neglect the grace gifts on his life (1 Tim 4:14). Paul said that grace was imparted to Timothy when the body of elders laid their hands on him. This intriguing and foundational doctrine of the laying on of hands mentioned in the book of Hebrews, teaches us that grace is imparted through the laying on of hands and faith. Sometimes grace for healing is imparted, sometimes the baptism of the Holy

Spirit, sometimes it is grace that appoints peoples to the position in the church of the Holy Spirit's choosing, sometimes the impartation of grace gifts. Paul says that we are not to neglect these grace gifts. They are grown in us as we use them and we grow in our experience as we do.

FAN THEM INTO FLAME

Paul says in 2 Timothy 1:6 that we should fan into flame these grace gifts on our lives. Astute attention should be given these gifts so that they are aflame in our lives. Again in that scripture Paul speaks of the gifts being imparted by the laying on of his hands, attention and care is needed for these graces to remain at optimum efficiency and power.

CAN I GET MORE GRACE OR GIFTS?

The scriptures teach us that we have gifts according to the grace God gives us. This may sound like He has already predetermined an apportioned grace to us and that's the end of it. Yet in this context, the humble receive more grace. Humility is a key factor in the release of more grace and grace gifts.

Romans 12:3 For by the grace given me I say to every one of you: Do not think of yourself more highly than you ought, but rather think of yourself with sober judgment, in accordance with the faith God has distributed to each of you

James 4:5 Or do you think Scripture says without reason that he jealously longs for the spirit he has caused to dwell in us? 6 But he gives us more grace. That is why Scripture says: "God opposes the proud but shows favor (gives grace) to the humble."

WHICH WAY IS GRACE FLOWING?

If the leaders of a church are not careful in their administration, ensuring each member's administration of their personal grace, then we will often find grace flowing the wrong way. For example, someone gets up on Sunday morning in the main service and asks to sing a song because they feel like God gave it to them. Let's assume they have a deeply passionate and committed heart to Jesus and their life is honorable. Yet when they start to sing it becomes apparent that they are tone deaf, While they kill us softly with their song, grace does not flow from them onto the congregation. The congregation must be gracious to them while they finish. Grace flows from the people to the person "ministering". Now, let's take that song with another person of equal fervor and valor in the church. This person however, has a great voice and musical ear. They start to sing with great skill. Grace flows from that person onto everyone within the sound of their voice. Grace is flowing the right way.

This principle is true with each grace gift. Someone who has been asked to fill the leadership seat that does not have a leadership grace on their lives will suck grace from everyone he or she is trying to lead. Anyone with leadership grace in the meeting will find it especially hard to endure that person's lack of grace in this way. Someone who has the grace gift of leadership will be frustrated, because what seems obvious and intuitive to them will be completely missed by someone who does not have this gift. Likewise, someone who has a teaching grace can communicate in a way that creates clarity while those teaching without it will likely cause more damage and confusion than blessing. If we do not attend to this basic truth, we not only cause grace to flow the wrong way but will require more grace to fix what has been skewed.

There are obviously examples of this principle for each of the grace gifts, but the glaring responsibility that leaders of churches must acknowledge is that we must be careful to assign the right people to the right seats on the bus. Let the leaders lead, the servers serve, the teachers teach and the prophets prophesy. When we arrange peoples service within the body in recognition of the grace gifts on their lives, we ensure that great grace flows to everyone in the church. If we get this wrong then we assign our church members to frustration and confusion. This is made confusing because of the earnestness of peoples hearts and the purity of their motives. Yet success does not come by integrity or earnest longing alone but by skill as we have previously noted. Churches seldom thrive at this snail's pace.

grace will constantly be required from everyone if leaders do not have the courage to manage this "seating arrangement" on the bus. This is not because there is anything necessarily wrong with people's hearts, it is because they are being asked to serve in areas that they are not skilled in. Get the people in the right seats on your bus. This is the for the eldership team to ensure.

The following question is for church leaders. How many people on your senior leadership exhibit great leadership grace? It is an unfortunate observation of mine that in many churches those who are in the leadership seats are often people with low to mid range leadership grace. We have marginalized the stronger leaders because to enfranchise them would mean relinquishing our personal control. Many high powered leaders do not yet understand that God graced them with high capacity primarily for use in His body. They are still under the illusion that the gifts on their lives are for their enrichment. We do them a great disservice by not pointing out to them that they will give an account to God for the administration of the grace gifts He gave them. Teaching them accurately of God's intent and winning them into an understanding of grace based service in submission to God's vision and appointed leaders will bring freedom and blessing to them and the body.

THE GREATEST JOY

The great secret of grace gifts is that when I function faithfully in the grace God gave me to serve others, not only does grace flow to them from my life, but I get charged as I serve. When I find the seat I'm supposed to be in, I see my contribution blessing others and I am invigorated by it. Grace flows through me to them and brings with it a satisfaction not found elsewhere on earth. Often we see people serving in their grace space with shiny eyes and hearts aflame because they are making a difference in the kingdom. I don't want people serving because its their duty and they are faithful no matter what. I want members who are so excited to serve because it blesses them and all they minister to. The role of elderships in releasing grace gifts

HELP THEM DISCOVER THEIR GIFTS

This is one of the primary purposes of elders. Presupposing we have understood the role of grace gifts and have taught them to our congregation. First, there must be a system whereby we recognize peoples' gifts. Very seldom will people step forward to ask for a position. Most will feel arrogant in doing this. We must ask people and help them discover the grace gifts God assigned them. I have asked my elders and deacons this question often at the beginning of the year; "If you were me, and you knew yourself like you do, where would you deploy yourself this year in this church to have the maximum kingdom affect?" Whatever system or mechanism you find or devise, make a way for people to discover their gifts in a safe environment.

CREATE PRACTICAL EXPRESSION FOR THEIR GIFTS

This will require preplanning and thought. Prepare opportunities for people to serve in teams in your local church. Currently, in our church we have 29 teams where people can serve in an aspect of the grace gift on their lives. Each team has a leader, often not on eldership or diaconate and each team also has an overseer who is usually one of the elders. We ask people for a one year commitment to that team after which everyone automatically comes off that team and we give everyone another option the following year to sign up for teams the next year. Some of our teams are by invitation only (Elders, deacons, finance). Other teams are available for sign up but will require some screening (worship teams require auditions, Youth and children's church require background checks etc). Most teams require no other qualifications than a willing and grace-gifted member. We aim to provide equipping for each team during the year. This requires a good working relationship between the leader and overseer of each team. In our church culture, if we do not have a leader for the team we assume we do not have a team. The grace to lead is the gateway gift to grace gifts.

EXERCISE AND CELEBRATE THEM

Ask team leaders for testimonies of the grace that is released through the teams. We have been amazed at the creativity and excitement released when people in the body start to bring their strength. We exhort people to bring their strength to our church, which is code for "use the grace God has given you." Welcome and greeting done by a team of people with hospitality gifts has excelled far beyond the practical need for people to be welcomed to our church. The people who help us with our projection have launched us into an audio visual arena far beyond the time when it was a team of volunteers who were willing but not necessarily graced. Conference management and organization has been easy when those with gifts of administration are given the reins. Without exception, every area of our church that has been released to people graced to see it done has exploded in excellence and motivation beyond our previous standards and expectations.

There is little doubt in my mind that massive grace and energy resides untapped in the body of Christ that God intended to be aflame. Grace ought to be flowing all around our churches through people operating in their grace gifts. Sadly in many churches, this grace not only lies untapped but more detrimentally, frustration is unleashed on the body through unwise or immature leadership assigning roles to people uniquely unsuited and not graced for them. This is probably one of the most important areas of development that will emerge in the upcoming days in the body of Christ.

Let us investigate the grace gifts individually.

GRACE TO PROPHESY

Romans 12:6 We have different gifts, according to the grace given us. If a man's gift is prophesying, let him use it in proportion to his faith.

We have investigated this gift before as it is mentioned along with the 'phanerosis' gifts. Here the gift is mentioned as a grace on people's lives. Some scholars have tried to separate this gift from the one of exactly the same name mentioned elsewhere in scripture hoping to make of this one merely the ability to preach. This is neither good Biblical interpretation nor logically valid.

People who have this grace gift find it easy to function prophetically and are the ones often hearing from God. They are people who naturally understand the delivery of truth. For them, hearing from God for others with a certain degree of distinct detail is almost a natural ability. They seem able to perceive truth about others around them and have an almost constant sense of what God is saying.

The guiding principle supplied with the description here is that those who bear this grace to prophesy should do it in proportion to their faith. Some of the great motivations of those who prophesy is to encourage, stir up the faith, and lift the heads of those around them that are suffering or downcast. This grace to prophecy often produces these results. As such it is sometimes a temptation to say what we hope will lift people up, even though we did not specifically hear from the Lord. This is prophesying beyond our faith. Whenever we say things that are hopeful and not faithful we do this. We are not called to prophesy in hope but in faith. If the person with the grace to prophesy does not have faith that what they are saying is from God they should rather be quiet or quote scripture, which we know is the word of God. When we prophesy beyond our faith and people accept it as though it is from the Lord, we can set them up for disappointment and it ultimately damages their faith. We ought to avoid this kind of immature response to the grace of prophesying.

However, those who faithfully administer this gift bring tremendous blessing to the body. They do more than bring encouragement to people although this is a foundation for all prophecy. Through their grace to prophesy, they also partake in the following administrations of God's grace;

IMPARTATION OF GIFTING

People who have a governmental office in the church and who share this grace, will be used to pray and minister to people by this gift. They should prophesy about other callings and impart grace to people in line with what God has said.

1 Timothy 4:14 Do not neglect the spiritual gift within you, which was bestowed on you through prophetic utterance with the laying on of hands by the presbytery.

ENCOURAGEMENT IN THE FIGHT OF FAITH

Those who are faithful in this grace often give direction, and work to strengthen resolve and a foundation for faith others. This gift is often more than just a word in the moment but an understanding and insight which they declare and hold others accountable to.

1 Timothy 1:18 Timothy, my son, I give you this instruction in keeping with the prophecies once made about you, so that by following them you may fight the good fight, 19 holding on to faith and a good conscience.

STRENGTHEN BELIEVERS

The gift functions as a sign for believers who have lost sight of the kindness, greatness or compassion of God. This gift serves as a sign for them of all that is still true about God. Often this grace to prophesy will lead people to remain true to what God has said. Built in to the gift is the ability to draw people closer to the Lord. If the gift draws people from Him or is discouraging from God or godliness it is not being administered well.

GRACE TO SERVE

*M*any have been gifted with the grace to serve. They find satisfaction in serving, preparing, or supporting others, often times remaining out of sight or at least out of the spotlight. They are the people God said He would never forget and whom Jesus said would be the greatest of all in His kingdom. Theirs is an indispensable place in the body. Their efforts create life and provide vital services for some who are more visible. Both scriptures in Romans 12 and 1 Peter 4 mention this grace of serving and have guiding principles for this grace.

Romans 12:7 If it is serving, let him serve

1 Peter 4:11 If anyone serves, he should do it with the strength God provides, so that in all things God may be praised through Jesus Christ.

The Romans scripture shows that if serving is your gift, go to it. There don't seem to be any long lessons, deep explanatory notes or places to be carefully avoided. If you can serve, then serve. Keep serving wherever you can, because inevitably that is what it takes for the body to be built up. While each member of the body must serve the others by faithful functioning, there will be some especially graced in serving. By their attitudes and their actions they set an example for believers in this particular field.

1 Peter adds the qualification that those who serve should be serving in dependence on the strength God supplies. This introduces two specific guide rails for this gift. It infers that our service needs go beyond our own strength. Second, if God is not supplying strength to our endeavors we must ask the question

whether He is in support of them. If we run out of grace in a specific context we ought to hand over the service graciously and in a manner that does no harm. Here are some additional scriptural pointers for those who serve.

THOSE WHO SERVE HAVE GREATER AUTHORITY IN THE KINGDOM

There are many volunteers for rulership, but few for service. Jesus made rulership and service synonyms in the kingdom. If you want to be great, serve. Faithfulness in service is the kingdom's defining factor for authority in leadership.

> *Luke 22:26 But you are not to be like that. Instead, the greatest among you should be like the youngest, and the one who rules like the one who serves. 27 For who is greater, the one who is at the table or the one who serves? Is it not the one who is at the table? But I am among you as one who serves.*

SERVICE IS DETERMINED BY THE MASTER, NOT THE SERVANT

Jesus said that if we were going to serve Him we must follow Him and go where He leads. Fundamentally in our service we must surrender to the mastery of Jesus. His right to command us must be matched by our recognition of His station, and ours in relation to Him. Although He has elevated us to more than servant status when He called us children, there is a distinct service element to those who respond to His call. Paul understood this from practical experience and called himself a bond slave of Jesus.

> *John 12:26 Whoever serves me must follow me; and where I am, my servant also will be. My Father will honor the one who serves me*

> *Romans 1:1 Paul, a servant of Christ Jesus, (doulos- a slave, bond servant)*

Servants tend to be empowered by their service to others and especially when their service has made a distinct difference in elevating the person or situation they served.

GRACE TO TEACH

*T*his is the grace God gives to some to make truth plain to others. These are the people often given to insights and perspectives useful for understanding. They are the ones helping the teacher at school convey the concept or explaining details to those who will listen. They are not necessarily called to the office of a teacher as we saw in the doma gifts section. These are people who are able to clarify aspects of truth and make them understood by those around them.

> *Romans 12:7 If it is serving, let him serve; if it is teaching, let him teach*

As with all grace gifts, teachers learn best from the faithful administration of their grace gifting. Grace gifts that are well used will build muscle and maturity which serve to make them even more effective. The scriptures do give us a few more guiding principles for those who have this grace;

IT IS NECESSARY TO HAVE EXPERIENCED WHAT YOU TEACH

Many people teach theory from the scriptures but have never experienced what they are teaching on. While the scriptures stand alone as truth and can be declared as truth without reference to the mouthpiece, many teach assumptions, traditions or perspectives that are not cemented in experience. Thus they do not teach accurately. Experience brings understanding and tempers the teaching with compassion. We have all heard the saying, "I used to have 5 theories on child raising and no children, now I have 5 children and no theories."

John 3:9 "How can this be?" Nicodemus asked. John 3:10 "You are Israel's teacher," said Jesus, "and do you not understand these things? (NIV11)

STUDY UP AND KNOW WHAT YOU ARE TEACHING

The more we have studied, and the more we know our subject the more confident we are in teaching it. We must not beg the question when we cannot make the argument. It is fine to have our own opinions but let those opinions be formed through a broad understanding of the topic and the reasoned positions of those who know their subject. We honor our audience when we have taken time to study, learn and research our subject. Too many people declare truths that their lives prove are not their own.

1 Timothy 1:7 They want to be teachers of the law, but they do not know what they are talking about or what they so confidently affirm.

TEACHERS WILL BE JUDGED BY A STRICTER STANDARD

What we teach people about the Lord creates a picture in their minds about Him. Our teaching creates boundaries of limitation or gives them space to live well. We can place people in bondage and diminish their expectations of God or we can show them who He is and bring them to the great liberty of the sons of God. We will be held accountable for what we teach.

James 3:1 Not many of you should presume to be teachers, my brothers, because you know that we who teach will be judged more strictly.

This principle was an established understanding in the culture of Jesus' day. Teachers of the law would interpret the Torah's words by making practical applications. What they exhorted their followers to do they called "loosing". What they forbade their followers was called "binding". If, as a Rabbi, I told my followers that to remember the Sabbath meant that they were not allowed to cook anything on the Sabbath then I bound it in their lives. If I believed that taking the animals out to graze and be watered on the Sabbath was an acceptable practice then that was "loosed" to my followers.

Matthew 18:18 "Truly I tell you, whatever you bind on earth will be bound in heaven, and whatever you loose on earth will be loosed in heaven.

New Testament teachers bear a responsibility for what they bind and loose over people's lives. When people choose to follow and listen to teachers they are placing them in a trusted role. Those who teach will give an account for the perception of God their teaching created and the expectations of Him that their teachings formed in other people's hearts.

This is a vital grace to the body that helps create a community who believe God and who live according to His word. It is evidenced in the early church that after receiving this grace of teaching they were first called Christians or a community "like Christ". Paul, before he was set aside into the apostolic office, was recognized as a teacher.

Acts 11:26 and when he found him, he brought him to Antioch. So for a whole year Barnabas and Saul met with the church and taught great numbers of people. The disciples were called Christians first at Antioch.(NIV11)

Acts 13:1 In the church at Antioch there were prophets and teachers:

May God fill our body with people who are faithful in the administration of the teaching grace on their lives.

GRACE TO ENCOURAGE

Romans 12:8 if it is encouraging, let him encourage;

*T*his is the ability to intuitively know or sense how to be encouraging to others. All of us are blessed by this vital ministry. In fact, much of the kingdom seed needs this kind of attention to bring it to maturity and full fruition. The original script from the verse above has also been translated "another who is a comforter, in his consolation". Paul the apostle came into his ministry because he was encouraged by Barnabas, who believed in him and stood up for him when others didn't.

> *Acts 4:36 Joseph, a Levite from Cyprus, whom the apostles called Barnabas (which means "son of encouragement"),*

> *Acts 9:26 When he (Paul) came to Jerusalem, he tried to join the disciples, but they were all afraid of him, not believing that he really was a disciple. 27 But Barnabas took him and brought him to the apostles. He told them how Saul . . . .*

> *Acts 11:25 (When Paul was languishing in Tarsus) Then Barnabas went to Tarsus to look for Saul, 26 and when he found him, he brought him to Antioch. So for a whole year Barnabas and Saul met with the church and taught great numbers of people.*

Those who walk in this grace often see potential where others see only ruin. They give themselves in encouragement because that is the grace on their lives. They are warned by those without this grace that people will take advantage of them and sometimes people do. There are many who are helped to great exploits because someone in the background encouraged them in God. Barnabus helped Paul to become the man he was called to be. When Barnabus saw potential in John Mark, Paul did not see it and their dispute over him separated them on their ministry journeys. Later on we see the fruits of Barnabus' ministry of encouragement when Paul acknowledges that John Mark is helpful to him in his ministry. It is also believed that this John Mark wrote the book of Mark. Those with this grace may be able to win people that others believe are beyond help. Some people with this gift will be called of God to lavish it on a few specific individuals.

The entire church is urged to join in this grace, but those who have this gift on their lives should be especially faithful to do it. We are urged to make it a daily discipline and habit;

Hebrews 3:13 But encourage one another daily, as long as it is called Today, so that none of you may be hardened by sin's deceitfulness.

Hebrews 10:25 Let us not give up meeting together, as some are in the habit of doing, but let us encourage one another--and all the more as you see the Day approaching.

IT IS COUNSELED AS A NECESSARY PART OF INSTRUCTION OR REBUKE;

At different times we may need either rebuke or encouragement in order for us to grow in our walk with the Lord. We all prefer the encouragement of Barnabus to the shouts of the sons of thunder James and John. Even when we know we deserve to be corrected it is best received when brought by someone also graced to encourage. Encouragement is always linked with rebuke in the New Testament.

Titus 2:15 These, then, are the things you should teach. Encourage and rebuke with all authority. Do not let anyone despise you.

1 Thessalonians 5:11 Therefore encourage one another and build each other up, just as in fact you are doing.

1 Thessalonians 5:14 And we urge you, brothers, warn those who are idle, encourage the timid, help the weak, be patient with everyone.

2 Timothy 4:2 Preach the Word; be prepared in season and out of season; correct, rebuke and encourage--with great patience and careful instruction.

IT IS A HALLMARK OF GOOD THEOLOGY, SOUND DOCTRINE AND AUTHENTIC PROPHETIC MINISTRY

This vital grace will oil the otherwise dry theology some people profess. Those who teach, lead or set vision for churches are well served by someone who brings this strength to the ministry. It is a necessary attribute of those who declare God's truth. Theology taught to Christians which does not encourage them ought to be held in high suspicion.

1 Thessalonians 4:17 After that, we who are still alive and are left will be caught up together with them in the clouds to meet the Lord in the air. And so we will be with the Lord forever. 18 Therefore encourage each other with these words.

Titus 1:9 He must hold firmly to the trustworthy message as it has been taught, so that he can encourage others by sound doctrine and refute those who oppose it.

Acts 15:32 Judas and Silas, who themselves were prophets, said much to encourage and strengthen the brothers.

IT MAY BE ADMINISTERED THROUGH ACTIONS

It is not always words or doctrine that brings encouragement. A helping hand, a supporting friend, a loving smile or a gesture of solidarity can be immensely encouraging. This grace of encouragement does not only function with words.

Philemon 1:7 Your love has given me great joy and encouragement, because you, brother, have refreshed the hearts of the saints.

Ephesians 6:22 I am sending him to you for this very purpose, that you may know how we are, and that he may encourage you.

1 Thessalonians 3:2 We sent Timothy, who is our brother and God's fellow worker in spreading the gospel of Christ, to strengthen and encourage you in your faith,

As with all other gifts, it is best used maturely and in dependence on the Holy Spirit. It does not rely on the flattery that appeals to sinful nature, which has, at its core, selfish motives. This grace of the Spirit rejoices with other people's advancement in the faith. Just as with love, encouragement has optimum efficacy when it is sincere.

GRACE TO GIVE

Romans 12:8 if it is encouraging, let him encourage; if it is contributing to the needs of others, let him give generously;

*T*his is the grace to give generously to others. Here again we realize that although generous giving is a mandate the entire church shares, there are specific individuals God has graced to give in a way that supersedes the norm. Each of the members of the body of Christ shares the responsibility of looking after their own relatives, their church family and the poor. In this, we emulate our Father whose great love for us compelled Him to give us His own son, and along with Him, all things. In view of this generosity how can we allow stinginess? In fact, the scriptures declare that "tightwad" stinginess cannot cohabit with God's love.

1 John 3:17 If anyone has material possessions and sees his brother in need but has no pity on him, how can the love of God be in him?

Jesus is eager to see His Father honored and beloved as supreme ruler of our hearts. A love of money threatens this supremacy. Those who make it a habit to give generously will find their hearts free from the love of money.

Luke 16:13 "No servant can serve two masters. Either he will hate the one and love the other, or he will be devoted to the one and despise the other. You cannot serve both God and Money."

The people with the grace to be generous ought to administer their gift as faithfully as any of the gifts mentioned so far. Embedded within this grace is the ability to generate wealth in order to be more generous. Generous givers are told to administer this grace with guidance. Be generous in your contributions to those in need. Some churches became known for their excelling in this grace of giving and are marked by heavens commendation, as Paul exhorts the Corinthian church. God's people are supposed to excel in this grace of giving.

Romans 12:6-8 We have different gifts, according to the grace given us. . . if it is contributing to the needs of others, let him give generously

2 Cor 8:7 (To the whole church) But just as you excel in everything--in faith, in speech, in knowledge, in complete earnestness and in your love for us --see that you also excel in this grace of giving.

The scriptures teach we should give in the following manner; Generously (2 Cor 8:2, 2 Cor 9:6,13), Willingly (2 Cor 8:3), According To our Ability (2 Cor 8:11), Cheerfully (2 Cor 9:7), Systematically (1 Cor 16:2), Proportionately (1 Cor 16:2) and sometimes Secretly (Mat 6:3).

A generous heart and a cheerful giver are pleasing to the Lord. I believe the Lord wants people who are wealthy and generous so that the gospel can spread to all the earth. It is not a ministry of compulsion but rather a ministry of freedom and grace.

2 Corinthians 9:7 Each man should give what he has decided in his heart to give, not reluctantly or under compulsion, for God loves a cheerful giver.

2 Corinthians 9:11 You will be made rich in every way so that you can be generous on every occasion

Deuteronomy 8:18 But remember the LORD your God, for it is he who gives you the ability to produce wealth, and so confirms his covenant,

The people who have this grace are no less spiritual than those who have the grace to teach or encourage, and they are no less necessary. If you know of some people like this encourage them in their gifting. Many have backed off from provoking people in this particular gift out of a misunderstanding of what James says.

James 2:2 For if there should come into your assembly a man with gold rings, in fine apparel, and there should also come in a poor man in filthy clothes, 3 and you pay attention to the one wearing the fine clothes and say to him, "You sit here in a good place," and say to the poor man, "You stand there," or, "Sit here at my footstool," 4 have you not shown partiality among yourselves, and become judges with evil thoughts? (NKJV)

Peoples welcome and worth in the kingdom are not to be judged by the demonstration of their worldly goods. Favoritism in such circumstances is evil judging according to the scriptures. Yet a clear understanding of the grace on peoples lives is not this evil judgment. Encouraging someone to be a generous giver in line with the grace placed on their lives is as important an encouragement as to any other grace gift.

GRACE TO LEAD

Romans 12:8 if it is encouraging, let him encourage; if it is contributing to the needs of others, let him give generously; if it is leadership, let him govern diligently;

The word used here for "lead" is the word proistemi – to stand in front of, to preside, maintain, be over, rule. It is the same word used of the head of the home and by inference is a similar role. Those who do not lead their families well are disqualified from leading the church.

1 Timothy 3:4 He must manage his own family well and see that his children obey him with proper respect. 5 (If anyone does not know how to manage his own family, how can he take care of God's church?)

No-one would dispute the indispensable role that leadership plays in all of human existence. We are drawn to leaders. The scripture, celebrates the role of leadership and expects that we do too;

1 Thessalonians 5:12 Now we ask you, brothers, to respect those who work hard among you, who are over you in the Lord and who admonish you. 13 Hold them in the highest regard in love because of their work. Live in peace with each other.

Unfortunately, unwise, unbiblical and immature leadership have done harm to God's people. The answer does not lie in appointing no leaders while allowing those with the strongest opinions or harshest voices to lead. The answer is a more Biblical approach to leadership. Biblical leaders were clearly defined by Jesus Himself;

Matthew 20:25 Jesus called them together and said, "You know that the rulers of the Gentiles lord it over them, and their high officials exercise authority over them. 26 Not so with you. Instead, whoever wants to become great among you must be your servant, 27 and whoever wants to be first must be your slave Mat 20:28 just as the Son of Man did not come to be served, but to serve, and to give his life as a ransom for many." . . . . . 2 Corinthians 1:24 Not that we lord it over your faith, but we work with you for your joy, because it is by faith you stand firm. . . . . . . 1 Peter 5:2 Be shepherds of God's flock that is under your care, serving as overseers-- not because you must, but because you are willing, as God wants you to be; not greedy for money, but eager to serve; 3 not lording it over those entrusted to you, but being examples to the flock.

They should show the following attributes, serving as examples to God's people;

1 Thessalonians 2:10 You are witnesses, and so is God, of how holy, righteous and blameless we were among you who believed. 11 For you know that we dealt with each of you as a father deals with his own children, 12 encouraging, comforting and urging you to live lives worthy of God, who calls you into his kingdom and glory.

Hebrews 13:7 Remember your leaders, who spoke the word of God to you. Consider the outcome of their way of life and imitate their faith.

Philemon 4:9 Whatever you have learned or received or heard from me, or seen in me—put it into practice. And the God of peace will be with you.

1 Corinthians 4:17 For this reason I am sending to you Timothy, my son whom I love, who is faithful in the Lord. He will remind you of my way of life in Christ Jesus,

314

which agrees with what I teach everywhere in every church.

2 Timothy 3:10 You, however, know all about my teaching, my way of life, my purpose, faith, patience, love, endurance,

These kinds of leaders are indispensable and ought to be celebrated. The scriptures exhorts these leaders to govern diligently. The Greek word spoude is used here meaning – speedily, dispatch, eagerness, earnestness, earnest, care, diligence, haste. Dilligent attention to the body is the requirement of those with the gift of leadership.

DEFINITION

The gifts of grace are those gifts distributed to us by God and are often thought of as our 'strengths' or 'abilities'. They are gifts from God in line with the grace He places on each life.

We are all called to prophesy, but there is a gift of prophecy. We are all called to be witnesses, but there is a gift of the evangelist. We are all called to serve, but there is a gift of helping others. We are all called to be hospitable but there is a specific gift of hospitality. It is God's grace apportioned to our lives that allows some to experience a specific area of giftedness. Here they will find joy in service, a fulfillment in the work, and a greater effectiveness in ministry.

GRACE TO SHOW MERCY

DEFINITION

*A*s we know from the parable Jesus told below, receiving mercy is a wonderful gift that is not always matched by our giving of mercy. The gift of showing mercy is the God-given grace to care for people who are suffering. It is compassion in action. Its purpose is not to make the afflicted feel sad or to cause them to think they owe some type of debt; but to raise their spirits and to bring freedom from their pain or bondage.

> *Matthew 18:26 "The servant therefore fell down before him, saying, 'Master, have patience with me, and I will pay you all.' 27 Then the master of that servant was moved with compassion, released him, and forgave him the debt. 28 "But that servant went out and found one of his fellow servants who owed him a hundred denarii; and he laid hands on him and took him by the throat, saying, 'Pay me what you owe!' 29 So his fellow servant fell down at his feet[a] and begged him, saying, 'Have patience with me, and I will pay you all.'[b] 30 And he would not, but went and threw him into prison till he should pay the debt. 31 So when his fellow servants saw what had been done, they were very grieved, and came and told their master all that had been done. 32 Then his master, after he had called him, said to him, 'You wicked servant! I forgave you all that debt because you begged me. 33 Should you not also have had compassion on your fellow servant, just as I had pity on you?' (NKJV)*

The gift of showing mercy covers a wide variety of actions including visiting and attending the sick; caring for the poor; showing love and compassion to orphans and widows; showing kindness to believers who are suffering emotionally, encouraging and helping those going through a personal crisis, forgiving of debts whether material or spiritual.

Showing mercy often involves a sacrifice of time and money. Flowers or food or sending cards cost money. Visiting takes time. The good Samaritan had to backtrack to Jericho (Luke 10:34) and pay the innkeeper to take care of the brutalized victim (10:35). It is not merely sentiment or prayer.

Theologians talk of two types of mercy, consequent and judicial mercy. Consequent mercy is having compassion for those who are currently suffering and then working to relieve their suffering. This mercy is shown while a person is suffering. Most often, this kind of suffering is accidental and undeserved.

Luke 10:33 But a Samaritan, as he traveled, came where the man was; and when he saw him, he took pity on him. Luke 10:34 He went to him and bandaged his wounds, pouring on oil and wine. Then he put the man on his own donkey, took him to an inn and took care of him. Luke 10:35 The next day he took out two silver coins and gave them to the innkeeper. 'Look after him,' he said, 'and when I return, I will reimburse you for any extra expense you may have.'

Judicial mercy is the second type of mercy we must show. This is compassion for those who are about to suffer and then acting in attempt to prevent it. It is mercy shown before the suffering begins. The first scripture above regarding the slave who was to be thrown in jail but was then shown mercy is a good example. Our salvation is the best example of judicial mercy. As sinners, we deserve to suffer in the Lake of Fire forever, but God has shown us mercy before we ever suffer by commuting the sentence (Eph. 2:4; Titus 3:5 see below). Most often, judicial mercy is given to people whose suffering is not accidental or undeserved.

Ephesians 2:4 But because of his great love for us, God, who is rich in mercy, Eph 2:5 made us alive with Christ even when we were dead in transgressions--it is by grace you have been saved. (NIV 11)

Titus 3:5 he saved us, not because of righteous things we had done, but because of his mercy. He saved us through the washing of rebirth and renewal by the Holy Spirit, (NIV 11)

THE TONE IN SHOWING MERCY

Scripture gives us two attitudes that should accompany this gift of grace.

Romans 12:8 if it is showing mercy, let him do it cheerfully.

Jude 1:23 snatch others from the fire and save them; to others show mercy, mixed with fear--hating even the clothing stained by corrupted flesh.

The first is a cheerful administration of this gifting. Begrudging, grumbling mercy is not a good reflection of the gracious and merciful God who has shown us mercy. We get our English word hilarity from the Greek root of the word used here for cheerful. It denotes happiness, joy and cheerfulness. It is the most accurate reflection of our God who delights to show mercy.

Micah 7:18 Who is a God like you, who pardons sin and forgives the transgression of the remnant of his inheritance? You do not stay angry forever but delight to show mercy.

The second is a showing of mercy that is mixed with fear of the contagion of sin, not lightly celebrating it, or making light of the consequences averted in its forgiveness. Showing mercy is a vital ministry for the release of many in the church, especially those with sensitive consciences. People with tender consciences can often be bound with heavy chains by legalistically driven Christians or heavy-handed leaders. It is the accusers of the brothers who despise this great grace. It is precisely this quality that drew sinners to Jesus.

Matthew 9:10 While Jesus was having dinner at Matthew's house, many tax collectors and "sinners" came and ate with him and his disciples. 11 When the Pharisees saw this, they asked his disciples, "Why does your teacher eat with tax collectors and 'sinners'?" 12 On hearing this, Jesus said, "It is not the healthy who need a doctor, but the sick. 13 But go and learn what this means: 'I desire mercy, not sacrifice.' For I have not come to call the righteous, but sinners."

GRACE OF HOSPITALITY

*H*ospitality is the grace to share our home, our lives, our personal space and resources with others, without communicating a need for performance or an expectation of return. It is not self serving but seeks to focus the attention on the guest, and to meet the needs of an individual who may never be able to return the favor. It has clear boundaries and is not a complete service to the excesses of others. Henri Nouwen says that there can only be a welcoming space where there are boundaries.

The Greek word for hospitality is philozenia. It comes from two words, one is love, and the other is stranger. Biblical hospitality is the love of the stranger. This is particularly foreign to our culture, where strangers are often threatening figures. Our reaction to strangers is captured in another word that comes from the Greek, xenophobia, the fear of strangers. We rightfully stress to our kids not to talk to strangers.

In New Testament days, there were few hotels or motels. The majority of inns were brothels. So one of the first practices that the early church set up was the practice of hospitality so that those in the Christian community who traveled, whether for business or for preaching and spreading the gospel would have safe places to go to. Later, during the crusades this idea spread to looking after the sick. Modern hotels and hospitals can be traced back to these roots in Christian hospitality.

Hospitable people have a unique grace to place others first. Most people are preoccupied with their own needs, worries, tensions, and interests that prevent them from giving their full attention to others. Those gifted with hospitality seem to be able to communicate, often without words, that it is their privilege to have you in their home and that they like having you there with them. Their lives have space for others, a place where you can belong, and play a significant part. People gifted with hospitality demonstrate deep value for Biblical community.

SCRIPTURAL MANDATES

Romans 12:13 Share with God's people who are in need. Practice hospitality.

Literally it says, "Pursue hospitality." and the verb implies continuous action. So the command in Romans 12:13 is that hospitality not be a once a year or occasional chore, but a constant attitude and practice. Our homes and apartments should stand constantly ready for strategic hospitality--a readiness to welcome people who don't ordinarily live there.

1 Peter 4:8 Above all, love each other deeply, because love covers over a multitude of sins. 9 Offer hospitality to one another without grumbling. (NIV 11)

Ungrudgingly! That means, be the kind of people who do it and like to do it! The command to be hospitable is not just a command that can be legalistically fulfilled with a quota of guests. It is a command to be a certain kind of person, namely, the kind that doesn't resent having to be hospitable. "Practice hospitality ungrudgingly to one another." Without murmuring. As the next verse (4:10) implies, let your hospitality be an extension or an overflow of God's hospitality to you.

Hebrews 13:1 Keep on loving each other as brothers. 2 Do not forget to entertain strangers, for by so doing some people have entertained angels without knowing it. (NIV 11)

The instruction to "not forget showing hospitality" implies that forgetfulness in this arena happens even to people who engage in it. One of the important qualifiers for choosing widows who were to be cared for through provisions provided by the church was that they had themselves practiced hospitality.

1 Timothy 5:10 and is well known for her good deeds, such as bringing up children, showing hospitality, washing the feet of the saints, helping those in trouble and devoting herself to all kinds of good deeds.

It is commended in the church and was a sign of honor and recognition.

3 John 1:5 Dear friend, you are faithful in what you are doing for the brothers, even though they are strangers to you. 6 They have told the church about your love. You will do well to send them on their way in a manner worthy of God. 7 It was for the sake of the Name that they went out, receiving no help from the pagans. 8 We ought therefore to show hospitality to such men so that we may work together for the truth.

Hospitality is especially encouraged for those who preach the gospel. The faithful practice of hospitality is one of the repeatedly mentioned qualities required to be an elder.

Titus 1:8 Rather he must be hospitable, one who loves what is good, who is self-controlled, upright, holy and disciplined.

1 Timothy 3:2 Now the overseer must be above reproach, the husband of but one wife, temperate, self-controlled, respectable, hospitable, able to teach.

GRACE TO HELP

The word used for helping in 1 Corinthians 12:28 is "antilempsis." This word for helping, in its verb form means "to take a burden upon oneself." People with the grace to help can stand by someone who is called to ministry and take care of their specific needs. They do this by taking certain responsibilities on themselves in a way that releases others to concentrate on the things they have to do. If they say they will take care of something then you can rest and relax about it because they are high functioning doers whose competence brings relief. It's similar to having a personal deacon or having someone with serving grace committed to helping you.

These are not wallflowers incapable of doing anything themselves. They are destined to help others with vision and drive. They are gifted and focused people who have been given grace to help others. They derive joy from their helping role, satisfied in the knowledge that without their strength, the project would have been much more difficult and far less enjoyable. Behind all great achievement and leaders we will find these people serving faithfully.

The scope of what they help with is as diverse as the opportunities we have in life. Some people can help with practical details like paper administration or sourcing of goods for the best prices. Some can help by managing events.

Help graced people seem to recognize needs quickly. They move deliberately to assure that those needs are met often on their own initiative. In this, they provide great comfort to those they are helping because they move beyond merely supplying peace but provide material needs as well. People with a strong helping gift find their greatest release under secure leaders who know how to define targets and set boundaries.

Joseph is a great Old Testament example of someone who functioned in a helps ministry wherever he went. He was a help to his father with his flocks. He was a help to Potiphar in his entire household until his wife lied about him. He was a help to the jailer by running things well. Finally he was a help to Pharaoh in the administration of the accumulation and dispersion of grain.

GRACE TO ADMINISTRATE

*T*he grace to administrate is an ability that can produce great results and bless many people's lives. If managed immaturely, this grace can cause general frustration. When managed well, it blesses everyone involved. The Greek word for "administration" comes originally from the word "kubernetes" who was a helmsman who kept his ship on course. It was this helmsman's job to evaluate his crew, understanding their strengths and limitation. He was to navigate the waters and keep the ship from being hurt by the rocks or stranded on a beach. He had to evaluate the tides and the wind speed and keep them all in mind in order for the ship to steer a straight course. Then the word administrator or (kubernesis) is understood to mean "piloting or steering." The administrator is the person that we entrust a task or a project to in the hopes that they will produce an excellent finished work.

There are different aspects to administration and not all administrators are graced with each part. Some administrators who have a great ability to connect with people will intuitively know how to motivate groups of people for the tasks they need to do. These people do not necessarily understand how to administrate finances or paperwork. Some administrators who are great with paper systems and run an extremely efficient office, do not work that well with people. Implied within administration is a leadership ability that can manage people well and even coordinate leaders within their specific spheres of influence. The greater the project, the greater the need will be for the administrator to employ leadership.

Examples of different types of administration can be found in Exodus. The first is when Moses' father-in-law sees him burning himself out and suggests a course of action that frees Moses and involves other people (Exo 18). Later, as the Lord tells Moses to build the tabernacle, He gives Moses two men skilled to work with all kinds of materials and the ability to manage the workmen (Exo 31:1-11)

Unfortunately, in some circles a weird doctrine has developed that whenever people start to administrate anything they are "quenching the Spirit," as though by their gift of administration they could erase God's power. These people believe that somehow we should not apply ourselves to accomplish anything. They assume that God's Holy Spirit will do it all for us. Why does God give the grace gifts of leadership and administration if He did not expect us to be leading and administrating? Why does He give us overseers if He doesn't want anyone interfering with what He does? No, my friends, God loves to work with us in the church. He likes to share His heart and hear us share ours. We should take great pains to encourage the administrators to use their gifts and to hone them into excellence. When they do, they will create space in which people find opportunities and safety and with which the Holy Spirit will Co-labor.

Every temple God had built had detailed blueprints. To ensure His will is brought to life on earth He graces some people with gifts of administration. He does not operate on whim but is the consummate planner and administrator. God kept His plan secret for ages and then revealed it through the apostles and prophets. If you desire to see all that God has for your church, the administration gift will be pivotal.

OTHER GRACES

I believe that the list of graces is primarily illustrative and is not exhaustive. There are therefore other graces currently operating in the body of Christ

GRACE TO SPEAK

This is a communication ability that goes beyond the conventional perspective on preaching. It is the ability to form with words the perceptions, environments, cultures and responses that honor God. It is the ability to bring peace into turmoil by speaking. Sometimes, this ability finds expression in speaking out public prayers for a congregation. People with the gift of speech can speak in a meeting and bring clarity to the body. Their words carry healing, insight, peace and joy to their audience.

1 Peter 4 alludes to this grace just after it exhorts the church to faithfully administer the graces God gives us.

1 Peter 4:11 If anyone speaks, he should do it as one speaking the very words of God.

The tongue has power to light fires, steer our course and bring healing. People who learn how to harness its power for the kingdom, can bring tremendous blessing to the church even outside of a formal sermon.

Proverbs 15:4 The tongue that brings healing is a tree of life, but a deceitful tongue crushes the spirit. (NIV 11)

WRITING

The ability to write is a grace that is similar to speaking, though perhaps not as publicly acknowledged. My theory is that Paul the apostle was jailed so that he would be forced to write. I doubt we would have had nearly as many New Testament scriptures had Paul been free to travel and minister in that time. Toward the end of his life, Paul asks for more writing materials.

2 Timothy 4:13 When you come, bring the cloak that I left with Carpus at Troas, and my scrolls, especially the parchments. (NIV 2011)

God has accomplished considerably more through Paul's writing than by any of the miracles he performed while on earth. Success in the moment is dependent on many issues but longevity of ministry, that which goes beyond your life, is almost always associated with what you have on paper.

God graces some people to create language that forms the expression of His kingdom in their generation. It is an extraordinarily important aspect of the kingdoms advance. The "it is written" must come before "so I say." Truth, emotion, anointing and revelation can all be transferred through the written word.

Additionally, there are those who write songs and poems and parables. They are incredibly influential. If we ask our members to recite the main points of our sermons a month after they were given most would be hard pressed. Ask those people to recite the words to the current worship songs we sang that same week and most of them would have them all memorized. Song writers have great power to shape Christian thinking and worship.

Throughout church history the newest moves of God are always attended by new music and words which form the vehicle for their sustenance. God graces some people with this ability and it should be encouraged and applauded.

The scriptures say that the angels sang while God created. This means that before there was a physical realm, music existed. Around God's throne there are angelic choirs singing songs of worship to Christ that are recorded in the book of Revelation. Music is therefore eternal and spiritual and is able to connect our spirits to the spiritual realm. The sons and daughters of Jubal (the first musician) have an amazing opportunity. By their craft, they can create a mood that fosters the presence of God. Musicians who are in vital relationship with Jesus are able to mirror the mood of the Holy Spirit in a meeting and sustain that atmosphere by their music.

The more faithful they have been to master the grace on their lives, the more they bless the church. When they play with skill, spirits are stirred to godly action and are also released from malignant influence. Like every other area in the body, when gifted people express their gifting maturely and in team with others, they produce a synergistic blessing that is greater than the sum of its parts. Few things can compete with the blessing of gifted musicians who know how to respond to the Lord and play in team.

DANCE

Dancing is one of the expressions of worship that the Psalmist exhorts. It can express emotion and devotion to the Lord that unleashes victory and rejoicing.

Psalm 149:3 Praise his name with dancing accompanied by tambourine and harp.4 For the Lord delights in his people; he crowns the humble with victory. (NIV 11)

Psalm 150:4 Praise him with the tambourine and dancing; praise him with strings and flutes!(NIV 11)

It is true that the environments where dancing and movement are not allowed, tend to be formal and restrictive. Churches that allow dancing tend to be more relaxed, open and free. This is both obvious and important, because care must be taken to oversee the sheep by the Spirit and not by rules. Where we set up preconditions to what the Lord can and cannot do, we limit our experience of Him. Clearly God has consistently amazed His people with His endlessly creative ways of encountering them. Environments that limit the expressions of worship will often miss valid expressions of God or extinguish fires that the Spirit of God is starting in people's lives.

Dancing is not a personal preference for me as an expression of worship. I always feel like watchers will think I am being attacked by a bee hive when I dance. Yet I know that there are expressions of freedom, victory and praise that are heralded best through dancers. To not allow or celebrate this is shortsighted and limiting. Let victory reign in the praise and dancing of the redeemed.

ARTWORK

Many forms of visual art exist and are God given graces. Artists are at the front-lines of change. Sociologists have long recognized that the culture of tomorrow is depicted in the art of today. Artists are on the forefront of expression and have a heightened social radar and sensitivity that can often seem out of place. When all others are seeing one thing, artists tend to plainly see something else. This often contributes to their sense of otherness.

If we can learn to see what they are straining to express, we will be well-served. Each day has enough troubles of its own and if we can find artists who can express the kindnesses and grace of Jesus, our lives are blessed through them.

Graphic art, performance art, video craft, photography, poetry, decorating and many other art forms bring beauty and truth to our lives. A remarkable surge of energy is often released into the churches whose leaders take the time to engage artists who are graced by God.

Conclusion

*L*eadership is the pivotal gift that the life of the church depends on. Leaders in God's church must take their leadership model from Jesus, emulating His humility and commitment to do His Father's will. It is in this seemingly obvious point that many of us fall short. We have developed the leadership gift, studying, reading, and talking about leadership, yet have not moved into governance as God desires. Leadership can bring immense benefits but cannot lead people into all of their inheritance, nor will it be able to transition into spiritual realities relying on natural gifts.

We aspire to be like political leaders, coaches, theologians and sometimes even celebrities when it comes to leadership. Undoubtedly they have something to offer and aspects of their lives ought to be emulated. In Jesus though, we find perfect theology and practice to emulate. Despite this truth, the church is for the most part unclear about the great emphasis Jesus and the New Testament place on governance. Tensions and seeming paradoxes exist, in that we are called to be the servant and the leader at the same time. Being the least and the greatest in one person. Having no executive authority yet bearing the approbation of heaven's authority. These tensions are often not worked through in the context of scripture, but are often made to fit a more worldly leadership paradigm. Thus, we try to fit a worldly structure on an eternal revelation. This never works out and always robs the eternal of its supernatural effects on the earth. Paul said the cross was emptied of its power when treated like this.

The overarching reality is that God works through leaders, so wherever leadership is established and celebrated, life will result in the people. Good leadership brings good to people. Strong yet evil leadership brings evil to people. As Proverbs affirms

Proverbs 29:2 When the righteous thrive, the people rejoice; when the wicked rule, the people groan.

When good leadership arises, and they learn God's governance as well, people are not only blessed but launched into eternal destinies. This governing of God's people brings growth to everyone it oversees because it carries the breath of God's revelation and is fed by Kingdom power. Oh how we need this governance in the church, dead to selfish ambition and conceit. How desperately we need men and women who give their all, pour out their lives as drink offerings on the sacrifice and service of the faith. Disorder and confusion are unleashed where envy and selfish ambition are allowed in leaders' hearts. The opposite is established in their absence. Godly government brings order, clarity, and space for the church.

James 3:13 Who is wise and understanding among you? Let him show by good conduct that his works are done in the meekness of wisdom. 14 But if you have bitter envy and self-seeking in your hearts, do not boast and lie against the truth. 15 This wisdom does not descend from above, but is earthly, sensual, demonic. 16 For where envy and self-seeking exist, confusion (disorder) and every evil thing are there. (NKJV)

In these pages I have tried to outline a system for the establishment of godly government in local churches. I hope that they will act as catalysts to a greater exploration of these topics.

There remains a cry in the heart of the Spirit in these days for the emergence of godly leadership, which is like rain falling on a mown field, like the rightness after rain that brings forth growth from the earth.

I pray your leadership gift develops in sync with your heart for the Bride to the place where God can trust you to bear His presence in your generation.

To each governor in a church I send out this encouragement. You are busy with a great and noble task. The Bride of Jesus the King, is under your influence. Her preparation and beauty are your responsibility and therefore you are watched over by the most faithful bridegroom in the universe. He is also the wealthiest and most willing to see your job completed. Call out to Him for help and wisdom and you will receive it in abundance. Let me say it again, yours is a noble task and for all eternity those who have served Jesus and His Bride well, will have an honored place and name. Stay strong and clear on the task. Do not be discouraged or defeated. There is a victors crown waiting for you along with the words, "Well done! My good and faithful servant."

Grace and peace to you.

71601121R00183

Made in the USA
Columbia, SC
01 September 2019